The Power of Good Deeds

The Power of Good Deeds

Privileged Women and the
Social Reproduction of the Upper Class

Diana Kendall

ROWMAN & LITTLEFIELD PUBLISHERS, INC.
Lanham • Boulder • New York • Toronto • Oxford

ROWMAN & LITTLEFIELD PUBLISHERS, INC.

Published in the United States of America
by Rowman & Littlefield Publishers, Inc.
A wholly owned subsidiary of the Rowman & Littlefield Publishing Group, Inc.
4501 Forbes Boulevard, Suite 200, Lanham, Maryland 20706
www.rowmanlittlefield.com

PO Box 317, Oxford, OX2 9RU, UK

British Library Cataloguing in Publication Information Available

Library of Congress Cataloging-in-Publication Data

Kendall, Diana Elizabeth.
  The power of good deeds : privileged women and the social reproduction
of the upper class / Diana Kendall.
     p. cm.
Includes bibliographical references.
  ISBN 0-7425-1975-9 (cloth : alk. paper)—ISBN 0-7425-1976-7 (pbk :
alk. paper)
  1. Upper class women—Texas—Social life and customs. 2.
Debutantes—Texas—Social life and customs. 3. Women—Texas—Societies
and clubs. 4. Charity organization—Texas—Case studies. 5.
Voluntarism—Texas—Case studies. 6. Social stratification—Texas. I.
Title.
  HQ1905.T4 K46 2002
  305.4'09764—dc21

                                              2002003764

Printed in the United States of America

⊛™ The paper used in this publication meets the minimum requirements of
American National Standard for Information Sciences—Permanence of Paper for
Printed Library Materials, ANSI/NISO Z39.48-1992.

Contents

Acknowledgments

Although I am solely responsible for the contents of this book, it would have been impossible to research and write about this study without the encouragement and assistance of many people. At the risk of forgetting to include everyone who has assisted my thinking, data collection, and analysis, or the completion and publication of this book, I would like to mention several individuals who have been most instrumental in this process. From my graduate days at the University of Texas at Austin, conversations with and the work of sociologist Joe R. Feagin have informed my thinking about the significance of race, class, and gender in all aspects of social life, including those areas in which power issues such as domination and subordination are defining factors in everyday life.

At Baylor University, I have received much encouragement regarding my work from all of my colleagues in the Department of Sociology and Anthropology, especially from its current chair, Charles M. Tolbert, II, and its former chair, Harold W. Osborne. Wallace L. Daniel, Dean of the College of Arts and Sciences, and Larry Lyon, Dean of the Graduate School, have been instrumental in helping me coordinate my teaching and research interests so that they could culminate in publications. I would be remiss if I did not mention the excellent graduate students who have helped me with literature reviews or other aspects of my research. Among the students I would especially like to thank are Mikele Cayton-Woody, Heather Frye, Nina Heckler, Diana Karafin, and Alex Trouteaud.

I am indebted to Dean Birkenkamp and Alison Sullenberger for their strong support of this project, and to the others at Rowman & Littlefield who helped turn my manuscript into this book, including Jehanne

Schweitzer, production editor. I appreciate the prompt and accurate work of Mary Bearden, who did the copyediting on the book.

I want to thank Susan A. Ostrander, professor of sociology at Tufts University, whose insightful comments about earlier drafts of this book put me on the right path for marshaling my data and interpreting them in a more effective and forceful manner.

Finally, I would like to thank the women who participate in the women's voluntary organizations in the cities in this study. I appreciate their efforts on behalf of the communities in which they live, but also I appreciate their insights and comments during my participant observation. Without their perceptions regarding the matters discussed in this book, my study would have been incomplete.

CHAPTER ONE

Introduction

One of the most special nights in the lives of some social elites in this nation is when their daughter is presented as a debutante or their son serves as an escort to one of the young women being presented to Society—society with a capital S. Rivaled in pomp and circumstance only by the upper-class wedding, the debutante presentation has been declared dead by social historians on numerous occasions, yet it remains an important upper-class rite of passage in cities across the nation.[1] Young women, decked out in full-length designer gowns, gather in an elaborately decorated ballroom to be introduced and take a formal bow in which their heads may be expected to touch the floor, then to arise jubilantly and gracefully after receiving a round of applause for their—and their parents'—accomplishments and to be escorted away by a marriageable, socially acceptable young man wearing a black tuxedo or "white tie and tails." The audience, comprised of elegantly coifed ladies and tuxedo-clad gentlemen, sipping wine, cocktails, or fancy bottled water and seated at tables whose closeness to the stage signifies the status of each table's occupants, is silent and respectful except when it applauds as, one after another, the young women are presented to Society. "Introducing Mary Louise [pause], of the House of Smith [pause], the daughter of Mr. and Mrs. Martin Smith. Miss Smith is escorted by John Doe the Third, son of Mr. and Mrs. John Doe, Jr.," the master of ceremonies announces.[2] Each takes her bow, her escort standing nearby.

At some debutante presentation balls, one young woman is designated as the evening's most important debutante, perhaps the Queen, signifying that her parents made a large contribution of money and/or time to the organization sponsoring the presentation or that they have extensive connections and social power within the group. Other debutantes may be designated as Princesses, meaning that their family's contributions are also significant to the organization, but less so than those of the Queen's family. It is all part of an elaborate social hierarchy, involving who is presented in what order.

Many of the social events of the upper classes, such as a presentation ball, are organized and orchestrated by elite women in their roles as members of prestigious women's volunteer organizations. These groups have a closed membership, meaning that new members must be "put up" for membership by existing members, go through a rigorous process in which they are voted on by a membership committee (and in some cases, by the full membership) of the organization, and be formally invited to join the group. Having a by-invitation-only membership guarantees members of elite women's volunteer groups that their organization will be comprised primarily of other women like themselves, even though the stated purpose of their group is to raise money for a wide diversity of arts, cultural, medical, educational, and charitable endeavors representing many sectors of the community. Elite women who participate in such invitational community service organizations gain strength in numbers whereby they can pool their considerable economic and social resources for a common cause—thus accomplishing more for that cause than any of them could do if acting alone—while, at the same time, enhancing their individual social power.

What is social power? A number of differing meanings have been given to this term, depending (among other things) on the context in which it is being used. By definition, however, *power* is based on privileged access to and control over scarce resources. If we think of power as being limited to such resources as political and economic power, then elite women today—even though they control more of the nation's wealth and hold more political power than they have in the past—generally have less power than do the men in their lives: fathers, husbands, and the other men with whom they associate. Feminist theorists have argued that elite women—like those in other classes—remain subordinate to men when power is viewed solely in that context. However, elite women *do* have power. Their power is based on a combination of the economic power that they hold either individually or jointly with other members of their families and the social power that they derive from influential social connections and prestigious organizational affiliations. Many of the elite women in this study own or have access to much greater economic wealth than do the people in other social classes. They also possess sufficient social power to have the upper hand in social transactions with other people, especially those outside their own class and racial/ethnic categories.

Previous research has identified a number of aspects, or roots, of social power. John R. P. French Jr., and Bertram H. Raven's typology of social power, for example, is particularly useful in explaining how women's social power may be different from that of men.[3] According to French and Raven, there are five different sources of social power that serve as bases by which people exert social influence: reward, coercive, expert, legitimate, and referent power. A person possesses reward power when others believe that he or she can provide them with desired rewards; conversely, a person possesses coercive power when others believe that he or she can punish them. Women who serve on boards of trustees of elite nonprofit organizations or who are in key positions as upper-class community volunteers, for example, have the ability to reward those who work hard for their cause. These rewards may include having their children honored by prestigious groups or being selected for presentation as a debutante or royal escort. Coercive power in nonprofit organizations, such as are discussed in this book, is more ambiguous because punishments typically do not take the form of monetary loss but may involve varying degrees of banishment from the inner circle of the group, including exclusion from membership, expulsion for nonparticipation or for behavior viewed as unacceptable by other group members, or remaining within the group but being treated as an outsider or virtual nonentity when it comes time for recognition and other social rewards.

Continuing with French and Raven's typology, individuals who are perceived as having expertise or knowledge in a specific field—or expertise and knowledge generally—are able to exercise expert power. For example, elite women volunteers often pride themselves on being specialists in specific types of fundraising or other event planning. Some are generally knowledgeable about philanthropy and possess information that is valuable to others regarding community resources that should be tapped to get a major project done. Linking their impressive array of social contacts with their expertise in raising money and getting people to donate their time and talents to good causes, some elite women are able to exercise expert power in the community.

An individual has legitimate power if other people believe that he or she has the right to exert influence over others and if those other people are willing to do what he or she suggests. Legitimate power may be conferred on those who hold a particular social role that commands respect or authority, or it may be linked to a feeling among others that they should—for some reason or other—defer to the wishes or demands of that individual. Like parents who typically claim to have legitimate power over their children, women who head up elite volunteer organizations or serve as the chairs of key fundraising activities claim legitimate power for themselves, thus giving them not only the status of being ball chair or president of the group as a whole, but also the ability to assign roles to others and, in essence, to tell them what to do.

Unlike other bases of power, referent power is based on an individual's or group's social attractiveness to others. Individual women may view one another as likeable and thus have referent power; likewise, elite women's organizations may have referent power with respect to those individuals who would like to join the group and receive the benefits that membership would offer them and their families.

The French and Raven model of social power is useful in studying elite women and their organizations because it views power as being based on the need or desire to maintain relationships. Unlike power elite models, for example, that relate power to the possession of external status or resources, such as those found in politics, the military, the economy, or some combination of these, referent power is much more personal and is based on a feeling of identification with others.[4]

As used in this book, social power refers to having some combination of reward, coercive, expert, legitimate, and referent power, such that a woman is able to reward others for doing what she wants done, or in having the ability to persuade others to do things they otherwise would not do, and in being respected for what she accomplishes. For elite women, for example, this may include getting one's child accepted into the "right school" when there are too many qualified applicants for the number of seats available, or in persuading other women volunteers to give hundreds of hours of their time for a specific charitable cause.

In The Power of Good Deeds, I examine how elite women, through the volunteer organizations in which they participate—and the very exclusivity of those groups—gain and utilize social power. By limiting membership in these organizations to other elites, privileged women accomplish two things. First, they bring other elite women into their organization—other women with good ties to wealth and prestige—based in part upon the group's elite reputation. Second, by organizing fundraising events that are designed to appeal to and bring in large donations from other affluent people—and the occasional event that is open to anyone who purchases a ticket—they give the group a purpose and a patina that are deemed worthy by their peers and by the community itself. In other words, they make belonging to the group appear to be an act of benevolence rather than one of self-interest.[5]

Participation in this type of elite giving and volunteerism has obvious class implications: It is not an option for women in other classes who do not have the same economic resources or the same access to the "inside players" in elite social networks. In other words, women in other social classes may participate in organizations that benefit worthy causes, but those other organizations will not raise the same levels of money, or provide the same level of social power, that elite women's organizations raise and provide. And women who do not have the "right" backgrounds and connections are simply not invited to join the organizations described in this book. Participation in these organizations also has past-in-present racial and ethnic implications. As a result of historic patterns of racial, ethnic, and religious discrimination, parallel (but not necessarily equal) elite women's organizations were formed—in some instances, more than a century ago. Over the years, most of these groups have changed in some respects, and others have been created, yet patterns of separation remain today: Different elite women's volunteer groups may have similar organizational goals but maintain racially or ethnically identifiable membership rosters. Throughout *The Power of Good Deeds*, I examine this class and racial-ethnic organizational exclusivity and its effect on the good deeds the women perform, the intended or nominal beneficiaries of those good deeds, and how these elite women's activities serve to reproduce the upper-class lifestyle and attitudes of entitlement across generations of elites.

As a sociologist and a member of several elite women's organizations in Texas, a number of years ago I began to notice the apparent contradiction between the stated philanthropic goals of these organizations—which typically include giving time and money to charitable causes that benefit diverse segments of the community—and the exclusionary membership policies and elite rites of passage that are maintained and perpetuated by members of these elite groups. I attended elite debutante presentations like the one I described above first as a guest, then as one of the members who helped in planning and conducting the event. After I had been an active member of one group for several years, my son escorted a debutante at that group's annual ball, and he later became a member of an elite men's organization that holds an annual debutante presentation ball. My husband remains an associate (older married) member of the same group. Because I had not grown up participating in such activities, I felt somewhat like "The Stranger," who was described by Georg Simmel as a person who is both an "insider" and an "outsider"—as an individual who engages in interaction that involves a combination of closeness and distance.[6] I believe my closeness to other women volunteers has helped me describe the inner workings of highly selective elite women's volunteer organizations, while my distance from the more competitive aspects of such endeavors has provided me with greater objectivity to describe the events that unfolded around me during my observation periods.

Over the years I watched as different elite organizations in various cities recognized the children of their members and contributors. As I attended a presentation ball one evening and noticed how few people of color (other than waiters) were present, I commented to a friend about the

limited number of women of color in our organization, which was sponsoring the ball. Her response set me to thinking. "You know that [our or-
ganization] is open to minorities," she said, "and they can join if they
want to, but they just don't. Maybe they have more fun with their own
friends and feel more comfortable at their own social events." If this had
been the first time that I had heard such a statement, I probably would
have thought little more about it, or about the fact that most white Americans do not seek to join predominantly African American organizations
or to participate in their social events. But it occurred to me that my
friend's comment was a recurring theme among many white elites,
namely that people of color do not want to be involved in elite white social circles, even if they are at least technically eligible to participate, to
join. And people of color—especially African Americans—do have their
own by-invitation-only groups and hold their own presentation balls.
Eventually, my sociological imagination went to work, and I began to formulate a series of research questions.

Why do many women from the upper classes join invitational volunteer organizations to do good deeds for other people? Are they engaged in
these activities for the benefit of the community and the less fortunate, or
are they seeking social power for themselves and to enhance the social and
cultural capital of their children? Is their motivation for giving and volunteering some combination of both of these factors? If their motivation is
the betterment of the community, why are so many of these organizations
organized along racial-ethnic and class lines? How do elite women use
prestigious organizations such as the Junior League (a predominantly
white group), The Links (a predominantly black group), and symphony
and opera guilds to accomplish personal and social goals? What effect, if
any, does the exclusivity of these organizations have on members and
their families, and on those—regardless of race or ethnicity—who are outside the upper classes? Finally, how might existing inequalities of race,
ethnicity, and class be exacerbated by seemingly innocuous elite practices
such as a debutante presentation?

This book describes the answers that I have found to these questions
after years of studying the subject of elite women's social activities. I show
how women of the social elite perform many good deeds through their
volunteerism, yet engage in (and justify) exclusionary practices that help
perpetuate the upper classes and maintain class-based privileges for
themselves and their families, all in the name of the good deeds that they
and their organizations perform. My study adds to our knowledge about
how women of the upper classes perceive themselves and their activities,
just as prior ethnographic studies of the homeless, the poor, the middle
class, and the elderly have contributed to our understanding of other segments of the U.S. class structure.[7]

The "Social Elite" in America

In order to look at both older and newer socially elite families, as well as to compare and contrast the experiences of more privileged people of color, it is necessary to have some sort of typology of the women I have studied and to establish categories that will help me explain where various of the women stand in relation to the length of time their families have had wealth and/or high income, the extent to which their social cohesion is based on participation in elite educational, religious, and social venues, and how they are perceived by others in the groups and communities of which they are a part.

Before I discuss the typology that I created, it is important to note that several factors were important in categorizing these women. First, the Texas cities in which this research was conducted are not "old" cities when compared to cities that were established much earlier elsewhere in this country (and where most previous studies of elite women have been conducted) such as New York, Boston, or Philadelphia. Nor are the wealthy women in this study members of well-known "old" money U.S. families such as the duPonts, Mellons, or Rockefellers.

Previous research on the white (Anglo) upper class in the Northeast and West has typically used certain criteria for determining membership in that class. Sociologists such as E. Digby Baltzell, G. William Domhoff, and Susan Ostrander have identified members of the upper class based on such factors as being listed in the *Social Register*, having attended select upper-class schools, and being members of a few elite clubs and organizations located primarily on the east and west coasts of the United States.[8] Typically, those members of the upper class were descendants of families that made their fortunes during the Gilded Age (1870–1910) and passed large amounts of wealth on to subsequent generations; however, throughout the United States there has been a significant decline in the use of listings such as the *Social Register* as an indicator of social status. For example, over the past twenty-five years in cities such as New York, appreciably fewer of the trustees/directors serving on arts and cultural organization boards are also listed in the *Social Register*.[9]

Unlike some of the states where most of the *Social Register* listees have resided, Texas has been a state for slightly more than 150 years and, although the wealth of some families here extends back several centuries and to other regions of the country, many Texas families would be considered to be self-made by comparison with "old money" families elsewhere. However, some of the women in this study are members of families that have had substantial wealth for several generations and, as such, they constitute "old money" for the southwestern United States.

Second, even among the cities involved in this research, distinctions must be made regarding how much wealth exists and what size the socially elite populace is: Many more families have "old money" in Dallas and Houston, for instance, than do most wealthy families in Austin. However, in each of these cities—as is true elsewhere across the country—there are people who are identified by others as being among the social elite, and regardless of the distinctions that can be made, social elites across cities typically engage in similar behavior and have somewhat similar outlooks.

Third, racial and ethnic differences must be noted among social elites. As previous researchers have pointed out, for example, the wealth (as contrasted with income) of African American families across the nation is nowhere near as large as that of their white counterparts.[10] African American, Latino/a, and Asian American families who are considered to be "old guard" or to have "old money" typically do not have the same level of wealth as "old money" Euro-American families. Likewise, as mentioned previously, many elite women of color—especially African American women—participate in separate, parallel social organizations as a result of historic patterns of racial and ethnic separation, and these organizations do not always have the same levels of prestige and social visibility as elite white women's organizations. However, some women in my study are "cross-overs," meaning that they are influential members of elite African American or Latina women's organizations as well as having a significant voice in the decisions made by boards of trustees of historically white elite philanthropic groups.[11]

To distinguish among the women in this research without revealing their identities, I developed a typology into which I could categorize each of the women as I observed or interviewed them, based on what I knew about them, what I learned from others about them, and how they self-identified in regard to characteristics such as the "age of their money"—whether it is older or newer wealth, how well known and well respected their family is in the community, for what length of time their family has resided there, and—where relevant—whether a woman is white (Euro-American), African American, or Latina:

Old Money Families

In the southwestern United States, this category generally consists of white (Euro-American) women who were either born into the older families in their respective communities or have married into such families and fully integrated themselves into the life of the old guard, monied families in their city. Some of these women are major contributors to philanthropic endeavors, having made major contributions to universities, hospitals, arts organizations, and other charitable causes they support. The women in this category typically have a large amount of social power as measured by their ability to get other people to willingly do things for them, such as write a check to their favorite social cause. By contrast, these women do not engage in a lot of hands-on volunteering: They write checks, get other people to donate large sums of money, and serve as honorary chairwomen of nonprofit fundraisers. In some cities, the second and third generation of elite African Americans have now moved into the Old Money category within the African American community; however, these individuals typically would not be viewed as having the same amount of wealth or family recognition as white elites in the same category.

Old Name Families
The primary difference between the women in this category and the previous one is the amount of wealth possessed by their families. Some women with old family names have extensive social power that helps them to get things done in the community, including providing their children with the best educational and social opportunities. Women in this category often have family names that are tied to the political, economic, and/or social positions that previous generations of their family or their husbands' family possessed, and the family name is still well known to current generations who reside in the community. Although women in these families have sufficient wealth to be socially acceptable, they are primarily known as members of "old Austin," "old Dallas," or "old wherever" society, and they are seen as wielding their influence over others in the community more than as being major contributors to charitable causes. Some women in these families zealously guard elite clubs and organizations within the community in an effort to keep out people with new money and those who have arrived in the community in recent decades. Some of the African Americans who would be classified as members of "old name" families are the descendants of black entrepreneurs who established businesses (usually serving the minority community) and attached their names to those endeavors. Examples include owners of businesses such as funeral homes, insurance agencies, and furniture stores, along with those in professions such as medicine, law, and teaching. Some of their children or grandchildren have gained greater economic resources and moved into the Old Money category within the African American community.

New Money Families
New Money families have accumulated vast economic resources during the lifetime of people in the current generation or have moved to the cities in my study from elsewhere, bringing with them substantial amounts of money from endeavors such as high-tech, banking, and top-earning professions. Women in New Money families have less social power in the community and are often largely unknown unless they and their husband

make a major donation to an organization, generating media coverage and a series of thank-you events hosted by the group that received their largesse. The women in this category are more likely to be accepted by "old" society if their families have contributed large sums of money to community endeavors such as the performing arts and activities that benefit children. In exchange for these donations, the New Money families often assume that their names will be attached to buildings, arts venues, clinics, and activities that receive their contributions. Consequently, New Money families are welcomed in many social arenas but not into some of the more prestigious social groups until they are able to build strong social connections with "old" families and thus enhance their social power. A classic example is the high-tech entrepreneur who made billions of dollars during the information boom of the 1990s, donated millions of dollars to various "high visibility" social causes in a Texas city, received a great deal of publicity, and then as a quid pro quo offered to donate yet more money to a popular community cause if the chair of that capital campaign would assist the high-tech entrepreneur in gaining membership in one of the city's oldest clubs, referred to by one person as a "bastion of male privilege."

Worker Bees
Some Worker Bees also are members of Old Money or Old Name families; however, most of these women come from upper-middle-class families and have worked their way into elite women's groups in their communities. Some Worker Bees have a college education and perhaps a professional degree that may help them interface with other members of charitable organizations in the community. These women usually start their rise in the social hierarchy by becoming members of organizations that expect their volunteers to contribute time and talent to fulfilling the mission of that group and therefore welcome such persons as new members. For women in this category (who are not members of Old Money or Old Name families), the rewards for their efforts typically come in the form of social recognition such as being made the chairperson of a key committee or being elected as an officer or by having their child honored by the organization. Worker Bees build their social power by donating their labor power and talents to prestigious organizations. Not only the women but sometimes their husbands are often unpaid workers at the various charity fundraisers and other endeavors supported by the women's organizations—a phenomenon largely unheard of in the other categories of elites.

How the Research Was Conducted

Ethnographic research was necessary in order to learn about the social power exerted by elite women. Other than "glitzy" newspaper and magazine accounts, which typically report the rituals of the upper classes, we have little information about the exercise of social power.[12] My research started in Austin, Texas. I was a resident of the city and became involved in local and regional elite arts and health-related organizations whose board members and major contributors were almost solely from the old-guard Austin families—the Old Money and the Old Name families—but included a few newcomers whose connections made them valuable to the "old Austin" elites. To some extent, I fit into both the Old Name and Worker Bee categories: My husband's family had lived here for several generations and, based on family ties, good friends, and my willingness to work hard on behalf of these groups, I found myself welcomed into their organizations and inner circles.

My initial involvement with two of those organizations—the Austin Symphony Orchestra and the Austin Lyric Opera—arose from my enjoyment of and appreciation for music and the arts, as well as being the parent of a child who was of the age where he could benefit from the activities of such groups. I learned from my own volunteer work that, if a woman with sufficient economic resources and family and social connections worked diligently for a group and helped produce a successful outcome for activities such as fundraisers or if her family gave a sufficient amount of money, other prestigious organizations would often invite the woman to join the group and (perhaps) to serve as a board member of the organization.

Although in the past men had been the primary participants on the more prestigious nonprofit boards in cities such as Austin, the greater involvement of women in all areas of social life beginning in the 1960s brought about greater diversity on boards of elite charitable, philanthropic, and similar organizations. In 1975, the University of Texas named a woman as its president for the first time; the presidents of both the symphony and the opera in Austin at the time of my study were women.

Women such as these were among the first generation to learn how to effectively use social connections that were now open to them more than previously. On a smaller scale, women found that connections across organizations brought them into an increasing array of diverse social and cultural groups whose membership was prestigious and where opportunities for greater visibility and social power in the community were possible. For example, after I was nominated for membership in the Women's Symphony League (WSL; a women's support organization for the Austin Symphony Orchestra), I was able by working from the ground up to move from a new (provisional) member of that group to serving as showhouse chair and in various elected positions on the league's board. From there, I was elected to membership on the board of trustees of the Austin Symphony Orchestra Society (often referred to as the "Big Board" by women of the WSL due to its greater power and influence than the women's group has). For elite women, however, networking and expanding one's sphere of involvement and influence is not restricted to one organization or type of nonprofit volunteer community endeavor. After serving as chair of one of the WSL's two primary fundraisers, I was invited to cochair a ball to raise "seed" money (initial funds) to mount the first season of the Austin Lyric Opera, where I participated for ten years on the board of trustees and served as a vice president. As I became more visible because of my involvement in symphony and orchestra events, other groups—including a hospital foundation and an organization that supports a home for children—also invited me to work for their causes and serve on their respective boards. I gladly accepted.

Networking likewise is not limited to one's own community: Regional and national groups exist that provide women with ties to other upper-class families across the nation. The Women's Symphony League of Austin, for example, provides the opportunity for some members to participate in and be elected to offices in the Texas Association of Symphony Orchestras. For a select few, the opportunity exists to become involved at the national level through the activities of the American Symphony Orchestra League. As I participated in such organizations and activities, I learned that my experiences and those of my peers in Austin were quite similar to those of many women from other cities, large and small, throughout Texas and the nation. As the regional groups would meet in one city or another, members of the host city's league would have the visiting delegates over to their homes for coffee and dinners, where we not only would discuss business-related matters such as membership and fundraising but also our own personal experiences regarding a wide range of other matters.

I believe that I have had a unique opportunity to systematically analyze the issues of race, class, and social power that are raised by this research because of my background in sociology and my unprecedented access to numerous elite women as they went about their roles as key players in high status social organizations. When I began my research, and as I now present my findings, I have found that the questions I initially raised and the answers I have found are very important: We need to know much more about how the U.S. class system operates and the specific part that women play in maintaining and perpetuating race- and class-related privilege in this society.

I began my research with participant observation in the organizations that are discussed above. The participant observation portion of this study took place in a variety of social and business settings: at gala benefits (such as balls, dinner parties, and style shows); at charity sales and thrift shops; at monthly meetings of leagues and guilds and their boards of trustees; and at private parties and social gatherings in private residences and elite clubs. In addition, I conducted extensive in-depth and informal interviews with women in organizations primarily identified with the upper classes in Texas. In one part of the research, 225 members of an elite organization—most of the women in that organization—responded to a questionnaire that examined the women's views on organizational power, socialization of children toward volunteerism, and their own participation in elite clubs and organizations. To protect the identity of all the women who participated, either knowingly or unknowingly, in my study, I have used pseudonyms throughout this book; however, the other information about the women is not fictionalized.

In addition to observations and interviews, I used content analysis that draws upon materials from biographies, journalists' reports, and publications such as *Town and Country, Architectural Digest, W, Fortune,* and *Forbes,* and regional publications such as *Texas Monthly, D Magazine, Park Cities People,* and *West Austin News* that chronicle the activities of social elites. These sources provided rich information about the activities of members of the upper classes and provided insights on how inclusion and exclusion operate on the basis of race, class, and/or gender. The integrated use of participant observation, interviews, and content analysis provides unique insights on how privileged women, in the process of doing good deeds and exercising their leadership skills, also embrace the concept of exclusivity and engage in activities that may re-create race- and class-based segregation on an intergenerational basis.

Commonalities and Differences among the Women

All of the women in this study share certain characteristics. Obviously, their gender is one common factor. The region of the country in which they live is another. Although their wealth may vary widely, nearly all of them are members of households with an annual income that would place them in the top 5 percent of households in this nation. Most of them are married and have children. The women range from 18 to 85 years of age, and most of them have attended or graduated from prestigious colleges or universities. In most cases, they were or had been members of one of the more exclusive sororities on their respective campuses, and some of them are members of alumni groups associated with those sororities. A number of the women married men who had been members of equally prestigious fraternities, and some of them now have children who are members of the same sororities or fraternities. All of the women hold memberships in one or more elite women's organizations and have extensive volunteer résumés.

Although the majority of the women in my research self-identify as white, more than one hundred self-identify as either African American (black), Hispanic (Latina), Asian American, Native American, or as some combination of these categories. Regardless of race/ethnicity, all of the women self-identify as being a member of the socially elite. They all have a "very clear sense of 'we-ness,' of a sense of belonging and consciousness of kind, of class cohesiveness."[13]

Another commonality that the women share, as scholars have previously noted, is the role they play, either intentionally or unintentionally, in preserving social boundaries and fostering cohesion among members of the upper classes. This activity is not accomplished by the individual women alone, however; it is maintained through their efforts to control prestigious institutions and associational arrangements such as schools, clubs and organizations, philanthropy, and the rites of passage reserved for privileged children.[14] To accomplish this control, it becomes necessary for the women to closely guard membership and participation in the organizations from which they gather their power. For example, whether a college woman is a member of Kappa Kappa Gamma (a predominantly white Greek-letter sorority) or of Alpha Kappa Alpha (a predominantly black Greek-letter sorority), she is likely to zealously guard privileged information about her sorority from outsiders, thus ensuring the group's exclusivity. An example of classified information is how one becomes a member of such a sorority in the first place. Some sorority sisters speak about how they are irritated by (or at least frustrated with) "wannabes" who ask questions about how to join their organization. Since membership is a guarded prerogative open only to a select few who are chosen by existing members, those who "have to ask" often are not good candidates for membership, according to one member of Alpha Kappa Alpha:

> I think some girls are too bold in expressing interest in our organization. If they fit in with our group, the Sorors [the sorority sisters] will know who they are. We don't need for them to get in our face and tell us all the reasons they should be asked to pledge. Frankly, some girls just want to wear pink and green and say, "I'm an AKA." They don't want to spend all the time we do in community service projects.

This was a recurring theme among women in elite organizations: Almost universally, they felt that it was very important for their organization to select other like-minded women for membership.

Although the women in my study share many commonalities, some of the most distinctive differences were along racial and ethnic lines. These are, of course, linked to larger issues in U.S. society arising from the historic exclusion of women (and men) of color from all aspects of dominant group social life, resulting in the creation of separate social structures to help those who were less fortunate and to recognize the accomplishments of members of their group.

Three specific differences existed between the elite white women and the women of color in my study. The first has to do with the academic, professional, and social credentials of the women. Most of the younger women of color in my study had more impressive academic, professional, and social service credentials than did the majority of the younger white women. Among the younger social elites in the cities that I studied, for example, African American women were more likely to have earned professional degrees such as a J.D., M.D., or M.B.A. and to have given more years of service to the community before they were invited to join the Junior League or other exclusive social organizations than were the white women. In other words, membership was something that appeared to have been *earned* by the women of color, whereas for many of the white women, membership was almost treated as a *birthright.*

The second difference was the women's level of inclusion in personal, primary group activities such as being invited to another member's home for a social event or being included in the other women's social networks. Some of the women of color indicated that, although they had been invited to serve on an organization's governing board or to participate in its fundraising activities, they felt excluded from the inner group friendships that existed among many of the white members of the same organization. As one woman stated, "They were happy to include me when we were raising money or going to parties in hotel ballrooms, but I would later hear of the Christmas party that someone held in her own home, where most of the members were invited but my husband and I weren't." My own participant observation tended to bear this out: If the entire membership was invited to a white woman's home, the women of color were warmly welcomed, but if only a few good "friends" were invited, the guests rarely included women of color, especially African American women. Although this might in part be attributed to the fact that the white women often had attended the same schools from kindergarten on, had been in the same college sororities and been presented at the same debutante balls, had often served as attendants in each other's weddings, and had husbands and children who were friends with each other; nonetheless, the limited inclusion of women of color in activities not directly related to the organization itself was a distinct area of differentiation.

A final difference between the white women and the women of color was the extent to which women of color who excelled in their community involvement and philanthropy were often seen as "exceptions to the rule" as a result of some unspoken but ingrained belief that people of color were different, were less likely to really be part of the group. Whereas it was assumed that a number of the privileged white women could be the chairperson of the ball, the president of the organization, and be recognized as the group's "volunteer extraordinaire" of the year, the same assumption did not apply to women of color. When referring to an African American woman who was actively involved in several elite organizations, other members would often comment that "Viola is one of a kind"—a distinction not usually made with regard to her white counterparts.

These differences, despite similarities in the women's class background, reflect that, even though sociologists view race as a socially constructed reality, that construct still has great significance with regard to how individuals perceive themselves and how they are treated by others. Although it is an imprecise term, "race" as used in this book will refer to a category of people who have been singled out as inferior or superior, often on the basis of real or alleged physical characteristics such as skin color, hair texture, eye shape, or other subjectively selected attributes.[15] Factors such as skin color and hair texture continue to be a form of distinction not only across racial categories but also within the African American and Latino/a communities, where some people may identify themselves as being in the "in-group" and others as being in the "out-group," based on physical characteristics that have been evaluated either positively or negatively by members of dominant non-Hispanic white groups.

The good deeds that women can do by working together, coupled with the elite social status that they hold in common, has drawn these women into the various organizations that are described in this book and that are typical of similar organizations throughout the country. Each of the organizations includes people who self-identify as white, people who self-identify as African American, Asian American, or Latino/a, and people who find it difficult to self-identify as primarily one of those categories or another. Each of the organizations has members who are active and members who are less active in the day-to-day affairs of the group. Some of the groups, such as the Junior League or the Women's Symphony League, limit their membership to women, whereas others contain both women and men. The focus of my research, however, was not on the organizations themselves but rather on how the women use their organizational affiliations to carry out their goals.

The "Power" of Good Deeds

In conceptual terms, the power these privileged women have is social power derived in large part from the strength in numbers that they gain by uniting to work toward common goals that further organizational, community, and personal needs. As that statement suggests, social power is exercised at the personal, organizational, and societal levels. Scholars have demonstrated that women of the upper classes use their social power to accomplish personal and group goals and, whether intentionally or not, to uphold the privileged position of the upper classes in the larger social order.[16] As Susan Ostrander points out in her study of upper-class women, power motivations "function on both a personal and societal level."[17] According to Ostrander, as women of the upper classes achieve a position of power for their own satisfaction, they also uphold the power and privilege of their class.[18]

One of the most visible examples of women working together is when they share their physical strength to achieve a desired outcome, such as when Worker Bees join together to do something that one of the women, by herself, would not be able to achieve. One day, while I was performing my own assigned tasks at a designer showhouse (a fundraiser in which designers decorate mansions and the general public pays to view the finished product), I could not help but notice as, at the request of the showhouse chair, various men (husbands of the Worker Bees) attempted to move a baby grand piano across the room to where the chairperson wanted it. One after another, the men failed to make the heavy piano budge. Then three of the Symphony League women came into the room, saw that the piano was still where it had been to start with, and—after a brief discussion—completed the task themselves by gathering around the piano and, in a very brief, concerted effort, moving it across the room to the exact location where it was supposed to go. When one of the women saw me looking quizzically at them, she commented, "After the years of experience the three us have had moving appliances and old sofas at the [name of organization] garage sale, moving that little piano was a piece of cake."

Although this example involves physical strength, it is analogous to the many situations in which women work together to accomplish the goals of their organizations. Frequently, these activities involve fundraising projects that benefit other people; however, the women also unite to further their personal goals, such as making sure that their own children are invited to join the "right" sororities or fraternities and to participate in the most prestigious debutante presentations and other upper-class rituals.

Even though the women may exercise social power somewhat differently, the common pattern that I (and other scholars) have identified is how socially elite women accomplish the seemingly contradictory goals of self-aggrandizement and (at the same time) achieving highly desirable outcomes for their charitable causes and the betterment of the community. The power that they exercise is not individual power: Their social power is derived primarily from memberships they hold in prestigious organizations. As previously stated, all of the elite women-only organizations that I have examined have a closed membership, which means that they limit participation to those women who meet certain subtle class-based, and sometimes race-based, criteria. By class-based criteria, I mean a woman's financial ability to pay dues, to buy high-priced tickets to the organization's events, to make large gifts to its fund drives, and to purchase the appropriate (high-priced) clothes, cars, and other accouterments that show that she is a member of the social elite. Race-based criteria are sometimes more difficult to pinpoint. They may include an unspoken belief among many whites that their elite white friends are simply deserving of membership; whereas women of color should have done something to distinguish themselves from others of their category. Gradations of physical features such as skin color may be another unspoken factor—the less different a woman of color looks in comparison with her Euro-American counterparts, the more likely she may be to be included in a group's membership.

Race-based factors may include who a woman knows. Unless an affluent woman of color has a number of friends who are in elite, predominantly white women's organizations, she is unlikely to consider joining such a group; if she is interested in doing so, she may find it difficult to gain adequate sponsorship in order to join and even more difficult to rise to a leadership position in that organization. Achieving a leadership position in a prestigious organization enhances a woman's social power and provides her with opportunities to pursue economic or political goals if she so desires. One highly successful real estate agent/former Junior League president provides this example, "In my years of volunteer work, I got to know the many lovely ladies—and their husbands—who continue to be my best clients. I count on them for word-of-mouth recommendations that bring me some of my best business." The "power" of good deeds is thus twofold: helping others and helping oneself.

Organization of the Chapters

Chapter 2, "Elite Women and Philanthropy," describes the relationship between philanthropy and the lifestyle of many upper-class women and explains why affluent women, who do not have to donate their time and/or money to others, are motivated to engage in acts of giving and volunteering in their communities. In this chapter, I examine how women seek to debunk existing myths about elite women volunteers and seek to build their social power through their involvement in various types of elite women's volunteer organizations—including those that benefit arts and cultural organizations, prestigious schools, hospitals, medical schools, "the diseases" and the "less fortunate," and those that work for the empowerment of racial or ethnic minorities. Finally, the chapter discusses reasons why some elite women—often on the basis of race, class, age, or other factors—participate in some groups and not others, thus demonstrating how these factors intersect with elite women's philanthropy.

In chapter 3, "Good Deeds and Fundraising: It Takes Money to Make (Big) Money," I show how members of elite women's volunteer organizations arrange a diversity of fundraising projects—some of which benefit low-income, minority constituencies—from within the safe cocoon of their prestigious by-invitation-only organizations. Because of their economic resources and social connections, elite women are able to perform good deeds that benefit diverse categories of people while, at the same time, maintaining their own upper-class lifestyle and enhancing their social power through connections with other elite women volunteers. Chapter 3 describes how elite women organize fundraising events, ranging from thrift shops and garage sales to lavish charity balls and multimillion dollar showhouses. It also explains how the women combine "highbrow" fundraising parties where elites can gather for a good time with the "low-brow" fundraising projects that are open to the general public. For example, an elaborate on-site preview party with food, open bar, and entertainment for elites is often held the evening before a Christmas bazaar or citywide charity garage sale is opened to anyone who will pay the price of a general admission ticket. In this chapter, I provide a close-up portrait of elite women as they organize various "society" events, including fashion shows, charity balls, designer showhouses, and elegant fundraising dinners in private homes. Throughout, I seek to show how these women do not see the incongruity between the norm of exclusivity and their desire to reach out by planning events that raise money to help others.

As a result of their early socialization, many elite women are so accustomed to the norm of exclusivity that they do not recognize or question its existence or the effect that it has on other people. In chapter 4, "Learning the Ropes: The Childhood and College Years of Elite Women," I use my observational and interview data to show the significance of the neighborhoods in which these women grew up, the way their friends were selected, the ways they were taught "appropriate" behaviors and beliefs, and their educational experiences in creating the typical elite community volunteer, and how these women raise their own children in much the same way—a process of social reproduction that virtually guarantees that the next generation of elites will come to see their privilege not only as natural but as justified. The latter part of the chapter specifically focuses on the social connections and social power that elite women volunteers derive from their sorority experience in college, and how the ritual of rush is the beginning of a lifelong process of organizational selectivity—often along class and racial-ethnic lines—that the women come to accept as a necessary and inevitable part of the groups to which they belong.

As I continue to track how elite women gain social power and acceptance of their role as community volunteers, chapter 5, "Take a Bow: Debutantes and Good Deeds," concentrates on a topic that has received little attention in the study of social elites in the United States: the debutante presentation and its significance to members of the upper classes. The chapter describes the relationship between the good deeds of elite women and the "bargaining chip" that these deeds give them in having their children gain prominence among the next generation of elites. This chapter describes how rituals such as this assist in the social—and sometimes biological—reproduction of the upper classes. I examine the class- and race-based history of the debutante presentation to show the elaborate process by which a young woman is selected for this honor, and how the goal of "maintaining tradition" is evoked when women are questioned about why this elite rite of passage is so resistant to social change. I distinguish between various debutante presentations based on the racial and ethnic identities of participants and show how elite women's social power is enhanced through their involvement in exclusive women's organizations and their "in-group" social events.

Chapter 6, "Members Only: Organizational Structure and Patterns of Exclusion," utilizes a Weberian analysis to show how members of elite women's organizations often use bureaucratic procedures to maintain the exclusivity of their groups and to control either intentionally or unintentionally the number and type of "outsiders" who are admitted to the organization. I examine how organizational bylaws serve as ground rules for membership, how the division of labor in the group helps to determine who will—and who will not—be invited to membership, and why the hierarchy of an organization at the local, state, or national level may have an influence on bringing about change in organizational structure and diversity of membership.

In chapter 7, "Societal Implications of the Contradictions in Elite Women's Good Deeds," I argue that, although elite women enhance their social power and perform many good deeds in prestigious, invitational volunteer organizations, parallel organizations of elite women of color and elite white women contribute to racial and ethnic segregation across generations. Elite women may use their social power as a mechanism for enforcing class and racial privilege, limiting the opportunities of outsiders not only with regard to the social activities of elites but also with regard to avenues that might enhance their social, economic, and political power. This chapter assesses the societal implications of classism and racial segregation in elite women's organizations and concludes that the philanthropic endeavors of these women serve to legitimate the privileged position of the upper classes, which continues to disadvantage subsequent generations of middle-class and working-class individuals.

This book is not just about the good deeds that elite women perform and the social power that the women gain and exercise by belonging to the organizations through which those deeds are performed. Even as it seeks to provide the reader with a fuller appreciation of how much work these women do and the kinds of money they raise from various fundraising projects, this book also seeks to raise pressing social questions about the persistence of racial and ethnic separation and the class-exclusive nature of the social reproduction of the upper classes. What difference does this make to others who might want to be socially mobile or to make connections that might help themselves and their children to greater social and economic opportunities? Privilege advantages elite women over others in that they have greater control over the life chances and opportunities of themselves, their children, and other members of their family. Elite women can also exert social control over those in other classes, whom they help with their volunteer efforts, hire as their household workers, or who serve in staff positions in nonprofit organizations. Similarly, elite women gain control over the social interaction process by determining who is invited to certain events, where they will sit, who will be near them, and what types of social networks may be developed, especially regarding their own children's inner circle as they grow up. By the time the typical elite child is an adult, he or she is accustomed to associating only with certain people, giving advantages to—and receiving advantages from—others within his or her own group, and having little, if any, social interaction with those who remain outside the comfort zone. Whereas public accommodations such as trains, planes, and buses have been long desegregated, the most exclusive private clubs and organizations reflect that our society remains staunchly divided along the lines of race, class, gender, religion, and other socially valued or devalued characteristics.

In sum, my research suggests that social mobility requires more of individuals than simply making significant economic gains—especially for women of color who continue to find themselves marginalized with regard to predominantly white organizations such as elite women's groups. This is an important sociological issue when we consider the fact that the activities of members of the upper classes today will have a significant effect on the America of tomorrow.

Notes

1. For a discussion of early debutante presentations and how they were modified to suit changing times, see Cable 1984 and Montgomery 1998. In regard to the supposed decline of the debutante season, Domhoff (1998: 95) found that, despite the media's suggestion that such events were out of favor even with elites, one of the latent functions of this upper-class rite of passage is to maintain and perpetuate the upper class from generation to generation.

2. All of the names of the women in my study are pseudonyms. To protect each woman's privacy and that of her family, I have not revealed anyone's true identity. As is true of all sociological research, it is the responsibility of the researcher to protect the identity of those who agree to participate in a study as

well as those who are the "subjects" in observational research. When I used a questionnaire on one occasion, my research assistant had participants sign a separate consent form. These women also are not identified by name in this book.

3. French and Raven 1959; Raven 1988.

4. Carli 1999 looked at the relative inequities in social power between women and men and how they exert influence by changing the opinions of others.

5. In her recent book, *Why the Wealthy Give: The Culture of Elite Philanthropy*, Ostrower (1995: 12) explores the normative basis of elite philanthropy and concludes that some wealthy women and men live in a "milieu in which giving is a norm" and philanthropy is "an obligation that is part of their privileged position." According to Ostrower, the wealthy donors in her study were more focused on how their peers would perceive their philanthropic endeavors rather than how those outside their class might view such activities. I believe this is true of the women in my study as well; they are more concerned about how their good deeds will look to "insiders" in the organization and frequently mask any self-interest they may have (such as the desire to see their daughter presented as a debutante) by stating another reason (such as a "helping the poor" or a "love for classical music") as a motivating factor behind their giving and volunteering.

6. Simmel 1971 [1908].

7. See, for example, Snow and Anderson (1993) regarding the homeless; Nelson and Smith (1999) on the working class in small towns; Newman (1999) on the working poor in the inner city; and Allahyari (2000) on volunteer work with the poor and homeless.

8. In this study, I have drawn extensively on the work of Baltzell 1958; Domhoff 1970, 1998; and Ostrander 1984 to formulate my research and organize my data. Although novelists and journalists have been fascinated with elite women for centuries, few sociologists have systematically examined the role that upper-class women play in the U.S. class system, particularly how they are able to build on the dimension of social status or esteem to perpetuate upper-class unity across generations of elites.

9. Ostrower 1995.

10. See, for example, Oliver and Shapiro 1995.

11. I borrowed the term "cross-over" from one of the African American women in my study who referred to herself in this manner. The term takes on additional significance in cities such as the one in which she lived, where a large proportion of the middle- and working-class African American population lives in an area that is divided by a highway, lake, or another structural barrier from what is referred to by this woman and others as the "white community" or "the other side of the tracks."

12. Domhoff 1998.

13. Ostrander 1980a: 82.

14. Baltzell 1958, 1964; Cookson and Persell 1985; Daniels 1988; Domhoff 1998; and Mills 2000 [1956].

15. Feagin and Feagin 1999.

16. Daniels 1988; Odendahl 1990; Ostrander 1980b, 1984; and Ostrower 1995.

17. Ostrander 1980b: 31.

18. Ostrander 1980b; 1984.

CHAPTER TWO

❧

Elite Women and Philanthropy

It's great helping to build the city. You want to have all the cultural aspects of a city. . . . It would be naive to say the economy will not affect philanthropy. But typically people who give for emotional and other reasons find ways to budget it into their lives.

—Susan Dell, wife of Dell Computer founder and CEO billionaire Michael Dell, discussing their $10 million donation to an arts center, one of many gifts totaling millions of dollars the couple has given to various cultural and religious organizations in Austin, Texas[1]

As philanthropists, the Dells are relative newcomers to a long line of wealthy donors who have given of their time and money to nonprofit organizations. Philanthropy, "the spirit of active goodwill toward others as demonstrated in efforts to promote their welfare,"[2] takes place at all levels of the class structure; however, it is uniquely identified with the upper classes, whose members have a greater ability to make large financial contributions than do those in the lower tiers of the class structure. Although in the past, the philanthropist was portrayed as an "old money" male from a well-known family such as the Rockefellers, Fords, Mellons, or Carnegies, today many generous contributors to philanthropic organizations are women and families whose fortunes have been made within their own lifetimes.

This book is about upper-class and upper-middle-class women who, through their volunteer efforts and the elite groups that they have organized to assist them with those efforts, engage in philanthropy. Giving and volunteering serve as major sources of elite women's social power because, through philanthropy, the women can reward or exclude others, demonstrate their own expert and legitimate power, or use their referent power to draw others to them and their good causes. In this chapter, I examine the relationship between philanthropy and the lifestyle of many upper-class women, noting how both the women (and their families) and the diversity of people served by their volunteer organizations benefit from that philanthropy. I then discuss the general categories of organizations to which these women belong and why different women—frequently on the basis of race, class, and age in addition to other factors—may participate in one type of elite organization rather than another. Finally, I provide an initial look (discussed in greater detail in subsequent chapters) at how the exclusivity that is a hallmark of most, if not all, of the groups, with regard to their membership practices has an impact on the women themselves and on the individuals, organizations, and communities that are the beneficiaries of their volunteer efforts.

Philanthropy and the Upper-Class Lifestyle

Although the term *philanthropy* is often used interchangeably with *charity,* some scholars believe that it is important to distinguish between the concepts. Charity is often thought of as a form of philanthropy that specifically benefits poor, disadvantaged, or disabled recipients; whereas elite forms of philanthropy may support institutions—such as prestigious universities or art museums—that may primarily serve the interests of the upper classes.[3]

It is no surprise that philanthropic activities are most closely identified with the upper class. For centuries, elite philanthropy has been a way of life for a subset of wealthy social elites who derive much of their identity from giving and volunteering. Specifically, philanthropy serves as a vehicle for the cultural and social life of the upper class, giving members of that class a sense of belonging and the ability to make connections, for themselves and their children, with other similarly situated people.[4]

As participants in the upper-class lifestyle, elite women have received less recognition for their efforts on behalf of charitable and cultural organizations because they have been overshadowed by the male image of the philanthropist, who historically has claimed legitimate power over the fundraising and disbursement endeavors of charitable organizations. In many wealthy families it is the father or husband who writes the large checks to institutions, ensuring that the family name will appear on a building, or at least on a printed program, acknowledging their contribution to the organization. However, beginning with the publication of several studies on elite community volunteerism by Susan A. Ostrander, Arlene Kaplan Daniels, Kathleen D. McCarthy, Teresa Odendahl, Francie

Ostrower,[5] and others, greater awareness of the role of privileged white women as philanthropists and community volunteers has emerged in social science and popular literature. Several common themes are found in such studies of upper-class women's philanthropy. First, the role of "community volunteer" is a central preoccupation for many upper-class women. Second, elite philanthropy usually benefits the wealthy more than it does the poor or the disadvantaged. And, finally, participating in highly selective volunteer endeavors helps privileged women develop their leadership skills and expert power and pursue their self-interests while preserving the privileged position of their class. My research builds on and extends the works of these scholars by providing a more in-depth analysis of the volunteer activities in which these women participate and by examining their philanthropy across racial and ethnic categories. This study shows how the social elite's accepted belief in the legitimacy of the norm of exclusivity not only contributes to the success of prestigious nonprofit organizations but also serves to perpetuate racial and ethnic segregation. By the *norm of exclusivity*, I am referring to the tendency of members of an organization from which other people are excluded to assume that the exclusion of individuals or categories of people who are not deemed to possess the attributes most highly valued by the current membership—often based on social, racial or ethnic, religious, academic, or economic criteria— is highly appropriate. By way of example, the students at an elite school are not likely to question the absence of other students who do not meet the school's admissions criteria.[6] By the same token, members of an elite women's organization are not—as a result of this norm—likely to question the fact that other people, who do not meet the spoken or unspoken criteria for membership, are not invited to participate.

The Increasing Role of Women in the Major Leagues of Philanthropy

At the national level, women have a rising influence in philanthropy. Some are giving inherited money to worthy causes and demanding accountability for the funds. Others are giving money that they themselves have earned to their favorite causes. In recent decades, "women's funds" have grown in number and in wealth, as money is raised and given out by women, often to causes that benefit women. The rewards—in the form of grants and other stipends—that women's funds give out may serve as a source of social power for the women in these groups. It is estimated that there were about one hundred women's funds at the beginning of the twenty-first century, as contrasted with only five such funds in the early 1980s.[7] However, women's influence is not limited to funds primarily by and for women: Old-line philanthropic institutions have also seen an increase in the number of women who run foundations such as the MacArthur Foundation and the Pew Charitable Trust.[8] Likewise, many nonprofit organizations have become more aware of women as potential givers and trustees, and some have zealously courted women's greater involvement in their institutions. Some women who have reached the top tiers of these organizations have enhanced their social power not only in the world of philanthropy but sometimes in the corporate sector as well.

The primary focus of my research is elite women's community volunteerism, rather than looking at the "check writers" who primarily give large sums of money to nonprofit organizations. Volunteer work is "unpaid work provided to parties to whom the worker owes no contractual, familial, or friendship obligations."[9] Scholars have suggested that volunteer work is productive work that requires human, social, and cultural capital for its fulfillment.[10] At the individual level, *human capital* refers to the "work-relevant skills and material resources (e.g., tools, transportation, credit) that individuals bring to jobs."[11] At the relational level, *social capital* is the groups and organizations to which a person belongs and the social networks (who people know) that arise as a result. Social networks are valuable if those within the networks act in a reciprocal manner to help each other out. Social capital is related to social power; however, as I am using these terms, social power is a more dynamic concept than social capital because it suggests the ability to have both *power over* other people and the *power to do* what an individual desires to do. Elite women have power over others and the power to get things done when it comes to community volunteerism. The third form of capital is what Pierre Bourdieu refers to as *cultural capital*—the ideas, knowledge, and cultural style that people draw upon as they participate in social life.[12] This concept has been widely accepted by scholars because it provides a framework for looking at how culture can serve as a form of capital that is acquired through learning activities and specific social experiences. In their study of volunteer work, John Wilson and Marc Musick state that, "Like any other form of capital, [cultural capital] can be 'invested' to yield 'social profits' in the form of symbolic goods, such as titles, honors, and club memberships. These 'social profits,' in turn, yield social esteem, which is denied to those who lack cultural capital."[13] Some elite women volunteers are rich in all three of these forms of capital, which makes it possible for them not only to have economic power but also to exercise various forms of social power.

As in many other forms of volunteerism, elite women's voluntary organizations are hierarchically arranged, starting at the top with positions held in particularly high esteem, such as being a board member or the chair of a high-profile fundraising event such as a ball or a showhouse. Although this also is true with regard to elite men's voluntary organizations, certain distinct differences are readily apparent. For example, for many affluent women, community volunteerism is related to their lack of employment outside the household.[14] In this case, volunteering may serve as an alternative to work or provide the women with an opportunity to do something worthwhile that will not interfere with their family life or other social activities. Volunteering provides these women with an opportunity to develop social power that otherwise is unavailable to them. By contrast, elite men typically do not view volunteering as an alternative to paid work or to doing nothing but rather see it as an additional activity in their lives.[15] For some men, serving on a prestigious nonprofit board is an extension of their leadership roles in corporate America or in a profession. As more women from the upper classes have entered professions or achieved greater visibility as members of boards of trustees for nonprofit organizations, some scholars believe that their views on philanthropy overall have become similar to those of elite men and that such views serve as a "bastion of class privilege and conservatism."[16]

The Ups and Downs of
Elite Women's Giving and Volunteering

Elite women in the United States have been involved in giving and volunteering since the founding of this nation. Even when all women were denied access to economic and political power, some women of the social elite chose to participate in philanthropic acts of giving or volunteering. The general assumption behind such acts of generosity was that they would help others, particularly the less fortunate, and that in doing such good deeds, the women themselves would benefit by developing their leadership skills and enhancing their social power. An early example was Jane Addams, a wealthy, college-educated woman who turned an old mansion in Chicago into a settlement house to help immigrants who lived in the slums. After Addams's graduation from college and a trip to Europe, she decided that her life was devoid of purpose apart from her charity work. Along with Ellen Gates Starr and a number of other privileged women, Addams opened Hull House in 1889, using both her own money and outside donations. This settlement house started as a single house but eventually became a large cluster of buildings where volunteers sought to bring relief to young women, the poor, and recent immigrants, including a large number of African Americans who migrated to Chicago from the southern United States. Addams also advocated social reforms such as the abolition of child labor, the regulation of working hours and conditions for women, and changes in juvenile law. Addams's work at Hull House has been described as reflecting the "subjective necessity of providing an outlet for the energies and benevolent impulses of wealthy, educated women" as well as dealing with the "objective necessity of relieving the sufferings of the urban poor."[17] With the work of Addams and other women like her, elite women's volunteerism started to be shaped as a "career" that involved addressing humanitarian concerns while opening up new opportunities for the women who participated.

Today, many elite women have created their own "volunteer career" that shares certain common characteristics with the careers of people in the paid workforce.[18] Through the development of expert power, elite women who are community volunteers can distinguish themselves in ways that women and men in other classes cannot. A volunteer career is uniquely open to upper-class women because of their class position, their family names, and the training they receive as members of the Junior League, The Links, or similar groups and through their service on nonprofit boards.[19] However, not all upper-class women are actively involved in philanthropy. Initially, I expected that the ones who *were* actively involved might somehow look down on those who *were not* involved, yet this wasn't the case. They simply accepted as a fact that some elite women weren't interested in such pursuits. On the other hand, the women did speak derogatorily of those within their volunteer organizations who did not spend sufficient time, money, and effort in furtherance of the group's goals.

Elite women who are active in volunteer work make a major contribution to their communities through the time and resources they invest in organizations that benefit other people; however, many also gain social power in the process. Although it is true, as some scholars suggest, that the work of these women preserves the privilege of the upper class and may help to take the rough edges off an abusive capitalistic economic system,[20] elite women typically do not acknowledge the class-based implications of their work and focus instead on the importance of their activities. As Jeanine, a 40-year-old white woman who formerly served as president of an elite women's organization, commented,

> Giving my time as a community volunteer is one of the most important things I do apart from taking care of my family. I love being with other hard-working, fun-loving women as we work on [our major fund-raising event]. Did you know that [our organization] donates more than 100,000 hours of volunteer time, not to mention over $1,000,000 a year, to projects in this city? I am extremely proud to be a member of this group! I am as close to the other members as I am to my sister, and I don't want to see my relations with others change because of new membership guidelines.

Jeanine's statement alludes to referent power, which is relationship-based. She gives the distinct impression that members of the group view themselves as family members, and that "outsiders" would like to join them in order to gain the benefits that might accrue from associating with "insiders," but that her group possesses the power to decide which women will—or will not—be admitted to the inner circle.

The ability to raise funds for an organization is central to the work of all volunteers, but it is especially true for women of the upper classes. Their organizations rely on rich, well-connected women—and men—to "bring home the bacon" (in the words of the development director of one arts organization). The pressure is often heavy on both paid staff members and elite volunteers to raise large sums of money and build an endowment that will meet the economic needs of the organization. One board member of a volunteer organization stated that her organization's informal motto is "Give it or get it." In other words, members should either give large sums of their own money or they should get their friends, families, and business associates—or people in general—to make substantial contributions. In fact, those socially elite women who want to be considered active participants in the organization should do both in order to demonstrate their commitment to the institution.

Whereas "giving" typically refers to writing a check or donating something that has some monetary value (such as shares of stock), volunteering refers to the commitment of time, energy, and talent to an organization. Some volunteer jobs require "face-time," meaning that the volunteer must be present for a specific number of hours, performing assigned tasks. Being a docent in a designer showhouse in an example: Docents must know basic facts about the showhouse and be able to explain to visitors what the designer has done in a specific room.

Jobs that involve working with clients from lower socioeconomic categories, such as indigent children and their parents, are sometimes referred to as "working in the trenches." Trench work may occur in many locations, including homes that serve children who are without parents, charity garage sales, or cleaning up after the ball at 2:00 A.M. Another term used to describe face-time and trench-time is "hands-on" work, which is contrasted with "check writing" (just writing a check rather than personally participating in the work). Since members may be able to "go associate" after a certain number of years of active service and thus no longer be required to work on group projects, volunteer organizations must continually invite a certain number of "acceptable" new members to join their ranks to have "enough bodies to get the work done," as Carleen, who served as chair of a large annual fundraising benefit, stated:

> If all our members stayed home and just wrote checks, we'd never make it! Most of the money we donate comes from fundraising projects that require members to participate. If they didn't show up to do the work, we'd never make our budget.

Even so, some members are permitted to stay in the "clean hands" category if they write large checks or have sufficient social power and economic clout with other members of the group. An example of a "clean hands" volunteer is Nicole. Carleen recalled conduct typical of Nicole (who was considered Old Money by most other members) as follows:

> Nicole agreed to bring some food to help feed the volunteers while they were setting up for [the major fundraiser]. She said that this was all she could possibly do because of her busy schedule. On the day when she was supposed to have her food there, she literally came running through the door with a large bowl in her hand, set it down quickly on the table, and said, "Sorry I'm late. My maid was running behind today, and she almost didn't get this made. See you later!" And with that Nicole was gone, . . . never to be seen again throughout the days that most of us showed up and worked a number of hours.

Because Nicole wanted to be a member of this prestigious group, she did the minimum to remain in good standing in that organization. Unfortunately, Nicole fits the negative stereotypes of elite women that many in my study have sought to overcome by their efforts on behalf of the community.

Overcoming Stereotypes of Elite Women Volunteers

Many elite women volunteers would be appalled at Nicole's behavior. They pride themselves on the time, energy, and talent that they personally put into their community endeavors. Previous studies show that upper-class women volunteers often use their work as a way to distinguish themselves from the stereotypes of privileged women as being either the *idle socialite* or the *Lady Bountiful*.[21] Dedicated volunteers have tried for many years to overcome the image of the first of these stereotypes, that of the idle socialite, a term initially used to describe women such as "Mrs. Astor" (Caroline Schermerhorn Astor), who was famous for giving lavish parties for her wealthy inner circle of socially acceptable New Yorkers in the late nineteenth century.[22] They also have attempted to distance themselves from the stereotype of Lady Bountiful, a "naive, but well-intentioned 'do-gooder,' sympathetic to the plight of the lower classes but not truly understanding. She has nothing better to do. The lady bountiful is utterly removed from the hardships of the world around her."[23]

These portrayals have served to stigmatize and trivialize women's philanthropy in the United States.[24] Although changes have occurred as more women have entered the economic, political, and social mainstream, vestiges of the earlier stereotypes remain, and in some cases the clichés are so prevalent that a few elite women may use the terms to describe others.

For example, in one of my participant-observation sessions, I listened as two women in leadership roles had a rather strong disagreement (in the presence of several other women) about an arts organization's ball they were planning. After the argument was over and one of the women had left the room, the other participant turned to her assembled friends and stated, "I get so mad at Marla. When she gets on her 'high horse' like that, she thinks she's Mrs. Astor." To which another woman replied, "Yes, with Marla it's 'my way or the highway.'"

These women's remarks demonstrate my point. For the most part, elite women volunteers work hard to dispel the myth that they are like either Mrs. Astor or Lady Bountiful as they perform their volunteer activities. Although their own sense of values—of what is right and wrong, good and bad—inevitably comes into play as they engage in their volunteer work, they try to avoid being well-intentioned "do gooders." They seek to better their communities and to be of service to the less fortunate. They know that, to accomplish such goals, they must work together. Most of them are willing to spend many hours in the hands-on and trench work described earlier in this chapter. In some cities, leaders of the Junior League and similar women's volunteer organizations have stated, "We are not a white-glove organization. We roll up our sleeves and get the job done!" This attitude is expressed by women who work in a variety of organizations and who consider themselves to be specialists in a specific area of community service. I will now describe some of the venues in which elite women's volunteerism and giving are most likely to occur.

Philanthropic Diversity and Women's Good Deeds

What factors motivate some elite women to join certain volunteer organizations whereas others are drawn to organizations with entirely different agendas? Although it is not possible to state all of the reasons, there appear to be four major motivating factors for the women in my study: First, class factors, including the woman's family and friends as well as her (or her family's) wealth. Second, the age of the woman and of her children. Third, the woman's race and ethnic background. Fourth, what might best be referred to as special circumstances—the woman being exposed to some stimulus such as an illness that motivates her to "do something" about a problem or to become an advocate for a cause. To show how these factors come into play, I have divided the elite organizations represented in this study into five categories: arts and cultural organizations, groups that work for the benefit of prestigious schools, foundations that support hospitals and efforts to battle "the diseases," charity organizations that help "the less fortunate," and groups that seek to empower members of racial and ethnic minority categories. Understanding the types of organizations to which these women belong, and what those organizations seek to do, helps us understand the relationship between elite women and philanthropy—why they belong to such organizations and what they seek to accomplish by belonging.

Arts and Cultural Organizations

Organizations that support the arts and other cultural endeavors continually look for new ways to raise money to support the group and its programs. Elite women are highly instrumental in raising money for these nonprofit organizations and, in recent decades, an increasing number of women have been elected to serve on the boards of trustees of major symphony orchestra associations, opera and ballet companies, and art museums.[25]

As previous studies have shown, women's motivation for volunteer service and charitable donations to arts and cultural organizations is tied to their class and family position.[26] Class factors—including a woman's family and friends and her ability to spend substantial amounts of money on membership fees, high-priced tickets, and designer clothing for a symphony or opera performance or gala—are important determinants in whether a particular woman is likely to join an elite cultural organization and actively participate in its activities.

The importance of contributing time and money to cultural organizations has been instilled in many of the women in this study since their childhood years, when they saw their parents participate in and benefit from such philanthropy, and when they themselves were provided with the opportunity to study music and art. Appreciation of the fine arts is an integral part of the elite girl's socialization. Elite women volunteers often have attended a prep school that boasts of having an outstanding fine arts curriculum. Most women in this study have traveled extensively to see the world's greatest art museums, and in their childhood and youth were honored as "royalty" at balls sponsored by a local cultural organization. Women with a long-term enjoyment of and commitment to the arts often follow through with this involvement throughout their lives, as Melissa—who was from a New Money family and currently serving as president of a ballet guild when I interviewed her—explained:

> I've loved the ballet since I could barely walk. When I was five, I started dance class, and Mother bought me a pink tutu that I insisted on wearing at all the wrong times. . . . My parents took me to see professional ballet companies in other cities. In the many years of our marriage, Tom and I have been regular contributors to the ballet, and we've had many fundraisers and parties honoring major donors at our home. I'm proud of our work for the ballet, and I want to encourage others to become involved.

Among women from privileged family backgrounds, interest in the arts cuts across racial and ethnic categories. Women of color, as well as white women, described their long-term interest in music, theater, and art. Most indicated that parents or teachers had introduced them to "the joys of" music or the visual arts in a manner that had "genuinely enriched" their lives. However, some women of color stated that one purpose of their current involvement in elite organizations was to bring greater diversity to the cultural activities and art exhibits that are available in their community. Linda, a Latina upper-middle-class Worker Bee in her mid-30s who was serving as an arts board trustee, for example, was interested in showing the Latino/a children in her community that they had a cultural heritage that they should be proud of, a heritage that she came to appreciate as a child:

> My passion is good art, especially works that show the cultural diversity of the United States. When my parents took me to art museums, I wondered why there were so few Latin American artists. It seemed like they always featured the paintings of Europeans or "Americans," so I thought Latinos weren't really in the artistic community. Thank heavens, I've learned differently. That's why I'm happy to be on the board [of trustees] of this museum: We make an extra effort to include high quality art from many cultures, and we consider gender when we are planning programs. The board and staff especially target children who attend [schools in predominantly low-income, high-minority population areas of the city]. We've introduced a number of traditions to the city, including the annual Dia de los Muertos [Day of the Dead] program.

As these comments suggest, elite women typically become aware of the arts at an early age and continue to pursue those interests in different forms throughout adulthood. The parents of the women usually had the financial ability to take them to arts and cultural events throughout the country and sometimes around the world so that their daughters could be exposed to "the best that the art world has to offer," as one woman noted. The women in my study, as is typical of elite women everywhere, had accumulated large quantities of cultural capital and possess the attitudes, knowledge, and preferences to which the word "taste" is often applied.[27]

The elite women volunteers in this study expressed a desire to share their appreciation of music, art, and other cultural forms with others. They describe their volunteer efforts as helping others, particularly "those children and young people who have not had much exposure to the finer things in life," as one woman stated. Elite women's work in arts and cultural organizations helps them fulfill several goals simultaneously: The women believe that they can enrich the lives of others while gaining personal satisfaction for themselves and social recognition for their families.

Although their comments about their motivations typically reflect their own personal interests, such as "I've always loved classical music" or "I want to see our city build a really world-class art museum," there is much more to the story than just this.

Love of the arts is one of many reasons why elite women participate in prestigious arts and cultural groups. According to Ostrower,[28] participating in cultural activities is an important component of the social life of many members of the social elite: "The enjoyment of cultural activities is more than an individual pursuit. Performances and exhibitions also provide settings in which members of the elite come together with their peers." Through check writing and/or giving volunteer hours, elite women and their families derive benefits from associating with others of their social class who support and attend cultural events. Although many of the exhibits and performances the women help fund are open to the public, social elites frequently gather at private functions before the opening of exhibits or performances and meet in other by-invitation-only "in-group" settings from which the general public is excluded. An example is a cocktail party and private viewing for major donors (typically put on by the trustees and staff of the museum) of a new art exhibit before the exhibit is open to the public.

Like the class- and race-based interests that motivate elite women to volunteer for cultural organizations, age is also a salient factor. The age of the women involved, as well as the respective ages of their children, may be a factor in why particular women become involved in these organizations and the types of activities in which they agree to participate. Women who have young children frequently are interested in giving to cultural programs that they believe will enrich their children's lives and give them an opportunity to associate with other children from similar family backgrounds. As one mother stated, the children "learn to appreciate the arts and also come to believe that this is a 'cool' thing to do because they see their friends involved in these activities."

When their children reach their middle school and high school years, the women work hard for organizations that honor children, showing them off at fashion shows and balls to other members of their social circle. An example of this is an arts organization that introduces onstage the formally attired children of those members who have worked the hardest for the group. When children are the age to be presented as debutantes or the escorts of debutantes, their mothers have already put in many years of work—often as much as two decades, if their children are to be chosen to receive "top billing" in a debutante presentation.

How active some of these women are in arts organizations may also relate to the ages of their children and even their grandchildren, showing greater devotion "to the cause" when their children are young or high school and college aged and again later when their daughters are the right age to join the group or their grandchildren are approaching the age at which they might be presented to society.

Prestigious Schools

Class, race, and age also are factors in determining the extent to which an elite woman will participate in organizations that support prestigious schools. The key factor, however, appears to be whether or not the woman perceives that she or her children have benefited (or stand to benefit) from those schools. The schools represented in this study range from prep schools (typically private day and boarding schools) to a number of "top tier" universities. Although the children of many wealthy families in the Southwest attend highly ranked public schools in affluent enclaves or suburbs, a number of children in the Old Money and Old Name categories attend private preschools and prep schools, where they are "legacy," meaning that an older sibling or at least one of their parents attended this school.

Many privileged women work on behalf of these schools because of the important relationship between the private school experience and the upper-class lifestyle. An elite education paves the way to a successful life in the U.S. upper class in that it teaches children the values and knowledge that will be expected of them in adult roles. Peter W. Cookson, Jr. and Caroline Hodges Persell, who studied elite U.S. boarding schools, state that, "To be accepted into a private school is to be accepted into a social club, or more generally speaking, a status group that is defined as a group of people who feel a sense of social similarity. People sharing the same status have similar life-styles, common educational background, and pursue similar types of occupations."[29] As a result, a shared experience binds generations in a family to a specific school and ensures that they will commit time and resources to maintain and perpetuate these institutions. A typical example is Virginia, a white pediatrician in the Old Name family category, who described her family's long-term connection with a prestigious prep school that her daughter attends:

> Sara goes to Hockaday because she comes from three generations of "Hockadaisies." When she was very young, her grandmother told her about "taking tea" with Miss Ela Hockaday [the school's founder and headmistress for many years] when she was a student there. . . . Now, I am happy to do anything I can to help out. I really like to work the auction. Volunteers get people to donate really great things for people to bid on, like a week at a resort or the golf clubs of a famous golfer that makes the dads go wild. Volunteers keep everything running smoothly at the auction, and we try to make sure that guests have a good time and come back next year. It's all for a good cause. We raise lots of money [for the school] while having one heck of a good time!

Virginia enjoys being part of a family tradition in which several generations have attended the same school. Volunteering at the school and giving money are also family traditions honored by many elite women.[30]

The elite women who volunteer at prestigious prep schools today are
more diverse than in the past as a result of the greater inclusion of more
students of color in the enrollment of these schools. Statistics made available by the Hockaday School, for example, show that minority students
comprised almost one-fourth (23 percent) of the student body in the
1999–2000 academic year.[31] Some women of color who may not have attended a prestigious prep school can become very loyal to a school and be
involved in volunteer efforts there if they believe that their children are
being treated with dignity and respect and that they are acquiring a high-
quality education. Carrie, an Ivy League–educated African American
mother who has volunteered for a number of years at a prestigious day
and boarding school, explained how she and her husband, a successful
physician, had decided to enroll her son (a first generation student) at the
school and why she has remained so loyal to the school:

> We bought a new house in a nice area of [city] when [my husband] came
> here to set up his medical practice. We were pleased with the public schools
> in the area. Since it was a relatively new subdivision, the schools were fairly
> new, and the teachers and principal seemed genuinely interested in the kids.
> Well, we had no more than moved in when the school district, under a
> judge's mandate, instituted cross-town busing, as they called it. The idea
> was to send white kids to predominantly minority schools across town, and
> to bring some of those kids to the white schools. Although I can see a lot of
> good reasons for doing something like this, given the racial segregation of
> the South, I couldn't see having George ride a school bus for thirty or forty-
> five minutes over to the other side of town just so that he could be with
> other black students like himself. Instead, we decided to put him on a bus
> to [an elite school] where the teachers were known for really caring and for
> helping their students to achieve success. George loved the school and re-
> ally excelled there, thanks to teachers who saw his potential and helped him
> reach it. Although he graduated a number of years ago, my husband and I
> will continue to support the school.

Like Carrie, other elite women of color who participated in volunteer
work at their children's prep school expressed satisfaction with the kind
of education their children were receiving, as well as how they, as parents,
were accepted by teachers, students, and other parents.

Elite women not only are actively involved in giving and volunteering
at prestigious prep schools, but also they contribute time and money to institutions of higher education. However, their contributions are not to just
any school: Major gifts and volunteer efforts are directly linked to the

woman's commitment to a specific institution she has attended or that has special meaning to her family, not to higher education generally.[32] The women in this study felt a sense of indebtedness and loyalty to schools that they believed had contributed to their sense of personal fulfillment and success. "I was born with [school colors] blood" is a frequent statement made by elite women who hold season tickets to athletic events, serve on alumni committees, and assist in the fundraising endeavors of their alma maters.

The good deeds of elite women in higher education benefit a wide diversity of people, including students who are *not* from upper-class families. The opportunity to graduate from college provides students with a source for upward mobility. However, elite women and their families also gain from their good deeds: They are invited to participate in exclusive by-invitation-only events, such as luncheons and dinners held at the university chancellor's residence or other special events that are not open to those who have not made generous donations of their time and money. Some women's good deeds, especially in the area of fundraising, receive great acclaim from university officials, such as the one who stated,

> Women with the "right" connections help us tremendously in our fundraising efforts. The development board is especially crucial. People give money to [this school] because their friends ask them to, not because our offices send out solicitation letters or have parties for donors. Sure, we want to thank those who have been helpful to us—a plaque or a luncheon is only a small token of our appreciation for their dedication.

Elite women's contributions to education do not always flow solely to traditionally white universities. Some privileged white women serve on boards of regents of historically black colleges and other institutions with large percentages of underrepresented minority groups in the student body. Likewise, some elite women of color are alumni of traditionally white institutions and may be active volunteers for alumni groups or involved in fundraising for specific colleges or departments within the university. An example is Marta, a Mexican American Worker Bee with a law degree from an elite, predominantly white university:

> I came from a wonderful family of migrant farm workers in South Texas. Without the outreach of this university, I would not be who I am today. Even though the school has many wealthy donors, I want to do my small part to show how grateful I am for the opportunities I've had.

One African American woman who attended a prestigious historically black college in the South stated that she had spent many hours raising scholarship money for her school and for the United Negro College Fund.

She believes that students attending historically black colleges should have the same opportunity to get an outstanding college education as those who attend predominantly white institutions:

> You've seen the ads for the United Negro College Fund—"a mind is a terrible thing to waste." Well, that's my motto, too. Whatever I can do to help young people have a chance to "make it," I'll try to do. Besides, it is *really* difficult to get wealthy white folks to contribute to [a historically African American college] because they see it as being on the "wrong side of the tracks," if you know what I mean.

Hospitals, Medical Schools, and "the Diseases"

Like philanthropy for arts and cultural organizations and educational institutions, hospitals, medical schools, and various diseases are popular causes among elite women. Women's motivation for working in medically related volunteerism can be placed in four general categories:

1. a special interest in health care and a perception that volunteerism in this area has greater significance—sometimes of a life-and-death nature—than in other areas of philanthropy;
2. family connections in the health care field, such as the woman being a physician or having a father, mother, husband, or other relative who is or has been a health care provider;
3. having had a personal experience with a hospital, doctors, or other medical personnel that was life changing, such as an institution that "helped save" someone's life; and
4. having had a personal brush with a disease, or having a close relative or friend who was harmed by that disease.

Betty, a 60-ish white woman in the Old Name family category, is representative of women who have a special interest in health care and see their contributions as very important to those who are "caught up in the health care system":

> I'm not a *community volunteer* in the sense that I am a member of a bunch of volunteer organizations. I'm a *specialist* who prides herself on years of service at [hospital]. As a matter of fact, I specialize in just one type of volunteer work here—I help families get information about their loved ones who are in surgery, recovery, or intensive care. I like this work because there is an urgency to what we do and our professionalism is of utmost importance to patients and their families.

Like Betty, many elite women involved in medically related philanthropic causes see themselves as "specialists" in the volunteer tasks they perform. Unlike Betty, however, most of the women view themselves as being fundraisers and check writers rather than as being hands-on workers. This is particularly true of women whose primary interest in health care is through family connections with a hospital or medical school. Marjorie and Sondra are examples. Marjorie, a white woman in her 50s, has been a volunteer for ten years at the hospital where both her father and her husband have practiced medicine. She was serving on the hospital board at the time of this study and previously had chaired the hospital's annual gala that raised a large sum of money. Sondra, on the other hand, gave her time and money to a medical school where her father had been an attending physician [a doctor who is affiliated with the medical school and its teaching hospital] for many years prior to his death:

> My father and mother established a tradition of philanthropy that my husband and I want to pass on to our children and grandchildren. This [medical school] is part of our family. When my father died, the church was full of administrators, doctors, med students, nurses, orderlies, and parking lot attendants. I'm talking about a friendship and love like I'll never forget. My husband and I are proud to endow the future of medicine at [the school] through our planned giving. I only wish that we could do more.

Elite women who have had positive experiences with a hospital may refer to these memories when describing their volunteer work. An example is Luci, a white woman in her late 30s to early 40s from an Old Money family, who explained that her children had all been born at one hospital in her city:

> [Name] hospital gives newborn babies a T-shirt that says, "I am a [hospital] baby." We have four of these tucked away from when each of our children was born. It was a natural for me, when the hospital needed more money for its neonatal intensive care unit, to organize a fundraising drive. One of our children was a "premie" and spent more than a month in an incubator before we could take her home, so I know how critical this kind of care is.

Like Luci, women who perform volunteer work for organizations that seek to eradicate or alleviate a disease often describe themselves as having had a personal experience—in this instance, with the disease—that got them interested in the particular organization. Some of them have lost a child, spouse, parent, or close friend to the disease. Others volunteer to work with local affiliates of national organizations like the American Heart Association, American Cancer Society, Arthritis Foundation, and American Diabetes Association because they view these efforts as worthy causes or because they know that there is a history of such medical problems in their family. Of course, as in other areas of volunteerism, some of the volunteers are drawn by the "glitzy galas" that are put on by some of these organizations as much as by the opportunity to support education, research, and treatment of various diseases. Regardless of the reason for their involvement, the women I spoke with prided themselves on their efforts on behalf of these causes.

Although women of all economic classes may join organizations that seek to eradicate diseases such as breast cancer, elite women have greater social and economic resources they can tap. Those privileged women who serve on the board of medically related causes typically begin their volunteer careers with a social power base that is already established by their families. However, some volunteers build their own power base through fundraising for "the diseases," hospitals, medical schools, and other high-profile causes in their community, or groups that help those who need financial assistance or that seek to empower minority groups.

Causes that Benefit the "Less Fortunate"

I found that elite women make a distinction between philanthropy and charity when it comes to their efforts to help the "less fortunate." As stated previously, the term philanthropy is usually thought to include charity, but it also encompasses a wider range of private giving for public purposes.[33] Charity specifically involves helping the "less fortunate," who are also referred to as "the poor," the "disadvantaged," or the "down and out." Unlike some definitions of charity that define these efforts as focusing on the "relief of severe and immediate needs,"[34] there is frequently no immediate relief for the problems that the women try to tackle, and their efforts typically do not address larger social inequalities such as how to reduce poverty or racism in the larger society. An example of trying to help specific individuals is the efforts of women's groups to provide a safe residential environment for children, usually from low-income families, who have been abandoned, abused, or neglected.

Elite women's motivation for helping the less fortunate usually comes from one or more of several sources: (1) associations such as the Junior League, The Links (an elite African American women's organization), or other prestigious women's organizations that have as their mission helping the disadvantaged,[35] (2) family and friendship groups that teach the importance of noblesse oblige—that those who "have" should give something back to the community by helping the poor,[36] (3) feelings of concern, especially for children or the elderly who are thought to be in need of assistance and not able to take care of themselves, and (4) a belief that women volunteers have greater knowledge—which they have an obligation to share with others—about child rearing, nutrition, how to dress for a job interview, or other information that might be valuable to someone who has had less education and fewer opportunities.[37] An example is

Julie, a white woman in her late 20s who comes from an Old Name family and volunteers with a well baby program through a women's volunteer organization:

> It's really amazing how little some of these women know about infant and child care. What especially surprised me was to learn that some of the women already had a kid or two before they came to our program. I don't know how these other children survived—maybe a grandma or somebody else who looked after them. Yes, our work is really cut out for us. I majored in family and consumer science in college and, believe me, that's been useful information.

Statements from two active members (the first identifying herself as a "full-time mom," and the second being employed full-time in addition to taking care of her own children) of a Junior League in this study show a similar desire to help the less fortunate:

> I feel a responsibility to help those less fortunate because I have the time and financial resources available to do so. Not everyone can do this, or would be good at it, no matter how financially successful. It depends on morals and character, not on finances. I think that no matter how difficult things might be for us—there are so many others who have less or poorer health, etc. We must use our blessings to help and be generous to others.

Many elite women not only are committed to helping the less advantaged but also to teaching their children to do likewise, as this member of the same Junior League noted:

> We need to explain to our children that *everyone* needs help, and some people don't have good families and friends to provide the help. Therefore other people in the community must step in to help these people, even though we don't know them, just like our family and friends help us. [I instill in my children a sense of responsibility toward the community] by explaining that some families are not as fortunate as we are, and that we must help them.

Most women in this study provided assistance to the disadvantaged in their communities through their service in organizations that supported programs for the less fortunate. Although there are many examples, I will focus primarily on local community foundations and women's organizations committed to helping abused or neglected children. Looking first at community foundations, these nonprofit organizations make grants to a wide diversity of community organizations, ranging from cultural and educational groups to organizations that primarily benefit the poor. Women who are involved with community foundations do not view themselves as being involved in one-on-one charitable activities; rather, they see themselves as "facilitators who make it possible for organizations that help the poor to get the resources they need."

Community foundations have outreach programs to identify groups that can be grant applicants. Diversity is sought in grant applicants so that foundations can provide seed money to groups that work throughout the community. Some foundation volunteers and staff also want to see greater diversity on the board of governors and the advisory council of the foundation. Although Old Name and Old Money families are well represented on foundation boards, some affluent newcomers and people of color have gradually gained access to positions in these organizations. Viola, an elite African American woman in her 60s who had been a Worker Bee for many years, stated that she believed that having African Americans and Hispanic board members brought "more people to the table" to talk about how grant monies should be allocated:

> This foundation is a worthwhile use of my time. The gifts, bequests, and donations it receives aren't eaten up by administrative expenses: The money goes to good causes that don't receive enough attention in [city]. Since the board of governors and the advisory committee members come closer to representing all of [city], you'll see groups like the Minority Health Care Network and Ballet Folklorico getting grants that they otherwise might not have.

Although elite women are frequently found on the boards of community foundations and other nonprofit organizations that benefit the disadvantaged, the most frequent focus of elite women's hands-on involvement with "charity" that benefits the disadvantaged is either (1) thrift shops and garage sales that require some knowledge of consumerism and retailing or (2) activities that help children in the short term, such as the annual Coats for Kids drive, or those that help children over longer periods of time, such as residential homes and therapeutic foster care settings for abused and neglected children. These and other fundraising events of elite women's organizations are described in greater detail in chapter 3.

Racial and Ethnic Empowerment

Groups that seek to empower women of color, among other activities, have been of great importance to many elite African American women.[38] A number of local, regional, and national organizations emerged during the civil rights and women's movements and their aftermath to examine how African American women might achieve their potential. Although most of these groups have a number of goals, including providing opportunities for community service, leadership development, and enhancement of career opportunities, they also seek to "uplift the race" and to empower African Americans, particularly women.

Elite African American women in this study frequently expressed a desire to improve the lives of people of color in the United States and to improve the educational and employment opportunities of low-income and poverty-level African Americans. Serena, an African American professional woman in her early 30s, is representative of the younger women who wanted to participate in activities that would benefit "other people like me":

> As I learned in college, many other people are disadvantaged because they didn't grow up in a family like mine, and they attended lousy schools. Since I've graduated, I've gone into [predominantly minority] schools in [a large Texas city] where the building was old and saggy, the books were all worn out, and it was flat depressing. The kids looked depressed, too. What I like about [organization] is the community outreach programs where we try to do something for those kids. We have programs to educate girls about teen pregnancy and [sexually transmitted diseases]; we have programs that deal with alcohol and drug abuse; and we do everything we can to encourage black kids to finish school and go to college, including raising scholarship money through our fundraising projects. I feel that my time is better spent in organizations that work with issues that relate to blacks: There are plenty of other fancy [white] groups that look out for "high culture" stuff like the art museum.

Many thousands of African American women, like Serena, have sought to overcome the effects of racial prejudice and discrimination that have created and perpetuated racial and ethnic inequality in the United States. Organizations such as the National Coalition of 100 Black Women, Inc. have chapters throughout the nation that are committed to addressing the needs of African American women. In some chapters, there are teen mother programs that teach parenting skills to young mothers, programs to collect back-to-school clothes for homeless children, and many other community service projects that benefit not only African American children but also other low-income families. More than most predominantly white elite women's organizations, one focus of giving by some African American women's groups is in another country or continent. For example, I learned that some chapters of the National Coalition of 100 Black Women made donations to purchase electric poles for a village in Ghana so that people living in this remote area would have electricity for the first time.

Although more African American women today are involved in fundraising for "mainstream" arts and cultural organizations, schools, hospitals, and other charitable institutions, there remains a distinct interest among these privileged women to "uplift" others of their racial or ethnic group who have not been able to "achieve the American dream" as these women believe that they have. As Viola stated, "Some of us have come a long way toward achieving the American dream, but we still have a long way to go. I won't think that we've succeeded until I know that African Americans are not routinely discriminated against because of their skin color."

Gender, Class, Age, and Race in Elite Women's Philanthropy

Gender, class, age, and race are factors in the types and nature of the philanthropic work of elite women in the United States. The discussion set forth above regarding the various categories of organizations in which these women participate has made note of some of those factors. However, the influence that these factors may have is more clearly visible when the factors are considered across, rather than within, the various organizations.

Gender-Based Distinctions

Although elite women may be drawn into giving and volunteering in one category or another of these organizations for any number of reasons, and the result may be that they bond with other elites who are similarly situated in class- and race-based societal hierarchies, a persistent gender gap exists that has made it difficult for the women to exercise power in the same ways that elite men—especially elite white men—do. Comparisons of elite women's philanthropy with that of elite men in previous studies have shown that certain kinds of philanthropy have been relatively open to women, but that women's endeavors have not always enjoyed equal stature with those of men.[39] These studies note that women have used their activities in charitable and philanthropic organizations as a source of power when they have had little opportunity to exercise other types of power. By creating parallel power structures through nonprofit institutions and reform associations, women have found an avenue for gaining public roles.[40]

Gender gaps on nonprofit boards have weakened; however, they have weakened unevenly in different fields. For example, in a study of nonprofit boards in New York City, Francie Ostrower found that a greater percentage of women were board members in areas such as culture, social services, and youth, but that women were not as well represented on hospital and education boards.[41] In all these areas of activity, Ostrower concluded that women are a considerable—but minority—presence, constituting less than 30 percent of the board even in those areas of highest representation. Ostrower partially attributes women's barriers within the elite to "their distance from the core economic institutions of their class, which have been dominated by men."[42]

Although the gender gap may have been reduced in philanthropic organizations over the past decades, inequality remains in both the unpaid and the paid positions in nonprofit organizations. At the time I was completing my research, GuideStar, a national database on nonprofit organizations, released a study in which it had examined the 1998 and 1999 tax forms of 75,000 public charities and found that the median pay of female chief executives lagged far behind that of male chief executives. Women also earned less than men in the top positions in every job category, including development, public relations, law, and technology.[43] If the staffing of nonprofit organizations has any relationship with the opportunities for women volunteers in these organizations, then gender equity remains elusive even for women of the upper classes.

In the present study, women and men were largely equal in number on the boards of symphony orchestra societies, opera and ballet associations, and other arts and cultural organizations; however, fewer women served on the boards of prestigious universities, hospitals, and medical centers. Most women who served in these categories had direct family ties to those institutions, or professional status that linked them to the particular organization. The most visible presence of elite women in leadership positions remains on the boards and committees of high-status women's volunteer organizations.

Gender-based distinctions exist even with regard to the women themselves. Elite women (across racial and ethnic categories) who serve on various nonprofit boards or hold membership in prestigious volunteer organizations in the cities in this study who list their occupation as "professional," "corporate executive," "entrepreneur," or "business owner"— positions historically dominated by men—or who are known to have inherited large estates are more likely to serve on the more prestigious nonprofit boards. These women typically interact with the men on these boards on a more equal basis and are far less likely to be asked to stuff envelopes or chair a ball than are those women who self-identify as "community volunteers" and rely primarily on their husbands' income to fund their involvement in philanthropic causes. Women in this latter category are more likely to be the party planners and the presidents of the women's auxiliary groups than they are to serve on the "big boards" of the symphony, opera, and ballet associations.

Women who are in the "community volunteer" category may follow their own interests in choosing one of the types of organizations described in this chapter; however, these women are also more likely to be involved in causes that are related to their husbands' career. Alice is an example. Her husband is an oncologist, and she has been actively involved for many years in raising money for the local hospice group. Although Alice has never spoken about the relationship between her husband's medical practice, which frequently involves the treatment of terminally ill patients, and her endless hours of volunteering and fundraising on behalf of a group that provides end-of-life support for patients and their families, many in her friendship circle assume that her interests spring from the nature of her husband's practice.

The women's potential for creating bonds with other women is strong as they work to produce some important outcome such as contacting potential donors or planning a fundraiser. However, their potential bonds with other women may be weakened by competition for scarce resources, such as whose daughter will get to be the "top" debutante at the next presentation. The men who participate in elite organizations, on the other hand, are more likely to see business or professional advantages in their association with the other men in those groups.

Women's associations and auxiliaries provide privileged women with a prime setting in which they can frame their volunteer efforts and assume leadership roles without the need to compete with the men of their class. Most competition among women in these associations and auxiliaries comes from other women. For some women, service alone is its own reward. For others, recognition for oneself or one's children is a crucial motivating factor behind the women's hard work and continued involvement. Sally, a New Money white woman who was then in her mid-40s, is an example. Having her daughter recognized as the top debutante by her organization was, for her, reaching "the brass ring" and an endeavor that put her in direct competition with another woman who had given many years of service to the organization:

> I'd served in nearly every office. I had chaired the ball several times and the showhouse once while Marsha [another woman in the organization] hadn't done nearly as much and thought she was going for the "brass ring" with her daughter. She talked to the [debutante selection committee] about making her daughter the [top debutante] that year. I couldn't believe it. What gall! A wise, older woman on the committee finally settled it by decreeing that my daughter should be the [top debutante] that year, and Marsha's daughter could be it next year.

Clearly, Sally is not typical of all volunteers in women's associations. Many women give their time and money without expecting any social return on their investment. From my observations, I have concluded, however, that those women's organizations that provide rewards or incentives, such as honoring the women's children or providing the women with social recognition, find it much easier to recruit women and to get them to donate money and many volunteer hours to the group. Organizations also have a "payoff" in terms of helping a woman to gain new, socially acceptable friendships or providing them with a prestigious organization they can list on their volunteer or business résumés.

Class Distinctions

Throughout this chapter, the class-based nature of volunteer endeavors has been evident. Although most elite women do not describe their activities as being class-related behaviors, the meaning of class is reflected by their choice of memberships and the kinds of volunteer work that they perform. As discussed in chapter 3, some of the organizations in my study engage in fundraising activities—such as operating a thrift shop or a garage sale—that bring their members into direct contact with people from lower socioeconomic tiers and other racial or ethnic backgrounds. Some women do not feel "comfortable" with such activities and, instead, choose to participate in organizations whose fundraising efforts are of an entirely different nature.

Doing volunteer work as a result of membership in invitational organizations, rather than those organizations that are open to anyone who wishes to join, reflects underlying class-based criteria for involvement in organizations.[44] The women often describe themselves as wanting to work with others who are "congenial" or "compatible," and these terms are used to describe why one person is acceptable for membership and another is not.[45] Class-appropriate behavior is also reflected in the activities that some elite women participate in, such as serving as a trustee on a nonprofit board or as an organizer of a high-profile charity gala but not spending much time as a hands-on volunteer in direct contact with the "less fortunate."

If the gender gap in elite philanthropy has grown more narrow, we cannot assume that a corresponding narrowing has taken place regarding class boundaries. The primary exception in the Southwest is the greater inclusion of New Money people, who do not have old family names and connections, but this inclusion is subject to the "newcomers" having sufficient money to make generous contributions to community organizations. The "dot-com bust" has had many ramifications in this regard. Several founders and executives of computer hardware and software companies who pledged large sums of money or stock to cultural, educational, medical, or other institutions are no longer able to fulfill their promises because of changing economic conditions. Relying on these pledges and partial contributions, several nonprofit groups placed individuals from these companies on their boards of trustees and gave them extensive publicity for their generosity. In the aftershocks of the "bust," administrators and trustees of several groups are in a quandary about how to remove those individuals from listings of major contributors and to make up the corresponding shortfall in the budget, as one administrator for an arts organization stated:

> There are times when "older money" is best. It is nice and stable, and you can count on it. We were really excited about the large gifts we received from more recent donors, and virtually all of them had been great about fulfilling their pledges. We love "newer money" too. We just hold our breath until it comes in.

Elite women are not a homogeneous category: Some have "old money," whereas others are in the newer money category, particularly those in families associated with the newer information and service technologies. Likewise, not all elite women in any particular city participate in the same exclusive social circles. However, the "top stars" in women's philanthropy, even in the larger metropolitan areas, are known to other elite women "by reputation" if not firsthand experience. For the most part, elite women share a unique form of status honor that is expressed through a distinctive style of life. According to Weber, *class* refers to a category of people who share common economic opportunities and have similar life chances, whereas *status* refers to interacting social groups that share a common lifestyle.[46] Status honor comes not only from sharing commonalities with those who are similar but also from maintaining an acceptable social distance from those who are different. How elite women do good deeds that benefit individuals, organizations, and communities while, at the same time, practicing *exclusiveness* is one of the central dialectic concerns of this study.

Although the women in this study generally do not show overt signs of class consciousness, they share certain *expectations* with other elites. One assumption is that social interaction with others outside their own social circle will be limited. An informal expression for this is that some people are "not our kind of people." A second assumption is that endogamous marriage patterns must be perpetuated by children and grandchildren. An informal expression for this is "Marriages are often family mergers." A third assumption is that the women have a unique responsibility to provide the stage (to use Erving Goffman's dramaturgical analysis of social life)[47] on which sons and daughters can act out their roles as young people seeking acceptable marital mates and the blessing of adults in upper-class social circles. For this reason, rites of passage such as children's presentations to Society and their marriages are rituals that bind members of the upper class together and weld two or more previously unrelated families together. Throughout this process, parents and grandparents have social and economic leverage that people in other classes do not possess. As one woman stated, "We control the purse strings." Similarly, Judith, a grandmother of three, was overheard commenting to her friend: "I've already told Bud [her grandson] that if he tries to marry one of those pierced-naval, bare-stomached, trashy girls at the mall, I'm cutting him out of my will without a cent!"

Perhaps Judith was joking about her grandson, but the idea of "cutting" someone out of one's will for "bad behavior" is not unusual among social elites. Lawyers who serve high-status families describe affluent clients who frequently change their wills, writing in or out certain family members as they deem appropriate, based on their recent behavior. While such actions may occur in middle- and upper-class families alike, the effects of being "written out" are most profoundly felt by potential inheritors of very large estates.

Age

Age is an important factor in women's involvement in philanthropy. The age of the woman, as well as of her children, is a central factor in determining the nature and extent of her involvement in various organizations. Different types of work are sometimes performed by women in different age categories, as previously discussed.

Age particularly intersects with gender and class in the volunteer experiences of older elite women. As they reach their late 40s, they become sustaining, rather than active, members of organizations such as the Junior League, and their contributions to organizations more often come in the form of money than from their labor power. The primary exceptions, which are discussed in detail in the next chapter, are fundraising events such as charity garage sales and some gala committees that rely heavily on older women, using the women's names and influence to draw in sponsorships and guests to purchase expensive tickets and merchandise at the auctions.

For the white women age 45 and older in this study, their connection to family wealth or affluent husbands remains crucial to their access to prestigious nonprofit organizations and boards.[48] Some younger white women bring a combination of family assets plus their own income, earned from professional or entrepreneurial careers. Maggie's family is an example: She and her parents owned a successful manufacturing plant that provided them with a large income. After the family sold the business to a major corporation, Maggie made generous donations to a number of nonprofit organizations and became a trustee on several elite boards.

Older elite women of color were likely to be involved in predominantly white organizations only if these organizations made a conscious effort to recruit people across racial and ethnic lines. Viola (the elite African American woman in her 60s who is quoted earlier in this chapter) described the thought process that she went through when asked to serve on a predominantly white arts board:

I'm already a busy woman. I own a business and have investments I need to watch out for. So when they asked me to join the board I checked around to find out if the trustees wanted "new faces" because they wanted to hear what we had to say or because they wanted to get grant money that otherwise might not be available. I also wanted to know how people across town [in a predominantly minority area of the city] would benefit from what I'd be doing if I agreed to serve.

Younger elite women of color expressed little hesitation about the motivation of board members who asked them to join their ranks. Most of these women had graduated from prestigious universities, where they had earned advanced degrees in business, law, medicine, or architecture by the time that they were asked to serve on corporate and charity boards.

Race and Ethnicity
The white women in this study typically do not think of themselves in racial terms. They are more likely to see other people, namely minority group members, as being affected by race. For this reason, few white women described the organizations of which they are members as serving the needs of a specific racial or ethnic group. Women of color were different in their responses. In surveys that asked about women's membership in community organizations, African American women frequently listed one or more predominantly black groups such as a sorority, Jack and Jill, or The Links, a pattern that appears to be typical for elite women of color throughout the United States. In 2001, when Deborah Brittain became the first African American to serve as president of the Association of Junior Leagues, for example, articles about her frequently listed the following as among the groups with which she was affiliated: National Council of Negro Women, The Links, Alpha Kappa Alpha [a predominantly black sorority], the NAACP Legal Defense and Education Fund, the National Urban League, and Jack and Jill of America.[49]

African American women with professional degrees who were members of organizations in my study frequently indicated that they held membership in professional groups such as the local bar association, the medical society, or groups such as the National Coalition of 100 Black Women (NCBW). White women, on the other hand, typically listed only socially prestigious, predominantly white groups. I found that African American women believed that white organizations overlook many of the needs of the black community and are too focused on showing others how to improve their life rather than listening to their issues and concerns. Organizations such as the NCBW attract women of color because of the issues they confront, as Deirdre, an elite woman of color in her 30s, explains:

Junior League has given me a chance to know [her city] much better. Believe me, there are areas of [the city] that I never knew existed until my provisional [first year] in the League. But, I'm also proud to be in the [NCBW] 'cause it is a group of women who learn leadership skills, get involved in networking, and address issues that I think are especially important to the black community. We've been studying problems that black families experience. We've also had career advancement speakers to help black women get ahead at work. These are topics that are of direct concern to women like me.

A comparison of lists where women stated the volunteer/community organizations in which they participated showed that African American women included organizations that specifically addressed the concerns of women of color, whereas those women who self-identified as Hispanic listed organizations that were more similar to those of non-Hispanic white women. Both African American women and Latinas were more likely than white (non-Hispanic) women to include their involvement in nonelite community organizations such as Big Brothers/Big Sisters, United Way, YMCA and YWCA, and area Girl Scouts councils.

Contemporary racial and ethnic division in elite women's volunteer organizations can be traced to earlier parallel social organizations that emerged in eras of segregation and overt discrimination, as discussed in chapter 6. Today, many of these parallel organizations remain not only because of the divergent interests of members across race and class boundaries but also because many people believe that separate organizations provide a "comfort zone." The idea of a comfort zone allows individuals to believe that being separate from those who are different from oneself is a natural and inevitable fact of life. Moreover, it is assumed that groups have the right to exclude those who might make existing members uncomfortable. This belief in a comfort zone is passed on from one generation to the next, perhaps without any conscious intention of perpetuating class, gender, and race-based inequalities, but the end result is the same regardless of the motivations involved.

Conclusion

In this chapter, I have described the significance that philanthropy, especially volunteerism, has for some elite women. I have identified five sources of social power (reward, coercive, expert, legitimate, and referent power) and have shown how elite women exercise power that is not purely economic in nature. The elite women in this study take pride in their activities and typically do not see the incongruity that exists between being members of exclusive invitational organizations (that some people view as snobbish or elitist) and doing good deeds that are intended to benefit the overall community—or even that specifically target the less fortunate as beneficiaries of their largesse. Because of long-standing acceptance of the norm of exclusivity, the women—and often their children—assume that it both is desirable and appropriate to exclude others from membership in their organizations on the basis of characteristics or attributes that, in actuality, have little or nothing to do with whether a woman could be a successful community volunteer. Although the financial ability to be a "player" in these groups—to be able to afford the "right" clothes and to be able to pay for tickets to the group's charity benefits, for example—may limit some women's ability to participate, finances alone cannot explain why these groups are so predominantly (and, often, exclusively) white and why affluent women of color have not been more actively recruited for membership in these elite women's groups.[50]

If, as previous research has indicated, giving and volunteering are ways in which people can enhance their social power and cultural capital, it appears reasonable to ask if some people—particularly people of color—are denied access to portions of power and capital in cities where the dominant arts, cultural, educational, and medical institutions and organizations remain largely controlled by a white establishment which, despite the greater involvement of white women and people of color in recent decades, remains largely unchanged in overall outlook and goals.[51]

At the bottom line, however, elite women's organizations are doing many "good deeds": They are raising (as we will see in the next chapter) billions of dollars through their projects and are committing hundreds of thousand of hours toward the betterment of their communities or funding projects that they believe are important for improving quality of life. Understanding these groups and the women who participate in them and serve as their leaders is therefore important to our understanding of the overall society of which they are a part.

Notes

1. Barnes 2001: A1.
2. *Columbia Encyclopedia* 2001.
3. See Odendahl 1990; Ostrower 1995. The most thorough distinction between charity and philanthropy is made by Ostrower (1995: 4) when she writes, "Charity is specifically directed toward the poor, and often focuses on the relief of severe and immediate needs. Philanthropy is a broader concept, which includes charity but also encompasses the wider range of private giving for public purposes. Thus, contributions to universities, museums, hospitals, churches, temples, mosques, environmental causes, social service institutions, parks, and research in-

stitutes all fall under the category of philanthropy, whether or not they are directed to poor recipients."

4. Ostrower 1995.

5. Ostrander 1984; Daniels 1988; McCarthy 1990; Odendahl 1990; Ostrower 1995.

6. For example, Cookson and Persell (1985: 63) found that the students at the elite boarding schools included in their study had "a high degree of self-esteem and efficacy." Most of the students believed that they were worthy of this position in the school and that they had the ability to "make things work." Students from legacy families (where other family members had attended the same institution) had a higher degree of self-esteem and sense of efficacy than other students.

7. Edwards 1999.

8. Edwards 1999.

9. Tilly and Tilly 1994: 291.

10. Wilson and Musick 1997.

11. Wilson and Musick 1997: 696.

12. Bourdieu 1986.

13. Wilson and Musick 1997: 696.

14. Ostrander 1984; Ostrower 1995.

15. Ostrower 1995.

16. Zweigenhaft and Domhoff 1998: 194.

17. Addams 1999: xvii.

18. Daniels 1988.

19. Ostrander 1984.

20. See, for example, Domhoff 1998.

21. Daniels 1995; McCarthy 1990.

22. Cable 1984; Montgomery 1998.

23. Odendahl 1990: 116–117.

24. McCarthy 1990.

25. Ostrower 1995.

26. Daniels 1988; Ostrander 1984.

27. See Wilson and Musick 1997 for a discussion of cultural capital and volunteerism.

28. Ostrower 1995: 94.

29. Cookson and Persell 1985: 22.

30. Daniels (1988: 7) states that upper-class women "uphold class expectations by sponsoring and actively supporting private schools . . . where their children can socialize with appropriate peers."

31. Hockaday 2001.

32. See also Ostrower 1995.

33. Ostrower 1995.

34. Ostrower 1995: 4.

35. Daniels 1988.

36. Odendahl 1990; Ostrander 1984.

37. Daniels 1988, 1991.

38. See Hine 1990.

39. See Daniels 1988; McCarthy 1982, 1990; Odendahl 1990; Ostrander 1984; Ostrower 1995.

40. McCarthy 1982, 1990.
41. Ostrower 1995.
42. Ostrower 1995: 83.
43. Female chief executives at the largest nonprofit organizations earned $170,180 a year, compared with $264,602 for male chief executives. Men filled three out of every four positions in organizations with budgets of $5 million or more and nearly nine out of ten positions at organizations with budgets of more than $50 million. By contrast, women chief executives were clustered in organizations with budgets of $500,000 or less a year (Lewin 2001).
44. Ostrander 1980a.
45. Ostrander 1980a.
46. Weber 1958.
47. Goffman (1959) suggests that social interaction, like a theater, has a front stage and back stage. The front stage is the area where a player performs a specific role before an audience. In my study, front stages include the venues established by elite women where their children interact with one another and with adult members of the upper classes. An example is a charity ball with a debutante presentation, where young people who previously have been unobserved by other elites literally move to the front stage and into the "spotlight" when they are formally presented to Society.
48. See Ostrower 1995.
49. Blomme 2001.
50. I also found little or no evidence that white (Anglo) women are actively recruited to participate in organizations whose membership is primarily (or entirely) comprised of women of color.
51. See Zweigenhaft and Domhoff (1998) for a discussion of how the business power elite now shows considerable diversity, as compared with the 1950s, but that its core group continues to be wealthy, white Christian males in the top classes. Moreover, according to Zweigenhaft and Domhoff (1998: 6–7), white women and people of color who have become at least a marginal part of the power of the elite "have found ways to signal that they are willing to join the game as it has always been played, assuring the old guard that they will call for no more than relatively minor adjustments, if that. . . . Class backgrounds, current roles, and future aspirations are more powerful in shaping behavior in the power elite than gender, ethnicity, or race."

CHAPTER THREE

~

Good Deeds and Fundraising: It Takes Money to Make (Big) Money!

I was driving down the highway, trying to get Mark to his appointment with the dentist on time. Little did I realize what I'd gotten myself into as a new member [of a by-invitation-only women's organization that sponsors the home where Mark was living]. As new
members, we are required to take the children to some of their dental
and doctor appointments and to do other things that help out around
the home. Mark was a young African American male, and he had a
whole bag of troubling tricks up his sleeve. He had no more gotten
into my car and I had entered a freeway when he started whistling
loudly while looking at me out of the corner of his eye. I tried to talk
with him about his friends, school, or something he might be interested in. It didn't work until I said that we might need to turn around
and go back to the home. Mark sat quietly for a minute, then unfas-
tened his seat belt and leaned over to turn on the radio and put the
volume on high. I did a poor job of communicating with him, but
somehow we got through the dental appointment, and I returned him
to the home safely. I know I'm not cut out for that kind of work.

With these words, Claire described the anxiety and frustration she experienced when she was asked to do something as a volunteer that
caused her to feel that she had lost control over a situation and was un-
able to assert her power over Mark, the young man—less fortunate than
she was—who was receiving the benefit of her time and efforts. Claire
stated that she was troubled not only by his behavior as she drove to the
dentist but also by the thought that other people might see "a well-to-do
white woman trying to correct an unruly black kid and not understand
what was happening." Consequently, she was also engaged in defensive

impression management, which typically occurs when a person experiences or anticipates a predicament that is likely to cause other people to attribute some negative or undesirable quality or identity to them.[1] Erving Goffman referred to this type of defensive impression management as the face work that is done to maintain or restore one's positive identity when threatened with a spoiled identity.[2]

Because Claire feared her loss of power over the situation with this young man and was concerned about impression management with other people, she asked the volunteer coordinator of her organization to shift her to some other type of work, such as fundraising. Although some elite women like to work with the less fortunate, Claire's situation is not unique. A number of the women do not have a great deal of hands-on experience with those who benefit from the efforts of their organizations and want to maintain a sense of social power over their volunteer activities (and, sometimes, over the recipients of their largesse). Previous research reflects that this is fairly common among such women. Susan Ostrander, for example, described how many upper-class women exercise social power by moving into leadership positions in prestigious volunteer organizations:

> Upper-class women are not, for the most part, involved in the direct service kinds of volunteer work. They do not, for example, push a flower cart in the hospital; answer telephones at school or library; staff the entry desk at the museum; or comfort sick, abused, or neglected children and adults. The few women who [have] done direct service activities [have] performed them early in their volunteer careers, for a relatively short period of time. Instead, upper-class women move quickly into leadership positions on the boards of their organizations. From these positions, they influence organizational operations and policy, and carry out what they perceive as their primary task—fundraising.[3]

As Ostrander suggests, elite women are uniquely in a position (compared with women in other social classes) to raise money in the community because they have "monied connections" and they can exercise their reward power to mobilize others to contribute.[4] Fundraising is a key activity of elite women volunteers due to most nonprofit organizations' need for a continual inflow of money and the widely held belief that women are "good at the soft touch when it comes to hitting people up for money or other donations" (as one male staff member at a nonprofit organization stated). The old adage that "it takes money to make money" holds true in elite philanthropy: Elite volunteers and affluent philanthropists are the magnets that groups use to draw in other wealthy people as donors.[5] Frequently, these women and their families are major contributors to the organization, a fact that makes it easier for them to approach others about making a major contribution to that organization. However, the personal touch of elite women is also important. Small—and seemingly inconsequential—rewards such as the gift of an expensive bottle of wine or a dinner invitation serve as rewards that the women can bestow on those individuals and corporate sponsors who generously contribute to their favorite charity or nonprofit organization. Although most elite women do not use coercive power to motivate potential major contributors, some women do make potential contributors aware of how unpleasant it would be to be "blacklisted" by the group or to have influential members of the community view someone as being a nonplayer. An example is one grande dame who frequently took new corporate executives and wealthy arrivals in her city to the most prestigious local private club, treated them to an elegant lunch or dinner, told them the "story" of her organization and its current financial needs, and then explained to them how much "becoming an integral part of the city" and its social power structure was linked to making generous contributions to her organization.

For this woman and many other privileged women, volunteerism is an "invisible career" in which the women exert various forms of social power. Arlene Kaplan Daniels described the attributes that are required for this sort of "career":

> All of these fund-raising activities, whether single or recurring events, require the engineering, mobilization, and plan of attack necessary for a small-scale war—or a major theatrical opening. In addition to preliminary negotiations with businesses, service people, publicity people, sponsors and helpers, these events mobilize energies, call forth entrepreneurial and creative skills, test the mettle of women under pressure to meet deadlines, solve last minute crises, and make large sums of money.[6]

In this chapter, I examine power differentials in elite women's volunteerism—and especially how the types of fundraising projects they pursue reflect underlying issues of race and class and show patterns of domination and subordination in the United States. Fundraising projects such as are described in this chapter reproduce social class inequalities by establishing the social boundaries that divide elites from nonelites. For example, at a charity thrift shop or citywide garage sale, interclass and interracial differences in the women volunteers and the low-income, often minority group "shoppers" at these events are readily apparent. The differences are also evident at high-profile, expensive fundraisers—such as a charity ball, dinner party, or gala—where affluent white guests and sponsors, along with selected minority-group members, come together to have a good time and raise large sums of money for "charity." Those who serve the dinners and clean up after such events typically are members of the working class and often are minorities. Such lavish events with high-priced tickets and sponsorships add allure to the elite women's organizations that arrange the events. In turn, an elite women's organization, if it has the "right" members, adds allure to the events it sponsors and constitutes a base of power, in this case referent power, for the women who participate.

The volunteer work of elite women reflects the racial and ethnic divide that persists even among people with similar economic status. Parallel white and African American women's organizations, developed in an era of overt racial segregation, survive today and can be seen in the events sponsored by elite women's organizations. In a single city, for example, members of the historically white Junior League may be planning a charity debutante presentation ball at the same time that members of The Links—a prestigious African American women's community service organization—are planning their own fundraising ball. Although the goals of these organizations and their fundraising projects may be similar, the people who plan and attend the Junior League's event typically will be white; whereas those who plan and attend The Links' event typically will be African American.

A great deal of energy and effort goes into the good deeds of elite women volunteers, and it is not my intent to belittle their endeavors. From my own involvement in such activities, I have seen firsthand how giving and volunteering in the community benefit both specific individuals (such as people who are poor, ill, or elderly) and major organizations such as symphony orchestras and hospitals. Instead, my purpose is to show how issues of race and class remain entrenched in social life, and how seemingly unimportant social activities help to maintain the advantaged position of social elites and provide elite women with a social power base that is unavailable to women in other classes.

In the following analysis of elite women's fundraising activities—including thrift shops and garage sales, balls and other galas, fundraising dinner parties, and fashion shows—the concept of exclusivity is important. Fundraisers sponsored by elite women's organizations serve as a social setting or "playground" where elites interact and solidify relationships that benefit both them and their children.[7] If it were not for these events, which clearly label the organization as the "in group" among social elites and definitely worth joining, some affluent women might not become involved in volunteer work. Most of the women in my study could easily choose not to do community service work, but they found intrinsic incentives (such as the personal desire to help others or to promote art, music, or ballet in their city) or extrinsic incentives (such as the rewards of membership—referent power—conveyed by the organization) that made them want to participate in such work.

My discussion of fundraising projects starts with those activities—including charity thrift shops and citywide garage sales—that are *least* associated in most people's minds with the upper-class lifestyle and in which elite women are most likely to come into contact with people in other social classes and racial or ethnic categories. I then examine fundraising projects—such as dinner parties in private homes, designer showhouses, charity balls, and fashion shows—that are *most* associated with the lifestyle of elite women and are best able to enhance their social power with other elites.

Getting in Touch with "the Common People": Thrift Shops and Garage Sales

Why would elite women participate in conducting charity thrift shops and garage sales that bring them into direct contact with people of other classes or of other racial or ethnic categories? The answer most frequently given by the women themselves is to help out those persons who are less fortunate than they are; however, many of them acknowledge that a form of expert power also comes with working in these major community service projects and fundraisers. At thrift shops and garage sales, elite women set up an arena in which low-income people are the primary customers, and the elite women take the role of collectors, organizers, and sellers of merchandise. Moreover, a number of the women serve as chairs of the events or of "departments" (somewhat like the departments in a department store), giving them authority over other volunteers and over those who come to shop at the events.

Charity thrift shops, which operate on a continuous basis as compared with an annual garage sale event, come in a variety of sizes and have names such as the Junior League Thrift Shop or the Bargain Hut. In many cities, members of the Junior League or similar organizations create these storefront operations that look like any other retail operation but with the difference being that both the merchandise and the hours spent by workers are donated. The time that the women spend working at the thrift shop counts toward the required number of volunteer hours that they must perform annually to remain as members in good standing. According to Jeanine, a white woman in her early 40s from an Old Name family and who formerly served as president of a Junior League:

> Thrift shops are a really good fundraiser for us. We can reach out to help the community and also raise money. The revenue our shop generates goes to our programs and projects. People with limited means can buy the clothing, housewares, and other things they need, at a price they can afford. We work with other community social service agencies by giving them vouchers they can hand out to needy families. The families then come in to our store and use the vouchers in place of money to make their "purchases." Volunteers

who work here must be good at organizing and selling, and they have to be able to communicate with people from all walks of life.

However, several of the women volunteers stated that they had "learned important lessons"—which appeared to mean about class differences—from their thrift shop experiences. Mary Beth, a white woman in her mid-30s from an Old Money family, described how she felt about working in the thrift shop in her city:

> Our thrift shop is one of many sponsored by [Junior] Leagues across the country. Our volunteers give more than 2,000 hours a year to staff the thrift shop and, remember, that figure doesn't include all the time they spend on other League projects. But, I will say that you have to be able to wait on people who, in another area of your life, might be waiting on you . . . you know, like the counter help at the dry cleaners or the water and chip server at the Mexican restaurant. This takes some re-learning on the part of some members, and some don't do this type of work at all. But we always have more experienced members on hand to make sure that things go smoothly.

Jeanine's and Mary Beth's comments show that the women are aware of the class and sometimes racial or ethnic distinctions that exist between them and their customers. Coded language is often used to describe their class- and race-based perceptions of the shoppers, such as one woman who stated that she "had never known how to spot shoplifters or potentially dangerous people—like somebody who's high on drugs, drunk, or carrying a weapon" prior to working at the thrift shop. Unstated was her assumption that the kind of people with whom she usually associated did not engage in such conduct, which she thought to be more common among customers at the thriftshop.

Other coded language related to the physical location of the thrift shop. Some women expressed concern about the location of the thrift shop and whether this area of the city was safe for them, thus demonstrating the social geography of race and class. American studies scholar Ruth Frankenberg states that "the notion of a *social geography* suggests that the physical landscape is peopled and that it is constituted and perceived by means of social rather than natural processes."[8] The social processes are important to many white women. Sarah, a white woman in her late 30s from a New Money family, explained how she and other women volunteers sought to "protect themselves" at the thrift shop because it was located in a "less desirable neighborhood":

> The thrift shop committee always emphasizes that our members have to protect themselves first because the shop is in a less desirable neighborhood. Based on the idea that there is strength in numbers, we have our shifts

worked out where there are always several of us there, and sometimes a husband or security guard, at any given time. We have learned how to deal with people, how to "watch our backs," and when to call the police. You need to feel safe while you're working [there], and the families that come to shop need to feel safe, too. The shop is located where people who need the stuff we sell can get there, and that's not in the "best" part of town by any stretch of the imagination.

Sometimes, women of color who join predominantly white elite organizations are offended by comments of long-term members regarding their concerns about their safety in "minority" areas of the city. Rashandra, an African American woman in her mid-20s who was a provisional (new member) of a Junior League, said that her white colleagues talked about an area of the city being "bad" or "growing worse" primarily because a significant proportion of the population in that area was made up of minority group members:

The idea of the thrift shop seems like a natural for [the Junior League]. After all, our purpose is to assist women and children who are poor. But I got frustrated when I heard one member say that our shop's current location was not good because it was in a "bad neighborhood," and that we should try to find a "better" area where we could relocate the shop. Having lived in [city] all my life, I knew that a lot of the families that live in the area where the current shop is located are the "salt of the earth" . . . [that] the only thing wrong with that neighborhood, at least in that woman's mind, I think, is that it's a black neighborhood. Oh, well, I guess we're making progress. At least we're talking about issues that have never been brought into the light before.

Despite a few women's concerns—based on class or race—about volunteering at thrift shops, most members who engage in such enterprises appear to strongly believe that these shops are a meaningful way to give back to the community by helping the less fortunate get the items they need while raising money to fund other community service projects.[9] A number of the women also see themselves as gaining leadership skills and becoming well known as a community volunteer through their efforts in the trenches. A woman who became president of the Junior League in a large city stated that she received her earliest recognition in the group for her "outstanding accomplishments" with the group's faltering thrift shop: "I couldn't have started as Chair of the Christmas Bazaar or the annual ball, but few women wanted to take over as Chair of the Thrift Shop Committee and get it back on a sound financial footing like I did."

Some elite women volunteers have found the opportunity to exert their leadership skills and develop expert power in a similar pursuit—charity garage sales. Like thrift shops, charity garage sales sell donated goods or recycled products such as old furniture or appliances to lower-income people and thereby raise money to fund their organization's projects. The primary difference in thrift shops and charity garage sales is that thrift shops operate year-round (with the exception of weekends and holidays), whereas charity garage sales are only held once a year for two or three sale days. Like thrift shop volunteers, charity garage sale volunteers work year-round to make their fundraiser a success. One volunteer described the yearlong process that it takes to have a successful three-day garage sale:

> The minute this year's sale is over, we will start to work on next year's sale. There is no down time, except maybe for a margarita, and then it starts all over again. In less than a month, members will be out in their Suburbans and pickup trucks bringing in donated stuff and organizing it according to department for next year's sale. Then they will be storing it in the warehouse, where other volunteers will sort it out, see if it needs cleaning, and put it in specially labeled boxes so that we will know what it is when sale time arrives. About two or three weeks before the sale starts, we take everything to [the place where the sale will occur] and we unpack everything we previously packed. We organize it by departments, just like a department store, and then we display it and put prices on each item. Believe me, this is time consuming and hard on the old back.

The social connections of the elite women are extremely important for obtaining a sufficient quantity of merchandise for each garage sale. The women contact local merchants with whom they regularly shop and ask them to donate "seconds" and products that do not sell well to regular customers. The women also contact their affluent friends, getting them to donate "outgrown, shopworn, out-of-season, dinged, overstocked, tired, or otherwise useless-to-you items," as one woman stated. These items may range from furniture, lamps, and appliances to exercise equipment, holiday decorations, books, CDs, tapes, and records. Hallie, a former garage sale chair, explained how the women in her organization recruit other members of the middle and upper classes to help out on sale days:

> We bring in husbands, children, neighbors, friends, sorority and fraternity members, and anybody else who's willing to lend a hand. We need volunteers to wrap twenty-five cent plates so they won't break on the way out. We need men who can help carry out large pieces of furniture and appliances. It's a *whole* lot of work, but it's worthwhile: The money helps cover the operating expenses for our residential treatment center and foster home agency, and every bit of the hard work is worth it when you look at the smile on one child's face.

Most women working at this charity garage sale are painfully aware of the disparity between their own lifestyle and that of the average sale shopper. Sometimes, awareness of these differences brings about a feeling that one should "hide" some aspects of oneself from the "audience" (to borrow from Erving Goffman's concept of dramaturgical analysis). There may be any number of reasons for having this feeling. Consider this comment by a former garage sale chair, for example:

> For safety reasons, we ask the women to leave their jewelry and expensive personal items at home. We all wear aprons, jeans, and tennis shoes and, other than our aprons, you can't tell us from the shoppers. We have been very fortunate some years to have a security company donate the time of some of its officers, so that we didn't have to pay for protection around where people pay out as they leave. On the limited occasions where we've had an "incident," these gentlemen have quickly taken care of the "problem" for us, and very few people even knew that anything went on.

Although the elite women volunteers modify their clothing somewhat, most of them have "tell-tale signs" of their affluent status, including nicely styled hair and manicured figure nails. Observations outside the arena where the sale is held show that the typical garage-sale shopper drives an older, much less expensive vehicle than the women volunteers, who frequently come to the sale in expensive vehicles such as a Lexus, Mercedes Benz, Cadillac, Jaguar, or Lincoln. However, there are the exceptions, such as the volunteer who stated, "I drive a beat up old truck out here, but there's nothing like it for garage sale 'pick-ups.'"

Most of the women who work year after year at this charity garage sale are Worker Bees who, regardless of their wealth, are committed to improving the quality of life for people who are less fortunate than they are. The first year that I worked at this charity garage sale in the household goods department, for example, I learned that some of the people who purchased plates, glasses, and silverware lived in households where there were not enough of these items for each person to have his or her own at mealtime. My field notes from October 1996 describe such a situation:

> We had dozens of large families of Mexican Americans come to the sale today. I was working in household goods, and we had donated plates for sale that were priced as low as twenty-five cents apiece. The dinner plates had small chips on the edges but were still usable, and one family appeared pleased that they could get a whole set of plates for several dollars. After I wrapped up the plates, the mother turned to a "display" of glasses, at which time, a small boy, about 3 or 4 years old, turned to her and said, "Mamma, does this mean I can have my own glass now?" She nodded her head in agreement but diverted her eyes from me, apparently hoping that I had not heard the child's question.

As I think back on this experience, I probably would not have recorded it if it had not been for the expression on the mother's face. I believe that the family had few material possessions, and this woman did not want me to know this.

Balancing "Low-Brow" Thrift Shops
and Garage Sales with "High-Brow" Parties for Elites

Although the apparent intended audiences of thrift shops and charity garage sales are low-income consumers, more-affluent people are invited to participate as contributors or party-goers. To attract individual and corporate sponsorships for the garage sale, for example, the women in this organization plan an event that will appeal to those in the upper classes. Therefore, the night before the garage sale opens to the public, the women hold an invitational "Preview Party" with food, entertainment, and a chance to preview the "treasures" at the sale. Each year's party has a theme, such as "Under the Big Top," and some club members dress up in appropriate costumes to sell raffle tickets or drinks. Party guests are local economic, political, and social elites who are seldom seen at the actual garage sale. By holding this more exclusive, invitational event, with expensive tickets, elite women members legitimize their organization's "charity" activity in the eyes of other social elites and encourage younger elites to see the party as "the place to be," as one woman commented. The referent power of the organization is also reinforced by the presence of high-status people in the community who otherwise would play no part in such an event.

Holding a "society" party in the midst of a garage sale is not a unique concept, however. Many groups find that it is necessary to balance "low-brow" volunteer projects with some "high-brow" events that will appeal to their members and other elites. One Junior League in this study not only owns and operates a thrift shop but also puts on an elaborate five-day Christmas bazaar attended by over 30,000 customers each year. The events at the bazaar are tiered, with some appealing to the general public while others are directed toward major contributors. The patron party, admission to which is about $125 per guest, is held so that members of the organization, their friends, and major contributors can enjoy a "black tie" evening of shopping and partying before the event opens to the public. Those designated as Underwriters will have made a contribution of $15,000 and above to the organization, while Benefactors have given $10,000 and Patrons will have contributed $5,000. Various categories of support, down to $500, are set up with additional perks being given at each higher level of contribution. In addition to the patron party, the bazaar also has a bistro, a tearoom, and hundreds of "shops" where merchants rent space and sell expensive items ranging from antiques and original artwork to designer clothing and children's toys.

This brings me to the central issue that I believe is demonstrated by this chapter: The power of elite women—both through their wealth and their good deeds—is essential for fundraising activities that raise large sums of money for good causes. They have the clout to attract the sponsorship by and participation of other elites; however, in return, the women must make elites feel special and provide them with opportunities to enjoy themselves in the company of others who are similar to themselves.

The Fashion Show:
Conspicuous Consumption for a Good Cause

Staging a fashion show or a charity ball is more in keeping with the social networks and class backgrounds of many elite women than is operating a thrift shop or a charity garage sale. The High Society charity fashion show is a popular fundraiser for elite women's organizations because members and their friends can enjoy a gala occasion while raising large sums of money. However, at these events, far more than women's and children's apparel is shown: The most lavish fashion shows dramatize the class position and the economic power of the audience, both as vicarious consumers (while they watch the production) and as conspicuous consumers (what they wear to the show and the items they purchase after the show is over).

The charity fashion show dramatizes Thorstein Veblen's argument that the wives of wealthy men ("ladies of leisure") participate in what he viewed as frivolous activities (such as fashion shows) that serve the ceremonial function of showing off their class position while demonstrating their husband's wealth and reputation.[10] According to Veblen, elite women's elegant clothing is not only a sign that the women can afford to dress in a manner that requires extravagant expenditures but also that these women are exempt from the necessity of any type of productive labor. Although many elite women today have a full-time career, the idea that such a woman has time to spend at a charity fundraising luncheon and fashion show—which is typically held in the middle of the work-day—suggests that she has far more leisure time and surplus money to spend than do most other women.

Charity fashion shows are sponsored by couture fashion designers or high-end department stores, such as Saks Fifth Avenue and Neiman Marcus, that want to sell the clothing and accessories on display in the show to women at the event. A nonprofit organization sponsoring such a show gets a portion of the receipts from the sales resulting from the fashion show. The class-based nature of this event is shown by the fact that most fashion shows sponsored by elite women's groups take place in a luxury hotel ballroom with an elevated runway down the middle of the room. Upon arrival, the women are offered appropriate noontime cocktails for "ladies" (such as mimosas or Bloody Marys), and when they enter the ballroom, they find a lavishly decorated arena in which large round tables are draped with elaborate cloths and napkins, and flowers and other decorations carry out a particular theme. At each place setting, there is a "goody bag" containing samples of expensive perfumes, cosmetics, and other small trinkets that the women will be able to take home with them as a souvenir and an enticement to go to the store to purchase the retail size of the items.

The elitist nature of the fashion show becomes more evident in situations where this show is held in conjunction with a debutante presentation ball. At this fashion show, the young debutantes are introduced, and they walk down the runway while the accomplishments of the debutante and her mother are described to the audience. One woman declared, "This was the proudest moment of my life," when describing such an event to me. For the most part, the fashion show is the exclusive gender domain of women, and the only men routinely present are the food servers, a few male models, and perhaps a fashion designer or the head of the department store underwriting the event.

After these introductions and presentations, the big show begins with a burst of music and a steady stream of youthful, very slim women strolling down the runway wearing the latest (and often most expensive) fashions from a designers' collection or a luxury store. To add "local color and interest," some organizations ask a few of their "best dressed" members to model in the show along with the professional models. A wide variety of clothing is shown to the guests over the forty-five minutes to an hour of the show, as a narrator describes the clothing in minute detail, including who the designer is and other "interesting tidbits" about fashions for the next season. Some fashion show organizers place lists of the clothing items on each table so that guests can mark the outfits, as the models display them, that they are most interested in purchasing. The grand finale is usually the arrival of the "bride," a model who wears one of the latest designer wedding creations and brings forth "oohs" from the audience. The show concludes when the designer or manager of the sponsoring dress shop or department store appears for a final round of applause from the assembled women.

Although charity fashion shows do not meet all the elements of Veblen's conspicuous consumption, which he thought was symptomatic of the superfluous lifestyle of the rich,[11] these events tie elite philanthropy and the volunteer activities of privileged women to a world that is far different from the everyday lives of most people. Sometimes, the women get caught up in the "unreal realities" of a world in which they assume that their exclusive activities are fully justified because of the good deeds they do for others. Many elite women would probably agree with the assessment of Helen, an elite woman who has attended many fashion shows in her city:

Call it conspicuous consumption or whatever you will, I am behind the fashion show 100 percent. As a realtor, it's what I call a "win-win situation":

The ladies love it, Neiman's makes a bundle, and they return some of it to us through their generous contributions and a percentage of their sales. The food is delicious, and we all have a super time! What's not to love about it? The women who come as our guests are already the best customers of the designers and stores that sponsor our show. We just help get them together.

Even with the changing composition of the population in various Texas cities, fashion show audiences typically are, in the words of one woman, "lily white" and "well-to-do." Unlike fashion shows that take place in middle-class settings, such as a PTA event to raise money for a high school prom, the fashion shows sponsored by elite women's organizations are distinct in that they are viewed by organizers and participants as being "upper class" social events. This perception is confirmed by observations that show that the ticket price for the event (ranging from hundreds to thousands of dollars per table) is one of the least expensive things that the audience purchases: The clothing they wear to the event, as well as the merchandise they purchase following the show, demonstrate to others in their class that they have an economic surplus and "good taste" and want to be part of the group.

As previously stated, fashion shows may be held as separate fundraising events but frequently take place in conjunction with other events such as a charity ball, to which we now turn.

Having a Ball

Charity balls are major fundraisers for prestigious women's groups, and the women who chair such events gain social recognition and intragroup power. There are various kinds of fundraising balls, depending on which organization is sponsoring the ball and what "cause" will benefit from the event's proceeds. Among the most popular charity balls are those at which debutantes are presented, and I discuss the race, class, and gender implications of these in more detail in chapter 5.

The balls sponsored by high-brow arts and cultural organizations clearly reflect the class and sometimes the racial or ethnic background of organizers and participants. When an opera association "puts on" a fundraising ball, for instance, the most frequent type of entertainment is opera singers performing arias from the best-loved operas. There is an assumption that guests are knowledgeable about opera and that they have the social refinement to appreciate an evening of arias. Pierre Bourdieu stated that opera performances "are the occasion or pretext for social ceremonies enabling a select audience to demonstrate and experience its membership of high society in obedience to the integrating and distinguishing rhythms of a 'society' calendar."[12] For some individuals, the opera ball is an extension of the social aura that they believe to be associated with high culture arts performances. It brings together not only opera lovers but also people of similar economic and social standing. The women who organize the event rely on their social connections, their cultural capital in the form of information about opera, and their organizational skills to conduct a successful event that is widely reported through photographs and newspaper articles. In this way, elite women volunteers gain status in the community and, perhaps more important to them, status in the opinions of other elites. Frank, the husband of Carleen—who has chaired Junior League and hospital foundation balls—described how he and his wife differed in their perceptions regarding the importance of elite balls:

> My wife loves to plan balls; she loves to attend balls. Okay, maybe I like going to see friends there and having a drink or two, but sometimes I tell myself, "I'm standing in the exact same place that I was last year and talking to the same people about the very same things that I talked to them about last year." Still, I get into my "penguin suit" and off we go because she says that being a ball chairman is what defines her place in the community.

Among social elites, some balls are viewed as high-brow; whereas others are seen as low-brow. How formal an event is and what clothing should be worn in order to conform to normative expectations are factors in determining which ball fits into which category. Balls at which formal attire is worn (black-tie events) typically benefit high-brow nonprofit organizations such as an art museum, symphony orchestra, ballet, or opera association, or high-profile institutions such as a prestigious university or medical school. Low-brow charity balls are more casual in clothing and appearance norms, and typically benefit an organization that benefits people across class lines or seeks to eradicate a specific disease. An example of a low-brow charity ball is the Cattle Barons Ball, which benefits the American Cancer Society. Originated in Texas, the Cattle Barons Ball is now held in a number of states, and it is the hope of ball organizers that middle-class as well as upper-class people will attend this fundraising gala. However, the class-based nature of this ball is evident in Helen's description of this event in her city:

> Sure, we want everybody to come. It will be at the Shady Oaks Ranch this year, and we have wonderful items for the raffle, like a new $40,000 Mercedes Benz, a $5,000 watch, and an $8,000 trip to a golf resort. The live auction will raise lots of money too: We have a cruise worth $17,000 and a trip to Scotland for people to bid on. We want guests to show up in their boots and jeans, but we ask them to be sure they put their checkbook or credit card in those jeans.

Even though less formal attire is worn to the Cattle Barons Ball, there is still an expectation that those who attend will spend money on raffle tickets and expensive auction items because it is for a good cause. Trudy, a Worker Bee, emphasized that this event is far more significant than what anyone wears:

> You can go like you want to . . . wear jeans, put on your hat and boots, and you're ready to go. Great entertainment too . . . like George Strait singing or getting to "bet" at a casino. There's a different theme each year, and it's a lot of fun. Of course, it's for a really good cause, too. Cancer research is vital for all our lives! My dad died of testicular cancer and one of my sisters had breast cancer.

The social connections that guests may cultivate at balls are sometimes mentioned in publicity about the event. The American Heart Association's Heart Ball is a black-tie gala that proclaims that "The who's who of [city] come out to enjoy this elegant black tie evening while raising the critical funds to support cardiovascular research and education."[13] Those who aspire to the upper classes are willing to pay to mingle with the right people, and this desire gives elite women volunteers the opportunity to leverage social power by either helping newcomers become incorporated into the inner social circle or largely ignoring them.

Formal events such as a black-tie charity ball generate criticism from some people who view these activities as elitist playgrounds for the wealthy, who use their contributions as a tax write-off. However, a different view emerges from people who benefit from the money raised by these activities. Consider, for example, the Crystal Charity Ball in Dallas, which is put on by an exclusive organization of "socialites" and "professional women" according to Helen, a 50-year-old white woman who has been a ball committee member and spoke with pride about the event:

> The [Crystal Charity] ball is always an extravagant affair. This year it had an elegant Parisian theme with gendarmes and cancan girls who looked like they came straight from Paris. It was well worth the ticket price. Auction items like chartering an airplane to go wherever you want sold for as much as $50,000 an item. We raised more than $4 million for charities like the children's medical center, Southwestern [medical school], and the retina foundation. I'm proud of our positive contribution, and I still resent the negative publicity we have received from the media over things like our old "Best Dressed List" and our annual fashion show. That's not really what this group is all about, but we have the right to have some fun along the way.

According to one administrator whose medical school benefits from the money raised by the Crystal Charity Ball committee, "We could never raise the kind of money from the community that these ladies do. We are extremely grateful for their hard work, and I don't want anybody to make light of their accomplishments." By way of example, the administrator pointed out that two "centers" at his school are named after the group: the Crystal Charity Ball Center for Pediatric Brain and Neurological Diseases and the Crystal Charity Ball Center for Research in Pediatric Critical Care, which are partially funded by proceeds from this annual event.

Elite women have unique social connections and resources to help them plan a major fundraising ball for thousands of guests. Regardless of which ball elite volunteers are involved with, the women on the ball committee work throughout the year to make sure that their ball is a "special evening" for guests and a financial success for the nonprofit organization that it benefits. Several ball chairs or former chairs described how much "psychological energy, as well as physical stamina," is needed to produce a major fundraising ball. Maria, a white woman in her late 30s from a New Money family, described the stress she experienced when planning a ball:

> I couldn't sleep for several nights after last year's ball was over. I was just lying there thinking about the theme for next year's ball [that she was chairing]. I knew "my ball" had to be wonderful, exciting, the best ever! I also knew we had to make a lot more money than this year, because that's the name of the game: Each ball chairman is supposed to outdo previous ones. What pressure! I didn't want to let anybody down, especially me. But I was the one who was putting myself under pressure . . . not the other wonderful ladies in our club.

Maria's concerns are well-founded: High expectations do exist for each year's ball, and women who take the leadership roles are held accountable for how well their event does. Women who excel in such roles are rewarded with intangible benefits such as positive name recognition and offers to serve in more prestigious positions. An example of how closely linked a ball is with the woman who chairs it is the fact that balls are often referred to among members as "Mary's ball," "Jane's ball," or "Louise's ball," depending on who chaired the event in a specific year. In return for their efforts, the ball chair and members of key committees receive recognition and more firmly establish their social position among the city's social elite. In this way, women from New Money families who attain the position of ball chair can further enhance their family's social and cultural capital. Their commitment to difficult and time-consuming tasks often makes the difference in whether or not daughters from New Money families are selected to be debutantes by elite organizations.

Even formal balls reflect the stratified social hierarchy in the cities in my study. One woman suggested that there is a "local social hierarchy of balls," with the most prestigious ones being the debutante balls of the "old guard" men's clubs, followed by the high-brow debutante balls sponsored by invitational women's organizations that raise money for charitable causes and provide a "stage" for the formal presentation of college-age daughters (and sons as escorts) to one's friends in Society. Lower in the social hierarchy of charity balls are the laid-back events such as the Cattle Barons Ball, which—although they raise money for a good cause—do not involve the presentation of debutantes and have tickets that are available to the general public.

Charity balls sponsored by elite African American women were not mentioned by the white women describing the social hierarchy of balls in their cities, thereby suggesting that only "white balls" were within the city's social framework. However, within the African American community, balls sponsored by the most exclusive black men's organizations are probably at the top of the "social pecking order," followed by balls sponsored by prestigious African American women's organizations such as Alpha Kappa Alpha sorority or Jack and Jill of America's Beautillion Ball, which acknowledges the accomplishments of young African American men and the young women who accompany them (in a reversal of roles as compared with a white presentation ball). Debutante presentation balls sponsored by elite African American women's groups are described in chapter 5.

Charity balls organized by elite women rely on the norm of exclusivity because guests must believe that not just anybody can attend and that the event is worthy of their time and money. Despite the money that is raised by charity balls, lines of class, gender, and race/ethnicity are deeply embedded in these events because they typically require a certain socioeconomic status and upper-class mind-set. There are class-based differences in the kinds of events that affluent people choose to attend and whom they expect the other "guests" to be. Many of these events in Texas are largely segregated by race and ethnicity even at a time when the state is becoming increasingly diverse.

Like "high ticket" charity balls, fundraisers held in private homes and lavish showhouses reflect the upper-class nature of elite women's philanthropy.

Charity Benefits in Residences: From My House to the Showhouse

Designer showhouses and elaborate fundraising dinner parties held in private homes are very popular events among elite women. These activities provide them with the opportunity to use their cultural capital and show off their expert power in high-end party planning. The major distinction between private dinner parties and showhouses is the site in which the event occurs: Dinner parties provide hosts with the opportunity to display their own home and lifestyle to others, whereas designer showhouses are more generic "stages" upon which social elites and outsiders can partake of luxury living.

Planning a fundraising showhouse is a very time-consuming job for the elite woman volunteer. First, it is necessary to obtain a site for the showhouse, which means that the women who organize this event must be able to persuade the owner of a mansion to make the house available to the group, or to persuade a homebuilder to build a house that the group can use as its showhouse. Next, the showhouse chair and her various committee chairs must establish connections with people who represent the entire gambit of the construction, remodeling, and interior design industries in their city. The women must also contact corporate and individual sponsors to gain underwriters for the event. During my years as a community volunteer, I was "promoted" over a three-year period from the showhouse publicity committee to the organization's liaison with the interior designers who were participating in the project, to the position of showhouse chair. I learned how much work and diplomacy went into planning and implementing a successful fundraiser such as this, and I quickly realized that I did not have as much social power or clout in the community to get things done as some of the wealthier, better-connected members of the group did. As a fundraiser, a showhouse is a very labor intensive endeavor for members of elite women's organizations because it requires that the women spend time serving as docents (who describe the various rooms in the house to ticket-purchasing guests), tearoom hostesses and servers, ticket salespersons, boutique assistants, and hundreds of other jobs in the showhouse division of labor. Victoria, a white woman in her 50s at the time she chaired this event, described the division of labor and what was required of her as a leader:

> As the showhouse chair, I set up a ton of committees and appointed chairs for each. We had the boutique committee, the tearoom committee, the docents' committee, the sponsor committee, the advertising committee, the housekeeping committee, the preview and gala opening party committee, the designer committee, and on and on. But one thing I learned, when anything doesn't get done, the chair or co-chairs had better be ready to step in and do it. If somebody falls in the tearoom, you need to be there to scoop them up and be sure they're all right. If the trash needs taking out, you may have to take it out. There's quite a bit of glory involved, getting your picture in the paper and being praised in the [organization's] newsletter, but you've really paid your dues as chairman by the time you've done a year or more of this kind of work which, for me, was on a daily basis. One Christmas Eve I remember talking on the phone to somebody about where to locate a future showhouse.

The efforts of women such as Victoria help the nonprofit organizations raise money, ranging from $30,000 to $40,000 for smaller cities and into the hundreds of thousands of dollars in larger ones, as a result of the showhouses. The showhouse is a popular fundraiser among elite women volunteers because it provides them with a class-specific arena in which to interact with other elite women. They can spend time in a luxurious residence, visit with other women, enjoy lunch (and sometimes fashion shows) in the tearoom, and shop in the boutique. Through these relationships, the women maintain an upper-class lifestyle. As Ostrander stated in her work on upper-class women: "As club members, upper-class women organize social and recreational life for themselves and their families, as do women of other classes. But their social life is the social life of a class, and their relations weave the fabric of upper-class life."[14] The social life of this class is evident in the types of fundraising projects that are selected by organizers to appeal to elite women volunteers as well as to those who pay to participate in the events.

Designer showhouses bring elite women volunteers into contact with middle-class people who come to view these mansion-sized residences that are opened to the public for the price of a ticket (ranging from $8 to $25 or $30 in large cities). To people who come to view the showhouse, it is typically a dream house, but for some of the elite women volunteers, the house is similar to the one in which they live. Fewer people of color are visible at designer showhouses, either as members of the sponsoring organization or as guests who pay at the door to see the house.

Elaborate charity dinner parties in private homes are another fundraiser that brings elites together. This type of fundraiser is a very lucrative affair for organizations that solicit contributions from established families in the community. Even those who have become tired of the "social whirl" will attend this in-group social event because they will know many of the other guests and "be away from the teeming masses," as one party organizer stated.

Using the language of Goffman, dinner parties provide a front stage setting for the interaction of social elites. Historians have documented that, as far back as the late 1800s, social elites in major cities embraced the dinner party as a social ritual. According to Maureen E. Montgomery's study of this social phenomenon, "Dining became a key social ritual in the development of New York high society. Private dinners were one of the most important forms of sociability for conferring social acceptance and cementing social bonds."[15] Obviously, the dinners of which Montgomery writes were not fundraisers; however, over time, the idea of the charity benefit dinner caught on as the social life of privileged people became increasingly commercialized, particularly with the relocation of many parties from residences to luxury hotels or private clubs. As this shift occurred, an invitation to dine at a private home became a symbolic gesture showing that a person might be included among the inner circle of the host's friends. As such, elite dinner parties have come to serve as an access ritual for affluent newcomers who are being considered for inclusion in top-tier social networks. This practice remains today, but charity dinner parties in private homes also help new corporate arrivals and other affluent people to establish bonds with long-term social elites in a given city. The dinner parties also provide a setting for established elites to have a good time and renew social relationships with friends who can assist them when their children need a letter of recommendation for college, a fraternity or sorority, or for other opportunities that require the imprimatur of a person who is well established in the social hierarchy.

Dinner parties are very time-consuming and expensive for hosts who put them on. They involve complicated logistics for the elite women who plan a series of them once a year. Marjorie, who chaired one foundation's annual benefit dinner parties, describes how these parties are planned:

> I think we borrowed the idea from the New York Public Library, and it's a great fundraiser. We work real hard to get the most gracious hostesses to "volunteer" their homes for this event. We have a series of parties that people can choose from, and we send out invitations listing the different kinds of parties people can pay to attend. Some feature wine tasting while others have an after-dinner entertainer or a celebrity author, for example. Host couples pay all the expenses associated with giving the parties, including hiring caterers, bartenders, florists, and other assistants to help them put on the party. Money from tickets and sponsorships goes to annual projects designated by [our organization].

The women apply the norm of exclusivity in subtle ways in regard to the guests at each party, as Marjorie further explained:

> With the invitation, we include a reservation card that asks people to list their first, second, and third choices of events to attend. The gala committee then decides who will go where, usually on a first-come-first-served basis. We let the host couples look at the lists to see if there's anybody they don't want to have come to their party. You know, somebody who might make them or other guests "uncomfortable," like a former business partner or an ex-husband or ex-wife of somebody already on the guest list. We don't think that's too much to ask. After all, the hosts are paying for the party, and we don't want to disturb anybody's comfort zone.

The "comfort zone" is a very important concept to elite women who ask other privileged people to open their homes to guests. As Barbara, who chaired another committee for this benefit, points out, the women are afraid that if a host couple has a bad experience one year this may cause the event to suffer in future years:

Everybody talks to everybody else. If word gets out that some guest was obnoxious or stole something, we'd never get host couples to hold another party. One year, we had a pushy journalist who wanted to attend a party (for free) so that she could do a write-up about the guy's priceless art collection. What a no-no! It ended up that she was mad, but she sure didn't get to go. [The man] and his wife said, "No way—we'll cancel the party first!"

Does allowing the host couples to exclude potential guests about whom they might feel "uncomfortable" ever exclude people on the basis of race or ethnicity? Barbara answered that question as follows:

Heavens, no. We don't have as many blacks or Hispanics participating in the event as we would like, so we certainly don't discourage them. However, invitations are sent to major contributors and people who've attended the parties in previous years, so we don't have too large a list of minorities because very few have been interested in attending. Invitations and reservations never have *anything* to do with race, but they do reflect friendships. The benefit committee members make sure that their friends are on the list.

Barbara's assessment of how decisions are made by those who organize prestigious fundraisers provides insight on why many women believe that their decisions are based on friendships and on "comfort zones," and as such, that these have no ramifications for race, ethnicity, or cultural diversity at such events.

Chairs of major fundraising events, such as of an annual series of charity dinner parties, possess legitimate power based on their status in the group and the responsibility they have for ensuring the success of the event for all involved, including those who host the dinners at their own expense. For elite women, this means that they must walk a tight line between status-asserting behavior and being the "ever gracious" society hostess and community volunteer.

Analyzing the racial and ethnic characteristics of women who plan elaborate dinner parties as major fundraisers and the patrons who attend such events, I identified a persistent pattern of racial and class separation. Attending a number of the events and conducting informal "headcounts" by race and ethnicity at a series of dinners sponsored by a hospital foundation, as well as examining hundreds of photographs taken at such parties, I found that few women of color are visible either as members of organizational committees or as guests at the benefit parties. One exception was a benefit where guests paid to attend a dinner honoring the local university's coaching staff, several of whom were people of color. When I discussed the issue of racial and ethnic diversity with one white woman who had served on the hospital's gala committee, she acknowledged that there was a lack of racial diversity but attributed it to the lack of minority physicians at the city's major hospitals. According to Amanda, "We don't have many black doctors, and doctors and their wives are the key sponsors and patrons at this event. That's why there aren't many blacks attending the parties." But when Viola, a woman of color who had served on the hospital foundation's board, was asked about racial and ethnic diversity at the same parties, she offered a different opinion:

> I'm glad we have these parties to raise money for the hospital. Most of them are *really* nice. But I'm not sure that we have reached out to the black community as much as we should. When I see all the black professionals in this town, I wonder why they haven't been contacted about getting involved. When I talk to board members about "minority outreach," they say, "Great idea! Why don't you do it, Viola?"

Like Viola, other elite women of color described themselves as "always being cast in the role of liaison between [a nonprofit organization] and the black community." When asked about how to get more people of color involved in high-profile charity activities, white elite women typically respond that "minority women are in a better position to reach out to others in their own community." Charlotte, a wealthy white woman in her 50s who has worked with the benefit dinners for several years, made a typical statement:

> Community outreach is one of the reasons we have committees. These committee members are supposed to use their connections to get other people to make donations and come for an evening of fun. I know that when I agree to serve on a committee, I'm going to be expected to get my friends to buy tickets. Why shouldn't everybody do this? I don't think race should even be brought up here: Motivating other people to become involved in *their* community is the central concern.

Charlotte pointed out that the women do undertake responsibilities when they "sign up" for a fundraising event committee; however, she failed to mention that few women of color serve on these committees or on this organization's board of directors. She also failed to mention that motivating other people to attend, regardless of what "community" they are part of, could be every member's concern, not just a concern for women of color.

Conclusion

This chapter examines how elite women use their social power to organize fundraising activities that benefit various segments of the community. Some of these fundraisers are similar in many ways to activities conducted by other volunteer groups—thrift shops and garage sales, for example. However, there are several very visible differences between these activities as conducted by elite women's groups and those conducted by other types of organizations. In a nutshell, those differences boil down to two things: money and prestige, which are directly related to the privileged position that these women hold in societal economic and social hierarchies. Although anyone or any group can conduct a garage sale, the amount of money raised by such an event when conducted by an elite women's organization is simply not in the same league with the amount raised by a less elite group. The same is true of a thrift shop, a showhouse, a fashion show, or a dinner party. Other, less-elite groups have such activities and raise money by holding them; typically, those other groups simply don't raise as much money, nor do their activities serve as a setting in which social elites interact and develop social ties that may be beneficial for their families.

Elite women's groups accomplish this through their referent power. The fundraiser is conducted by a group of women who have ties to other wealthy people, and they are able to obtain the support—and contributions—of these other people by virtue of the prestige of the organization itself. They conduct these fundraising activities in a manner that will appeal to these wealthy elites: Come to our party, which will only be attended by people like you. Perhaps the party is a preview party before a garage sale or designer showhouse. Perhaps it is an elaborate presentation ball or a series of fancy dinners at private residences. The elite nature of the organization itself is the guest's guarantee that the event will be attended by other elite people, that there will be high-quality, high-priced food and beverages available, customarily including an open bar that doesn't charge for cocktails. It is a guarantee that there will be entertainment of some sort—perhaps the presentation of debutantes, a "live" (an auctioneer taking bids) or "silent" (no auctioneer, just write down your bid) auction, or an operatic presentation. And it is all for a good cause— basically, what the guest pays (over and above the value of what the guest receives) is a tax-deductible donation. From a sociological standpoint, however, elite fundraisers serve to reproduce the upper class by providing a venue in which privileged people only associate with one another and in which the social boundaries between elites and nonelites are pronounced. Although individuals in the middle and working classes typically are not overtly reminded of their class position, those in the upper classes are reminded of their intraclass commonalities by coming together at social events that are open only to those people who fit well within the comfort zone of the elites who organize such benefits, particularly women of the upper classes.

Obviously, there is a circularity to this: To be elite and thus to be able to accomplish what elite women do in fundraising and event planning, the invitational women's groups to which they belong must have an aura of exclusivity; to remain "exclusive," the group must recruit new elites and basically exclude those persons who are not elite. This pattern of excluding those who do not meet either established or inferred criteria often means excluding people on the conscious or unconscious basis of race/ethnicity and class. In some cases, those who are excluded from membership are among the people the group purports to serve. I believe that this is how the norm of exclusivity works in elite organizations: The members of these groups believe that it is appropriate—and even necessary—to exclude from their groups individuals or categories of people who are not deemed to possess the attributes most highly valued by the current membership. They believe that the decision to exclude people is made out of commitment to the group and its goals, not to self-interest on their own part. They do not see, or at least do not acknowledge, underlying factors regarding race or class distinctions that may be embedded in the decisions they make regarding fundraising activities and social events.

The exclusivity of the volunteer organizations to which these women belong is part of the social power they exercise. Returning to the French and Raven model, women's social power has five typical bases: reward, coercive, expert, legitimate, and referent power.[16] Creating and maintaining an exclusive, elite women's volunteer organization gives those women who are active in—and, especially, those who are leaders of—such organizations all of these sources of power. Maintaining the norm of exclusivity gives these women the ability to exercise all five of these power bases.

How do elite women across racial and ethnic lines come to believe in the norm of exclusivity? Do they grow up with such a belief as a result of their early socialization? Is it something that they learn in school or during their college years? The following chapter looks at how elite women are socialized from an early age to accept the norm of exclusivity and how they respond to this socialization process.

Notes

1. Schlenker 1980.
2. Goffman 1967.
3. Ostrander 1984:112.
4. Ostrander 1984.
5. See Ostrower 1995.
6. Daniels 1988: 134.
7. Domhoff 1998.
8. Frankenberg 1993: 43.
9. It should be noted that not all customers of thrift shops are disadvantaged or poor. Although low-income families are the target audience for thrift shops and charity garage sales, middle-income and affluent women also shop there, looking

for bargains and finding gently worn designer gowns donated by members of the organization or costumes to wear to parties. One woman in this study described how she disguised herself so that she could go into a thrift shop in another city to see if they had anything she wanted to buy. Likewise, a charity garage sale may have a "preview party" at which the members and guests (all of whom have paid to attend the event) not only nibble on food that has been provided by sponsors of the event but also are allowed to purchase any of the items that, starting the next day, will be sold to the public.

10. Veblen 1994 [1899].
11. Veblen quoted in Diggins 1999.
12. Bourdieu 1984: 272.
13. American Heart Association 2001.
14. Ostrander 1984: 149.
15. Montgomery 1998:31.
16. French and Raven 1959; Raven 1988.

CHAPTER FOUR

❧

Learning the Ropes:
The Childhood and
College Years of Elite Women

Gay, a white woman—who at the time of these remarks was in her mid-20s—from an Old Name family, offered an interesting and informative personal narrative while we were discussing elite children's education:

> After the obstetrician told me I was pregnant, the first phone call I made was to my husband to tell him. The second call I made was to [an elite private school] to put my [unborn] child on the school's waiting list for four years down the road. I've been extremely happy with my choice and have enrolled my other children in the same school because they learn values that are in keeping with what we try to teach the children at home, and they develop playgroups and friendship with other children like themselves, playgroups that help them to know, from an early age, that they will be recognized for their hard work and their personal achievements. I also like it that [name of school] teaches cooperation and sharing, virtues that will be important when they start to be involved in the life of the community.

Some people might find it odd that Gay would have contacted a school about enrolling her future child even before she discussed her pregnancy with friends and other relatives, yet her remarks clearly illustrate an important point: Most elite parents strongly believe that, early on in their children's lives, the parents should start putting together all the right "building blocks" that their children will need in order to take their own places in the elite circles in which the parents live, and that the parents need to continue this process of social reproduction as the children grow into adulthood. Although biological reproduction creates new generations of children who are members of upper-class families, this does not guarantee that the attitudes, beliefs, and behaviors of the current generation of elites will be accepted by their offspring and employed in a manner that maintains the privilege of members of this class. For this reason, social reproduction—in this instance, meaning the replication of the social structures and class relationships that characterize a society and, especially, the right to maintain the privileged position of one's family within society—becomes one of the tasks of elite parents, particularly of elite women. Understanding the process of social reproduction of the upper classes helps to explain how the adult women in this study came to be the way they are, why they hold the attitudes and beliefs they hold, and how they bring up their children in a way that reproduces these characteristics in the next generation.[1]

This chapter looks at the childhood and school experiences of some elite women, and of their children, to show how these early experiences may contribute to the norm of exclusivity in elite women's organizations. Typically, elite community volunteers do not question their lifestyle, including the fact that privilege goes with their lives or that certain opportunities just "open up" for them that are not available to people in other classes. Consequently, elite women do not view themselves as having done anything that intentionally discriminates against anyone, such as whom they may—or may not—invite to participate in their clubs and organizations. Rather, they describe themselves as pursuing their everyday lives in a way that they have learned since childhood. Exclusivity and noblesse oblige are among the attitudes and beliefs that many elite women learn from an early age.

The ability to exclude others is a form of social power that privileged young women possess from an early age. Typically, the women in my study grew up in exclusive neighborhoods, attended exclusive schools, dined at exclusive private clubs, and belonged to exclusive organizations as a result of their parents' wealth and social position. Many women who possess this sort of privilege—by being an "insider" with regard to class and/or race—exercise the prerogative of exclusion without necessarily recognizing that they are doing so. Privilege is simply something that they have always had and that they envision they have the right to pass on to their children. One form of privilege is the ability to associate with those—and only those—people with whom one chooses to associate.

Elite women typically do not describe themselves as privileged or see their early childhood socialization as having been vastly different from that of girls in other social classes. In the words of Paula Rothenberg, these women have "invisible privilege" based on their class position, their race, their ethnicity, or some combination of these factors.[2] This invisible privilege, as Rothenberg has noted, provides those in the top tiers of society with advantages that other people do not have and gives their children a head start in life. It is so carefully woven into the fabric of their everyday lives that it becomes, at least to them, invisible.

Such privilege is particularly invisible to elite children, who are surrounded by others (except for servants) similar to themselves and who therefore are unlikely to notice that it even exists. Is this mere happenstance? No, the children are brought up in a social "bubble"—a term used by some of the women in this study to describe their neighborhood (or the neighborhood where they grew up) and the environment in which they desire to raise their children. This "bubble" exists based on a number of perquisites of privilege, including the elite geographic location of the family's residence (or residences), the early friendship groups and peer cliques that the children are allowed to have, the clubs and organizations of which they are members, and the schools—from nursery school through college—that foster their educational and social skills. It is a social bubble that the parents work hard to create and maintain. An example is Highland Park and University Park, wealthy adjacent enclaves surrounded by the city of Dallas. Many people who reside in these affluent cities refer to their neighborhood as "the bubble," a term that journalists have adopted for describing life in this small, exclusive area.

Whether the women in this study were employed full time in a professional career or were full-time moms, most of them were quick to acknowledge that they take—and feel that they should take—an active role in organizing their children's lives. Among the reasons for this belief is the widely held assumption among these women that, for their children merely to grow up in an affluent family is not enough. They typically believe that their children also need—and are entitled to have—accomplishments of their own. Among these accomplishments should be development of the right academic, professional, and social skills to fit into the next generation of the upper-class lifestyle and the accompanying concept of noblesse oblige, of helping the less fortunate. In other words, that the children should follow in the parents' footsteps, at least with regard to doing well for themselves and doing good for others. The unspoken belief or assumption is that the children will not—or will not be allowed to—fail.

Just as privilege and exclusivity are linked, so too are the concepts of control and achievement: Elite women typically believe that their children are most likely to "learn the ropes" for being successful as adults if the parents early on use their money and social power to control the circumstances under which their children grow up. This includes maintaining the social bubble described above—a safe and protective environment from which the children only emerge in supervised and special circumstances. This protective environment surrounds all aspects of the children's lives. In order to learn the concept of noblesse oblige, for example, children in some elite prep schools are encouraged to participate in closely supervised volunteer activities that help the less fortunate in the community in which the school is located Yet these same children would never be permitted (by their parents or by the school administration) to go alone to an inner-city school, an AIDS hospice, or a homeless shelter to engage in one-on-one volunteering. Doing good for others is always performed within the safe confines of the social bubble or under the immediate supervision of responsible adults who are charged with their care, a concept that is not forgotten by these children in their subsequent adult-life philanthropic endeavors.

Having the social power to control the interactions and early experiences of their children provides elite parents with the unique opportunity not only to ensure the exclusivity of their children's lives but also to make sure that the children have only limited and highly structured involvement with people of other social classes or racial-ethnic groupings. To both the parents and the children, this exclusivity—this form of social exclusion of those who are not considered beneficial to the children—is a matter of entitlement. It is an entitlement based on "good blood," good connections, and/or hard work (in the form of the accumulation of money and status by the parents). Controlling the social environment of the children and teaching them the concept of exclusivity is part of the parents' role in providing them with all the right "building blocks" for the upper-class lifestyle and part of the social reproduction of the upper classes.

Jenny, an active community volunteer from a white Old Name family and the mother of three daughters, introduced me to the building block concept in elite child rearing and of its importance to many elite parents:

> The symphony has a program called Building Blocks of the Orchestra, where children are introduced to instruments, music, conductors, and other things that it takes to make up a symphony orchestra. I got to thinking about this during a program one day and realized that children's lives are like building blocks. That, as a mother, I have a responsibility to take one block after another and help my children become the human beings that they have the potential to become. I know that my children have started with more of these blocks than some children have, and through the [Junior] League and other organizations, we try to help children who have fewer blocks than our children do so that they, too, can get a good education and have a happy life. But my primary responsibility is my own kids. It's important that I help them know who they are and why they must be proud of the family of which they are a part. I want to be sure that my children know how to use the building blocks that they have been given.

Previous research[3] has suggested that Jenny is correct: Elite families use the building blocks that they have been given in creating an exclusive environment—a social bubble—for their children and themselves. In the discussion that follows, we will examine some of those building blocks for elite young women and the effect that those blocks have on people both within and outside the social bubble. They include the neighborhood of the family's residence, the young women's friends and in-groups, the behaviors and beliefs that they are taught are appropriate, the educational institutions that they attend, and the Greek-letter sororities that they may join prior to graduation from college. We will also examine the effect that those building blocks have on the attitudes that elite women have regarding the good deeds described elsewhere in this book.

The Prestigious Neighborhoods that Elite Girls Call "Home"

The early socialization of elite women usually begins in a residential area that is among the most exclusive or prestigious in the city in which their families reside. Based on location, type, and quality, an elite family's residence may be both a showplace of conspicuous consumption and a part of the social "bubble": a safe haven that provides the family with comfort, safety, and isolation from those of other social classes. As E. Digby Baltzell has noted, elite families place great importance on their place of residence:

> The higher the social class, the more social distance is reinforced by geographical isolation. The social life of the upper classes, both children and adults, tends to be *exclusive*. . . . The exclusive neighborhood, then, with its distinctive architecture, fashionable churches, private schools, and sentimental traditions, is an indispensable factor in the development of an upper class style of life, system of personal values, and distinct character structure.[4]

Over the half century since Baltzell wrote about the desire of elites for geographic isolation, the concern for social distance has grown more intense among some elites in the Southwest as the cities in which they live have become more racially and ethnically diverse and as fear of crime has risen due to urban population growth and waves of immigration from elsewhere in the United States and from other countries. Geographic isolation and exclusivity may therefore be seen by elite parents as related to safety issues, and often are described to the children as such. A number of women in my study recalled being repeatedly told during their childhoods not to stray outside their own residential areas without the protection and supervision of their own or a friend's parents or household employees.

Elite residences tend to be in exclusive enclaves where housing costs prohibit all but the wealthiest families from acquiring a home. As a result, no middle- or lower-income families and few families of color will be the neighbors of elite white families, with the exceptions being top CEOs, celebrities, or sports stars of color, who are typically viewed as "the exception rather than the rule for minorities," in the words of one white woman. These exclusive residential enclaves usually fit into one of several categories, one of which is a fairly large older area of town with a high enough proportion of very expensive housing to promote the feeling of exclusivity and privilege. Some of these older areas are incorporated cities within the larger city of which they are a part, such as Alamo Heights (surrounded by San Antonio) and Highland Park and University Park (surrounded, as previously noted, by Dallas). These areas have their own school system and police department to enforce the rules, not only as they are set forth "on the books" but also sometimes as the residents see fit. I heard a number of examples of police being encouraged to stop and question people who drove older cars or did not look like "they belonged in our neighborhood," particularly after dark.

Other elite enclaves—such as the River Oaks area of Houston and the "Old Enfield" area of Austin—are located in exclusive older areas of a city rather than constituting an incorporated city in and of themselves. Often, the residents of such areas have been able to get the city to close certain streets, creating a cul de sac, or to create other barriers of one sort or another that discourage or prevent outsiders from driving through the neighborhood. If less expensive housing abuts such an enclave, elite parents may seek to dissuade their children from associating with children who live in the less expensive areas, as Nancy (a white woman in her mid-30s from an Old Name family) recalled from her childhood:

We lived in a large brick house on a tree-lined street, but several blocks away there were smaller, wood-frame houses with families living in them. I wanted to play with a child who lived in one of those houses, but my mother repeatedly said, "We don't play with the children who live on [name of street]." When I asked, "Why?" I always got the same answer, "Well, they are different from you and me, and there are plenty of children that you can be friends with on our own street." When I pressed her further, one day Mother blurted out, "Nancy, I wish you'd quit asking me about that. I've told you time after time that 'They are not our kind of people,' so will you kindly hush up about that?" I have really tried to raise my children to see that we should treat everybody the same regardless of wealth, race, creed, color, national origin, or anything else about them that may be different from us, but I'd have to say that how I'm teaching [my children] is different from what I learned in my own family.

To prevent their children's exposure to those they deem unacceptable, some elite parents choose to live in more closely guarded enclaves than the neighborhood where Nancy grew up. Gated communities located within the city proper and affluent suburbs in outlying areas are examples of such exclusive residential areas. Regardless of the specific geographic location of their residences, the goal of elites—particularly those with children—is sufficient social distance and geographical isolation (to use Baltzell's terminology) to separate themselves from people of other classes, races, or ethnicities and to be in the proximity of others from their own group. Whether parents and significant others explicitly use such terms or not, elite children across racial and ethnic lines quickly learn that some people are "our kind of people" while all of the others are not.[5]

Social geographers such as Stephen Richard Higley[6] have shown how the upper classes shape and control residential land use for their own benefit. Restrictive covenants regarding land use are an example: Affluent suburbs are established beyond central cities and their problems—including high crime rates, deteriorating housing and public schools, and high rates of unemployment—and residential neighborhoods in these separately incorporated suburbs have land use restrictions that specify what size house must be built, the size of the lot on which it can be located, and in some instances even what the minimum cost of building the house must be. Practices such as these protect property values and ensure a certain lifestyle for residents; at the same time, however, they have the effect of excluding families that cannot afford to live in an area with such requirements. Along with upper-middle-class professionals, many of the Old Name and New Rich families in Texas prefer to reside in these wealthy suburban enclaves rather than in the areas historically associated with elites in their geographical area. Wealthy suburbs located near the cities in this study (suburbs in which a number of the women discussed in this book live) include West Lake Hills (near Austin), The Woodlands (near Houston), and Plano and Frisco (near Dallas).

As discussed later in this chapter, the location of a family's residence may have some effect on whether elite parents in the Southwest choose to enroll their children in private schools or in well-regarded local public schools, but another of the building blocks involved in the social reproduction of the upper classes needs to be discussed before reaching that topic.

Parental Selection of Elite
Children's Friends and In-Groups

Consciousness of kind is a central factor when elite mothers help their children establish their first playgroups and friendship networks. Although some friendships may emerge from neighborhood settings, many of the women described how their children's playgroups are more closely tied to the mother's own friendship groups and social networks. As one mother stated, "I like for my kids to play with my friends' children. That way I know I can trust that they will be safe and that they will be around kids with whom they attend school or are involved in other social activities." A number of the mothers were rather outspoken about the fact that they do not encourage their children to find their own friends, sometimes even when the children are teenagers. Nancy, whose recollections regarding her own youth are stated above and who is the mother of several young children, is an example of an elite woman who sees it as her responsibility to help her children choose their friends:

> My children don't really select their own friends. They decide who they like most or have the most fun with in playgroups that we set up for them. Young children don't really know how to go out and find friends of their own, but they enjoy doing activities together that the mothers have set up or that are like playday in the summer at the country club. On those days, the kids get to use the club and the facilities, and they don't have to worry about whether they are in the way of adults. My oldest daughter met her friends at some of those activities along with the children of mothers who do volunteer activities with me.

Nancy, like other mothers in this study, provides her children with opportunities to play at the country club and at a private club in their neighborhood, where the only children with whom they will associate are the children of other club members. Neither the women nor their children see this as any form of exclusivity or "snobbishness," but instead view it as going about their everyday lives "just doing what we always do."

Elite mothers typically do not acknowledge that allowing their children to associate only with children of their own class or racial/ethnic group separates them from children of other backgrounds or that this may make it more difficult for the children to interact with those outside their own social circle as they grow up. Rather, the mothers are quick to describe how much diversity exists in the lives of their children, frequently noting the one African American or Asian American family that lives nearby or belongs to some organization of which the parents are members, and how their children have exposure to children from those families.

It must be noted, however, that elite white parents are not alone in promoting class-based (and sometimes race-based) separation of their children: Elite African American parents, for example, also tend to make decisions about their children's schools and playmates that separate their children from young people of other classes, regardless of race. In his best-selling book about the U.S. black upper class, Lawrence Otis Graham describes how children of the black upper class are members (along with their parents) of the exclusive by-invitation-only organization known as Jack and Jill of America, which provides "a great opportunity for [African American] professional parents to introduce their kids to children of similar families." According to Graham, Jack and Jill has served for generations as a "network for parents who want playgroups for their children, as well as a network for young adults who want companionship, dating relationships, and ultimately marriage partners."[7]

The consciousness of kind among African American children that Graham describes provides children of color with a race- and class-based identity as well as giving them a group of people with whom they can associate throughout life. In my own research, Tamara—an affluent African American college student—described the significance of Jack and Jill to her parents and in her own life:

> For my parents, missing a Jack and Jill awards banquet or party was as bad as if I played hooky from Sunday school. They thought that I might miss meeting somebody that I would really enjoy knowing or of seeing other black parents be good role models for their kids. I have to admit that when I came to [a predominantly white] University, it was nice that some of the people I had known at Jack and Jill were already in the sorority I wanted to join. Of course, it also helped that I was legacy because my mother had been in the same sorority at [a historically black university] in her day.

Organizations such as Jack and Jill provide African American families with a venue in which to recognize the academic and social achievements of their children. Like predominantly white organizations, elite African American organizations such as this may have the covert (and perhaps unintentional) effect of maintaining and perpetuating a class- and sometimes race-based consciousness that fosters an ingroup-outgroup mind-set even among young children.

Whether the process of inclusion and exclusion influences all children or not, many of the organizations that elite parents encourage their children to join (another of the building blocks of elite status) serve as a means of anticipatory socialization for the kinds of responsibilities that the children will assume and the honors and awards that they will receive for successful accomplishment of their responsibilities later in life. Sociological research has demonstrated the importance of anticipatory socialization—the process by which knowledge and skills are learned for future roles—for people of all classes and racial-ethnic categories, but this process is particularly important for those who assume that they or their children have significant leadership roles, economic responsibilities, and social obligations to fulfill on behalf of themselves, their families, and the larger society.

Teaching Elite Children
"Appropriate" Behaviors and Beliefs

Anticipatory socialization includes learning what behaviors and beliefs are appropriate for people in particular social locations. Among the elite women in this study, the most frequently mentioned behaviors and beliefs that they sought to teach their children at an early age were good manners, good communication skills, and loyalty. The mothers emphasized time and again the importance of preparing their children to be part of "polite society" and suggested that communication skills should be cultivated so that their children could interact with friends, family members, and other people who may be important to them in later life.

As early as age 5 or 6, some of the children in this study were enrolled in classes to learn good manners, just as their parents had been. The classes were typically taught by "socially acceptable" women who had many years of experience in arbitrating the social manners and customs of elites in their community. These women set up classes and "play" activities where children can learn to interact with other children, learn new social skills, and begin to establish networks beyond the immediate family.

By the time they reach 8 or 9 years of age, a number of the children are involved in junior cotillions, which are started by parents—particularly by mothers—who want their children to continue to learn about "the social graces." Typically held in settings such as the local country club, cotillion classes serve as an extension of earlier lessons in manners and etiquette, and they afford children the opportunity to interact with elite children of the opposite sex. The children in such classes frequently look like little adults, trying to do very adult-like things but lacking the physical stature to do so. At one of the "arranged parties" that a cotillion organizer planned, I saw that many of the children were short enough that their feet did not touch the floor when they sat in the adult-sized chairs in the room. However, the teachers and parental organizers did not see this as a problem: Rather, they issued directives to the children to "act like young adults," to "sit up straight in your chair," and, above all else, to "act like young ladies and gentlemen."

For girls, acting like a young lady includes, according to one organizer, "sitting cross-ankled but never with legs crossed." For young gentlemen, appropriate posture requires, among other things, sitting with their feet flat on the floor or, if they can't touch the floor, not wiggling their feet. My analysis regarding such classes being one of the building blocks of elite privilege is supported by previous accounts. For example, one prominent woman has noted that etiquette and cotillion classes are "a very long-term investment in a child's life. What they learn at cotillion is something they will have with them forever. It enforces the polite training they receive at home."[8]

Despite social critics who believe that the old upper class is dying out or that its social rituals are no longer important, the women in my study do not see it this way. Rather, they are busy encouraging their children (and grandchildren) to participate in playgroups and social learning experiences such as manners and cotillion classes that they believe will help the younger generation learn to live successfully an affluent lifestyle. Moreover, the women believe that what they and their children are doing is fun both for the children doing it and for the parents who watch them as they participate in these rites of anticipatory socialization. Charlotte, a white woman from a New Money family, described how she felt when she watched her son at junior cotillion classes:

> It is so much fun to see our young people all dressed up and having a good time. Children learn how to be polite and to interact with other children even though we have a few "casualties" along the way like the little boy who hid under the grand piano when he was supposed to ask one of the young ladies to dance with him. It all works, however. By now he and all of the other children are having a great time at the "little dances" we hold several times a year. You asked me what I think is most important about these classes, and I guess I would have to say that, early on, the children learn the answers to important questions such as "how does one eat hors d'oeuvres without messing up formal attire?" or "how much money should you leave for the maid who provides a towel after you wash your hands in the club's ladies room?" or "how can you make a full court bow in a debutante presentation without getting makeup on your dress?"

Children in socially active elite families learn the answers to such questions many years before they actually perform the activities involved. In addition, they come to see their parents as active players in elite social events even when the children do not attend adult functions. However, some of the women I spoke with about etiquette and cotillion classes don't have a fond recollection of that experience, Sherry—a white woman who at the time of this interview was in her 30s—being one example:

> I learned dance steps and I learned how to eat like a lady. That is true. But what I really learned is how to compete without appearing to be competitive. The underlying message that I got was that you have to compete for social recognition, you have to compete for boyfriends and for adult adoration, but you have to appear to be cooperative rather than aggressive. I also learned that you have to appear to be loyal to your family and your friends.

Although Sherry participates in volunteer work in her community and is active on the "social scene," she has distanced her children from some of the activities in which she was involved as a child, believing some of them to be superficial; however, one of the building blocks that she believes her early socialization provided for her, and which she believes is important for her own children, is learning the value of family loyalty.

Although not necessarily different from the behavior of people in other classes, the linkage between class and family loyalty is deeply entrenched in most upper-class families, where the children may become joint owners of the family's assets at some point in the future, or where children may believe that alienating their parents by behavior that appears to be disbelieving or disloyal might cut them off from the social and economic advantages that accrue from being closely identified with that family.

The importance of family as a social building block was evident in the frequent use of the word *legacy* by the women in this study. Legacy is a hereditary form of social power. Children may be informed at an early age that they are "legacy" when it comes to attending schools that their parents or other relatives attended or becoming members of clubs or other organizations where family ties may help a person receive an invitation to join. The term legacy particularly becomes meaningful to college-aged women, who often proudly note that being a member of a particular sorority is a part of their families' legacy. Across racial and ethnic lines, sorority women spoke of the concept of legacy as a "proud heritage." Some women who joined a sorority other than the one their mother had belonged to described themselves as feeling somewhat disloyal for their decision. However, many of the women joined the sorority of which they were legacy.

Family loyalty is also linked to the concept of noblesse oblige. Parents who have made substantial gifts to a particular charity, for example, may extract assurances from their children that the children will use their own money, or money they inherit, on behalf of that particular charity or at least for the betterment of the community. It is a family tradition, a family obligation. It has its rewards as well as its obligations. It also is one of the building blocks that the parents hope their children will utilize in their own lives—building blocks that are further cemented through the educational experiences of young elites.

The Early Educational Experiences of Elite Young Women

Previous studies have often indicated that children of the upper classes exclusively attend private preparatory schools, particularly boarding schools in the northeastern United States. However, this is not always true in the Southwest, where there are a number of highly regarded public schools located in wealthy residential enclaves and attended by many elite children. These schools are not "typical" public schools by any measure: Whether located in separate school districts maintained by wealthy "cities within a city" such as Highland Park, University Park, or Alamo Heights, or by wealthy suburban school districts such as the Eanes school district in Westlake Hills near Austin, these schools are considered to be top-tier schools for elite children who live within those districts' boundaries. Frequently, a "drawing card" for such a school district is a highly regarded sports program and a reputation for many of its graduates attending prestigious public or private universities.

The women in my study who enrolled their children in such public schools typically describe this as being important for the "democratization" of their children, but they also note that their children are receiving the high quality education that only a "special" public school or school district can provide and that the children are not missing out on any opportunities that might be available to children in college preparatory schools. With the exception of what is set forth above, however, I am going to focus primarily on elite girls who attend private schools, since most of the women in my study—at least at some point during their educational experience—attended an elite private day or boarding school.

The education of elite young women is a central factor in self-identity and class affiliation. As noted earlier in this chapter, some parents attempt to arrange—even before the child is born—for their daughters to attend certain prestigious schools. Which school or schools they will attend sometimes has an intergenerational genesis, with mothers (or even grandmothers) passing on tips regarding the selection of "the right school" to attend. Jenny described the system her mother had used in analyzing where she should attend school and stated that she had used a similar method when her own daughter was born:

> Mother kept a card file on schools in the area, beginning with nursery schools and continuing through private elementary and high schools and colleges. On the cards she wrote down, of course, the names and addresses of the schools, the name of the head of the school, and details such as what the school currently cost, who the alumni of the school were that she knew, and the names of people whose kids currently attended the school. I decided that these cards were a really neat idea because Mother always had references she could list on my applications for those schools, and she could jog her memory if she wanted to contact someone who might be helpful in getting me enrolled. The system worked well for my mother, and so far it's worked well for my children.

As Jenny's statement indicates, elite women are socialized as young children to understand not only the importance of attaining a good education but also that the particular schools a person attends are important building blocks for the lifestyle to which they have been born. Accordingly, elite women are very anxious to make sure that their daughters (and sons) will attend the right schools, beginning with the nursery school or pre-school experience. In some cases, parents in Old Money and Old Name families may feel that their children are entitled to attend a particular exclusive private school due to the family's longtime connection with that institution or with the church that sponsors it, but this is becoming more difficult—even as to availability of slots in schools they have considered to be "their schools" for generations of family members—due to increasing demands from New Money parents for similar educational opportunities for their children. As a result, new private schools come into existence, hoping to build their reputations over a relatively short period of time. Some parents, accordingly, place their children's names on waiting lists both for old and new schools, hoping for the former but being willing to settle for the latter.

Shared beliefs, values, and social networks are factors that bind many members of the upper classes together. Beliefs and values initially taught at home are strengthened in elite schools, where students are encouraged to develop a sense of collective identity that involves school, peers, and one's place within the larger society. As privileged young people create a web of affiliations in dormitories, sporting events, classrooms, and other settings within their schools, they establish ties that, because they are interwoven in such a way as to become indistinguishable from the students' individual identity, will grow and become even more important after graduation. Consequently, to develop solidarity with one's classmates is to develop a form of class solidarity because of the commonalities in beliefs and lived experiences that have been shared over a period of time, frequently without the students being exposed to countervailing belief systems or social networks. Over time, identity with others in the same class is a stronger link than merely some vague perception that they share similar values. As Baltzell stated, "The character of American upper-class institutions has usually been more a product of interpersonal networks than of ideological affinities."[9]

Cassy, a white woman from a well-connected Old Name family and who—at the time of these comments—was a college student, described how much an interpersonal network forged in prep school helped her and a number of her friends make a comfortable transition to an honors program at a prestigious state university:

> The friends I made at [prep school] gave me an instant on-campus network at [university]. I'd say our bond was strongest when we were freshmen because we were in the middle of a sea of strangers. In fact, several people who were not my best friends at [prep school] and I hung out together and went to dinners and parties. When I pledged [sorority], upperclassmen from [prep school] were there to cheer me on. They were very helpful and showed me what I should do and what I should expect.

My content analysis of the catalogs, school literature, and Web sites of eighteen elite prep schools (listed in Appendix 1) showed certain recurring themes at these schools that tend to create and reinforce not only academic rigor but also the development of communications skills and long-term upper-class networks such as Cassy described:

- Emphasis on tradition and the part that children and their families play in the tradition of the school;
- Focus on developing active, responsible citizenship and leadership skills among students;
- Emphasis on cultivating the individual interests and talents of the students while at the same time teaching them to respect the rights and opinions of others; and
- Stressing the importance of alumni and parent activities and associations as they relate to the networks that can be created by students, showing how the child becomes a significant link in the chain between the past, present, and future of that specific institution.

Elite private schools emphasize that they strive to educate the "whole child;" whereas public schools typically view this as the parents' responsibility.[10] The Web site of one elite private school in this study states the "whole child" or "whole person" mission as follows:

> Our mission to educate the whole person requires that attention be paid to virtues, ethics, character, and integrity. . . . [We are] committed to the idea that the proper goal of education is the shaping of free, responsible men and women. To this end, [the school] encourages intellectual curiosity and honesty, while cultivating a respect for the discipline required to pursue truth.[11]

In the process of educating the "whole child," even the simple fact of being accepted into an elite private school shows that the young person has been welcomed into a status group whose members feel a consciousness of kind or a sense of shared social similarities.

My content analysis of the catalogs and Web sites of elite schools also revealed that the schools emphasize how rigorous their curriculum is and how they pride themselves on using varied teaching methods and technologies to produce high academic achievement in a wider variety of courses than are typically available at other types of schools in the same geographic region. According to Peter W. Cookson Jr., and Caroline Hodges Persell, "Being comfortable in the world of ideas and being able to express thoughts in a concise and logical manner are not only the mark of a well-educated person, but are essential skills in the struggle for power today."[12]

Each of the schools included in my research emphasizes the building of the cultural capital that constitutes a source of social power for students who have been exposed to an education rich in the fine arts. As one school states, "In a unique way, experience in the arts promotes positive self-awareness in both the context of our community experience and the celebration of our diverse cultural heritage."[13] Like other elite prep schools, this institution not only wants to prepare those who might choose to become art professionals or to participate in art, music, theater, and dance for their own enjoyment, but it also wants to educate the next generation of active members of the arts audience who might also engage in volunteerism and philanthropy on behalf of their preferred arts organizations.

Previous research has noted how the education that elite children receive reflects the distinct lifestyle of the upper class, and that these schools transmit the traditions of the upper social classes to the next generation of elites.[14] In their study of elite prep schools, for example, Cookson and Persell described how boarding schools reproduce upper-class values and behavior in privileged children:

> Boarding school students . . . are taught that they should be moral and treat life as an exciting challenge, but what they often learn is that life is hard, and that winning is essential for survival. The "muscular Christianity" that so well describes the essence of prep pride is exactly right: speak like a man or woman of God, but act like a man or woman who knows the score and can settle a score without flinching. Preps are taught that right should prevail, but they learn that it often does not.[15]

As Cookson and Persell state, prep students learn that they must be competitive and that they must learn to live with seemingly contradictory concerns in their lives. Above all else, as Cookson and Persell note, prep school students come to believe that privilege is justified. This attitude is essential for maintaining an upper-class outlook, but it often limits the prep school experience so that the students' outlook may not stretch beyond the school's boundaries.[16]

In my discussions with one former prep school student, she referred to her years there as being an example of the "brick wall syndrome." I did not have a chance to follow up with her on this statement, but later came across the writing of another prep school student, Katie Hagedorn, who described the same phenomena in her boarding school experience. Hagedorn stated that the brick wall syndrome isolates boarding school students from the community that surrounds them, supposedly for the purpose of encouraging intensive studying, but that this isolation has another significant consequence for students: It limits their view of the world beyond the brick wall.[17] Thus, for some students at both day and boarding schools, the very educational institution that their parents are paying to enhance the children's cultural capital and broaden their social horizons may also create a brick wall—a wall whose building blocks foster the belief that exclusion of those outside the wall is normal rather than it being something arbitrary or discriminatory. The norm of exclusivity—whether learned in a prestigious private prep school or other elite educational institution—helps explain the exclusive nature of the women's organizations discussed in this book, and why the women who participate in them may not be aware of that exclusivity and the privilege associated with it.

Private schools—and the concept of exclusivity—have been important for children in both elite white and elite black families. Even among early black elite families, private schools were often considered to be essential for one of two reasons: For families living in southern cities, the segregated school districts provided little, if any, educational opportunities for black children; elsewhere, African American parents wanted to offer their children the opportunity to meet children from other high-income black families and to reinforce the idea of their own children's prominent lineage.[18] Although many black elite children today are educated in day schools or boarding schools that previously had primarily white student bodies, the transition for some African American students has not been without its tough times due to racial and ethnic differences in white and black students, including such factors as interests, politics, hobbies, or music, which may leave African American students out of the social groups established by their "overwhelmingly conservative white classmates."[19]

Elite education does not end with graduation from prep school. Upper-class children (whether they attended public or private schools), along with a carefully selected constituency of children from lower income backgrounds, attend prestigious private or state universities, where they not only further their formal education but also establish in-group ties with other members of their own class through by-invitation-only social organizations such as Greek-letter fraternities and sororities, further reinforcing the norm of exclusivity.

Elite Women and Sorority "Sisterhood"

For many elite women, having attended a prestigious college and having belonged to an exclusive sorority is an integral part of the background for members of their peer group, and they expect their daughters—and the daughters of their friends—to follow the same path. Such a background therefore becomes one of the requirements for entree into positions as community volunteers and board members of many of the most prestigious nonprofit organizations.[20] As Daniels states, "Perhaps the most effective introduction to the volunteer career comes from intimates: parents, other relations, the social circle approved by parents, close friends. Such influences are reinforced in private schools and sororities where well-to-do parents can place their children."[21]

Graduation from a top-tier college and membership in a prestigious sorority typically are prerequisites for entry into the inner social circles of Texas elites. *Not* having attended at least an "acceptable" college may be considered a sign that something is amiss, that the woman somehow simply doesn't have the right "background" to belong.

Although previous research has focused on upper-class women who attended Ivy League universities in the Northeast or highly acclaimed institutions such as Stanford University in the West,[22] and although some had attended such an out-of-state college, a majority of the elite women in my study (depending on age) either had graduated from or were presently enrolled in a few well-regarded state or private universities located within Texas such as Rice, Baylor, Southern Methodist, Texas Christian, Texas A&M, or the University of Texas at Austin. A number of factors typically went into the decision regarding which school to attend, one of the most frequently mentioned being the prestige of the particular university. Other factors included family preference (especially for a school that other family members had attended), a particular woman's proposed major field of study, and the type of career she hoped to pursue.

However, another recurring theme for a specific university within the state was the opportunity to join a particular sorority and to be "within easy driving or flying time to get back home for a special occasion." While many college students want to get home occasionally for the weekend, what these women were referring to was the ability to attend debutante presentations and the parties associated with them, as well as other "high society" functions such as the weddings of family friends or other social events deemed important for them to attend by their parents. Jana is an example of a college student from a wealthy family who maintained a multiple-city social network during her years as a student:

> I was very busy while I was in college. On top of my studies, I was presented [as a debutante] in Dallas, Austin, Tyler, and New Orleans. I went to teas and dinners and parties. It was really fun because some of my sorority sisters were also presented, representing other cities, and we could all be together at these activities away from school. When my parents had my deb party, there were dozens of my [sorority] sisters there. One December, my family and I went to New York for my International Debutante Ball presentation.

In my conversations with Jana and other sorority members, we discussed how, for many sorority women, their closest personal relations during college—and sometimes for years thereafter—are with other women in their sorority. Using a phrase borrowed from the "high-tech" workplace, one young woman referred to her friendship with other sorority members as "24/7"—a 24 hours a day, 7 days a week friendship.

Sororities are important to many elite women because the stated goals of these organizations include encouraging sisterhood, scholarship, leadership, and philanthropy. One of the first things that most sorority members and alumnae emphasize when discussing sorority life is how membership in such a group enhances a young woman's college experience by helping her develop friends and memories that will last throughout life. As Aimee, who had attended a large state university where she was a member of Pi Beta Phi, one of the most prestigious sororities at her school, stated:

> Some of my best friends throughout the years have been other Pi Phis. We remain friends in the alumnae group, where we have fundraisers that benefit low-income children. At a recent [alumnae] meeting, we talked about how important sisterhood had been to us. We learned how to work with each other; how to cooperate rather than compete; and how to always be there for each other.

Like Aimee, when most current or alumnae sorority members are asked to select a word that they think best describes sorority life, the one most commonly chosen is "sisterhood." Members of Greek-letter social sororities state that they enjoy a "special type of friendship" and the larger "Panhellenic Spirit" of sisterhood that bonds members of all sororities together. Mitzi, an officer in a prestigious sorority at the time of our interview, discussed her perception of this concept:

> Sisterhood is very special to me. It's a bond with other women that I'll have for the rest of my life. We help each other out when we need it. We are there for each other. We eat together and go out together. We study together; we go to [college athletic] games together. We party together . . . but we also work hard together. We have fundraisers each year and work on projects. Still, my sorority has one of the highest GPAs [grade point averages] at [this school].

Since Mitzi was a member of a sorority that some nonmembers described as "very hard to join," "snobbish," or "elitist," I asked her about her perceptions about exclusivity and exclusion of others within her chapter:

> *Query:* Do sororities such as yours get criticized for excluding other young women who might want to join your group?
>
> *Mitzi:* Well, there's always going to be someone who's critical of what you do. And I just say, "Whatever" and go about my own business. I've had to take that attitude since I was a cheerleader [in high school]. I think it's petty jealousy that motivates some people to say harmful things about other girls, if you want to know the truth. A girl sees you as having something she wants, whether you're a cheerleader or your boyfriend is an athlete, and sororities are the same way. Not everyone will be admitted to

their first choice sorority, but anyone at [university] can join a sorority; you just have to find the right one for you . . . you know, the one where you'll be the happiest.

Query: But aren't there some young women who would like to join your sorority and think they would be "happiest" there, but aren't invited to join?

Mitzi: Of course! But that's the thing. If you go through rush and do all the things you're supposed to, you are guaranteed a bid [a membership offer] from some group. In the end, rushees and actives who share similar ideas and goals will find each other. Legacies will find their places at Bid Day, and everything works out fine. I'll admit, it does help to be a legacy, a friend of a current member, or to know alumnae who have remained involved in the life of the chapter because they bring specific rushees to our attention. But, let me emphasize, we do have members who just walked through the front door [of the sorority house] at Open House without any of this and have been great pledges.

As Mitzi's comments suggest, membership in a Greek-letter organization provides some young women with the feeling that they are part of a unique and very important group. The use of specialized argot or language specifically associated with Greek life also gives rushees and members a feeling of being "insiders" while those outside the Greek system are "outsiders." For elite women, however, only some sororities are acceptable for membership: Membership in the "wrong" sorority is typically viewed as being "worse than being an independent" [not a member of any sorority]. Which sororities are the most "socially acceptable" for upper-class women remains relatively consistent among white Anglo Saxon Protestant young women in all the cities in this study. A major university with Greek-letter sororities (and fraternities) is located in each of these cities, providing me with the opportunity to study these organizations on both large, top-tier state university campuses and elite private universities as well.

Although there are some differences from chapter to chapter and campus to campus, Greek social life at these universities is more consistent than it is different. Participation in this social life begins with the process known as "rush," which has been renamed "recruitment" on some campuses.

The Ritual of Rush: Selectivity and the Process of Inclusion/Exclusion

College-bound middle- and upper-class young women who have indicated an interest in joining a sorority usually have been socialized regarding membership in such an organization for a number of years before they actually enter college. Especially for women of the upper classes, if one's mother, grandmother, and/or older sister were members of a specific sorority, the young woman frequently has decided in childhood which one she hopes to join when she enters college.

Some schools have implemented a guaranteed placement program, under which young women are guaranteed that they will receive a bid from some sorority if they attend all of the parties to which they are invited. However, it does not always work out this way, and a number of young women are less than pleased with the outcome of sorority rush or recruitment. Some decide not to pledge that group, and others have been known to transfer to other universities a semester or two later and to go through rush again in hopes of getting into their sorority of choice on the second attempt.

Being chosen as a new member of a prestigious sorority is less of a problem for some elite young women, particularly those whose sisters, mothers, grandmothers, or other blood relatives have been members of the organization, and who are therefore legacy. As a result, some women work for years to ensure that their daughters will receive bids to their mothers' sorority. The mothers may serve as chapter advisors or work on interior design committees for remodeling the campus sorority house or in other endeavors that not only will show their own extensive commitment to the sisterhood but will also call attention to the fact that they "have a daughter coming up who would like to join," as one woman confided.

The effect that being "legacy" has on a young woman's chances of being invited to "pledge" a prestigious sorority is reflected by how such information is conveyed to active members of that sorority. An example is Pi Beta Phi's Rush Information Form (see Appendix 2), which is designed to allow an alumnus of that sorority to provide information regarding *any* young woman who is going through rush at a particular school. It asks the alumnus to list (among other data furnished, such as the young woman's school and community activities and honors) any Pi Beta Phi Relatives (sister, mother, grandmother) and Other Greek Affiliated Relatives of the particular young woman. There is even a separate Legacy Introduction Form, that is to be used only for introducing legacy to the active members of the chapter and includes the statement:

This is to inform you that my: ___ Granddaughter ___ Daughter ___ Sister

Name: _____

From: _____

Will be/is a student on your campus as a:
____ Freshman ____ Sophomore ____ Junior ____ Senior

In other words, the "actives" are made aware that a young woman who is legacy is going through rush, and that particular notice therefore should be taken of that young woman.[23]

In discussions with elite girls as young as 7 or 8 years of age, I found that they often already used terminology such as "active member," "pledge," "rush," "bid," and "legacy" when discussing their plans for joining a Greek-letter sorority in college. They are aware that *rush*—a term that came into popular usage because potential members meet many so new people in a very short period of time—refers to the formal membership recruitment period held by sorority chapters on various college campuses. In the ideal sense, rush suggests that all young women are being "included" because they can go through the process. In actuality, however, it is a process under which a few select women will be chosen to join the most highly regarded groups, and the others will either pledge a less-esteemed group or drop out of the process altogether. The more recent name for rush—recruitment—suggests that an even greater process of inclusion is taking place, whether this is actually occurring or not.

Recruitment or rush typically begins with an Open House where rushees visit with active members of sorority chapters. At some schools, rushees visit every chapter on campus; at others, the young women visit only those chapters they might have an interest in joining, or which have invited them to attend a social event. During this process, some young women who "do not look like they would be a good match with our sorority are culled out" (in the words of one sorority rush chairman). After the first round, rushees receive a list of chapters whose members would like for them to come back for another visit. On the basis of those invitations, the rushee decides which chapters' parties she would like to attend for the next round. Those she does not attend will be eliminated from her list of potential chapters to join. After that series of parties, both the sororities and the rushees go through another round of who gets invited back and who accepts that invitation. "Bid day" follows, the day on which invitations to "pledge" a sorority are extended. Bid day is very important in the inclusion/exclusion process because it is on this day that a young woman knows that she either will or will not become a part of an exclusive sisterhood that she apparently desires to join. Mindy described bid day:

> Bid day was a big day for me. I have a picture of me and some of my sisters that has "Kappa Kappa Gamma Bid Day [year]" across the bottom of the photo. It was on that day that I knew I was becoming part of a new "family." [Singing:] Oh, Kappa Kappa Kappa Gamma, I'm so happy that I am a Kappa, Kappa Gamma, Nobody knows . . . how happy I am!

For young women who are invited to join the sorority of their choice, bid day is described as "one of the happiest days" of their lives. At this time they will begin to learn the "secrets" of the sisterhood, including passwords, secret handshakes, insignia, special ceremonial activities and rituals, and other attitudes and behaviors that are identified as being unique to their group. Learning the ropes of the sorority is an important pastime (and sometimes preoccupation) of young college pledges. However, the privilege of selectivity works within organizations and across groups, leading to the exclusion of those who are not among the chosen few. For many years, women of color were categorically excluded from white college life and sorority membership, leading to the development of parallel social organizations such as Alpha Kappa Alpha and to other social structures that remain in the twenty-first century.

Racial and Ethnic Distinctions in College Sorority Life
The reasons why elite women join sororities and the goals they hope to pursue in these groups may vary by race, ethnicity, and sometimes religion.[24] A brief look at the history of sororities is necessary for an understanding of their present-day consequences in the lives of elite women.

Sororities that would be identified as white, black, or Jewish have existed on U.S. college campuses for more than a century; more recently, several predominantly Latina and Asian American sororities have been founded on various college campuses, as will be discussed later in this chapter. The earliest white sororities were founded in the late 1800s and continue to have a membership that is white (Euro-American). For example, both Pi Beta Phi (founded in 1867) and Kappa Kappa Gamma (founded in 1870) were started at Monmouth College in Monmouth, Illinois, and were modeled after the men's Greek-letter fraternities. During a time when few women were admitted to colleges and universities, Greek-letter sororities created a "feeling of unity among pioneering women," as one sorority's Web site states.[25]

Because of prejudice and discrimination, some Jewish American young women organized sororities such as Alpha Epsilon Phi, which was founded at Barnard College in 1909. According to one of the original founders of this sorority, the goal was to choose girls not because of "any special scholastic preeminence, financial circumstances or other arbitrary standards, but a group who had common interests and were dominated by the ideals of true friendship."[26] However, unspoken in this statement is the fact that Jewish American college students, both men and women, experienced high levels of prejudice and discrimination at the institutions where they were permitted to enroll. Some were categorically excluded because of their religion; others were one of the few Jewish American students on campus because of restrictive quota systems that precluded similar students from enrolling. A recent study of college fraternities and sororities found that an entire Jewish/Greek "sub-system existed throughout the United States between 1895 and 1968 because of the exclusionary practices of the mainstream Greek system."[27] Among the "predominantly Jewish" sororities still in existence are Alpha Epsilon Phi, Phi Sigma Sigma, Sigma Delta Tau, and Delta Phi Epsilon. They are largely indistinguishable from other sororities, according to members, with the exception of such things as how they spend their volunteer time and phi-lanthropy. The national philanthropy of Alpha Epsilon Phi, for example, is Chaim Sheba Medical Center in Tel-Hashomer, Israel. Some chapters have fundraisers such as a spare change drive that raises money for that hospital. The organizations have other community service projects such as AIDS awareness programs, but the emphasis remains on helping oth-ers who are similar to oneself. Beth, a member of a prestigious, predomi-nantly Jewish sorority, described how she views her membership in that sorority as linked to her Jewish identity:

> I'm not sure if you want to call it a religious thing or a cultural thing, but throughout my entire life, I've known I was Jewish. Being a member of [sorority] is an extension of that identity. I think my [sorority] sisters and I have a unique focus—we are college women and we are also Jewish. We plan our projects accordingly by trying to do the things that will help out others in the Jewish community.

Like Jewish American sororities, a separate African American Greek system began early in the twentieth century. The earliest African Ameri-can fraternities were founded at predominantly white universities such as Cornell and Indiana University; others subsequently were established at predominantly black schools such as Howard University. Facing issues such as legalized racial segregation and discrimination perpetrated by hate organizations such as the Ku Klux Klan, black college men not only built a close bond and friendship but also warded off racial bigotry as best they could.[28] African American sororities were developed under the um-brella of the black men's Greek-letter organizations, with Alpha Kappa Alpha being formed at Howard University in 1908, followed by Delta Sigma Theta in 1913 and Zeta Phi Beta in 1920. In a book describing the history of Delta Sigma Theta, Paula Giddings notes that this sorority was formed to bring women together as sisters and to address the divisive, of-ten class-related concerns of African American women.[29] The only African American sorority founded at a white institution was Sigma Gamma Rho, which was formed at Butler University in Indiana in 1922.[30]

More recently, African American women on several prestigious, pre-dominantly white college campuses in Texas have described to me how they believe that membership in Alpha or Delta is vital for establishing social location in the minds of other students. Consider Cassandra's comments:

> At [name of private university], when you're black, other [white] students think you're here on an athletic scholarship. And not just the black men. To [black] women they say, "You play basketball?" Well, I'm not a jock, and I'm not here on a scholarship. To keep my dignity together, I really need to be

around my sorors—you know, my sorority sisters—other African American women who I know I can trust to support me when I need them.

The first Latina and Asian American sororities were formed on college campuses in the 1980s. The emergence of Latina and Asian American sororities, this much later than numerous white and black sororities, is partly attributed to the fact that historically black colleges had existed for more than a century in the United States, whereas few colleges have been identified as being predominantly Latino/Latina or Asian American. Increases in the numbers of Latino/Latina and Asian American students on previously white (Anglo) college campuses brought about an interest in developing organizations parallel to those previously established by white (Anglo) and black college students. The focus of Latina sororities such as Omega Phi Beta has not been exclusively on Latinas but rather on including "multi-cultural, multi-ethnic, and multi-racial women" in the hope that chapters on university campuses would "unify women of color who [are] dedicated to correcting the injustices that have and that continue today to affect our communities."[31] Similarly, "Asian American interest" sororities typically state that their purpose is to promote sisterhood, scholarship, leadership, and Asian American awareness in the university and community. Universities at two of the cities in this study had either a chapter or a colony (a chapter in formation) of Omega Phi Beta on campus.

Sororities and Philanthropy
The discussion of sororities that is set forth above helps in understanding several things about the women in this study, the elite organizations to which they belong, and the class- and sometimes race-related aspects of those groups. We turn now to another topic: Does sorority membership have any effect on elite women's postcollege philanthropy? In the college and postcollege years, some evidence suggests that there are some differences in the types of community service projects that are most often chosen by African American women's organizations as compared with those of white women. For example, a previous study of white and black sororities at two college campuses by Alexandra Berkowitz and Irene Padavic found that members of African American sororities placed greater emphasis on community service than do members of predominantly white sororities. According to Berkowitz and Padavic, "The black women described community service as a central and meaningful part of their sorority experience, while white women generally viewed it as a way to facilitate their social lives"; by contrast, many white sorority members placed greater emphasis on dating and romance ("getting a man").[32]

One reason for examining elite women's sorority experiences was to see if the women were aware of the seemingly contradictory nature of their sorority's exclusionary membership practices as compared with the group's desire for community outreach through service projects, and to see if, for many of them, this awareness or lack of awareness carried forward into their later work in elite women's organizations. From my discussions, I learned that most of the women did not view exclusionary membership practices as being at odds with the sorority's efforts to assist people from backgrounds different from their own. They see sorority life as providing them with an opportunity to help the less fortunate, including individuals and families from other racial and ethnic groups, but within the safe confines of Greek social life. One sorority member had this to offer:

> Do not venture outside the bubble to help the less fortunate. Take the bubble with you. Your sisters are the bubble. You go together to do things. You make plans with members of the frat your chapter "mixes" [at social events] with. That way you have a critical mass of people for a community project like painting an old person's house or working with children at a children's home.

As this woman's statement suggests, having been selected to join an exclusive organization may enhance one's opportunities not only to meet other people but also to use the strength of those social networks to help those who are outside their own social bubble.

However, whether sororities are actually a springboard for elite women's adult philanthropy, or whether they are merely a social clique, is a topic on which the elite women in my study had varying viewpoints. For some women, sorority membership fulfills its mission in helping them to do projects and fundraisers that benefit others. Amy, a white sorority member who was responsible for planning her sorority's service projects, was well aware of the importance of volunteerism:

> Greeks at [university] raise thousands of dollars for charity and provide many hours of service to the community beyond our campus. My sorority's causes are breast cancer awareness and a charity that helps out the homeless and poor families. I am philanthropy chair, and I coordinate fundraising activities with [a fraternity], and I know that our projects benefit the community and also promote Greek unity. I don't understand why some people are so negative about sororities and fraternities. I guess they either didn't want to join or were not able to become a part of their preferred group. But it doesn't mean that they should pick on those of us who are out helping other people.

Amy is a member of a white sorority; however, her statement is more similar to that of African American alumnae and sorority members who emphasized the importance of members' involvement in community service projects. One African American woman stated, "[sorority] membership gave me the opportunity to at least see what volunteerism is like. We always had a service project that had to be completed before an individual could become a full-fledged active member. As best I remember, all of us did this most willingly and enjoyed what we were doing." Another African American woman described how important she believed community service projects are for helping young women complete their education and become community volunteers: "I see so many young people who are so selfish. But when they belong and see that there are so many more people more unfortunate than them, it gives them more energy to successfully complete their education and keep giving afterward."

The white women I interviewed more frequently described fundraising activities of their college sorority as a form of camaraderie or as giving them "a feeling of belonging rather than being lost in a large student body." As one woman stated, "Sororities instill a sense of group involvement. This involvement, through good leadership, can be fostered to develop an awareness of community needs and volunteerism." Several women further noted that they appreciated the recognition that they and other sorority members had received from their local chapter, the national organization, and their university for the hours of community service they had given to the university and to the city in which their school was located. A few women mentioned how important they thought it was to have community service listed on applications for medical school, law school, and jobs that they hoped to pursue. According to Brenda, a white woman in her mid-20s,

> If you just list that you're a member of a sorority, people don't take you seriously; they have the mistaken idea that you just played your way through college. However, if you list volunteer activities (even though you've done them through your sorority), they say, "Oh, look, here's a person who's really interested in medicine because she did volunteer work at a children's clinic or has been involved in a breast cancer awareness project." Of course, we do volunteer work because we want to, but it's an added bonus that outsiders look favorably on the many contributions we have made during our college years.

Other elite women were less positive that sorority membership encouraged giving and volunteering. Some current and former sorority members stated that they believed Greek life encouraged "selfishness and self-centeredness." Rose Ann, a white woman in her late 30s at the time of the interview, but who had been active in her college sorority, is an example. According to Rose Ann:

> My collegiate chapter could only in the most generous terms be characterized as a group of snobbish and self-centered girls. In spite of our mission

statement that our purpose was to give back to the university and the community, most of us just shouted "me, me, me," except for an occasional few hours when we would have a fundraiser like a basketball toss, where the money went to a charity.

Statements such as this are not representative of the way many elite women might perceive their experiences in a sorority. They see sorority life as an opportunity to exert power over others or to gain the power to do for others through the philanthropic activities of the group.[33]

Sororities and Social Power

Prestigious Greek-letter sororities provide elite women with all five of the sources of social power. The most visible example is referent power: Women in the "best" sororities are extremely proud of their membership in the group and want their personal identity to be linked to that of others in the "sisterhood." The extent of their identification and closeness can be seen in their clothing and car decals, which are used as billboards to evidence the young women's affiliation with a particular sorority. At some universities, sorority members wear T-shirts with the Greek letters of their organization on designated days, particularly during rush (or "recruitment") and on days when the group is holding a meeting. To insiders and outsiders alike, the message is clear, as one sorority member stated, "I'm a Kappa, and this shows I'm proud of it!"

Being a member of one of the more prestigious sororities gives college women not only a consciousness of kind and a feeling of strength in numbers but other bases of power, as well. The structure of sorority life enables young women to learn how to use reward, coercive, expertise, and legitimate power over others in a nonthreatening environment where, as one sorority member stated, "there may be occasional competition *over* men, but there isn't competition *with* men like in the real world. This helps us to be high achievers in our own right and prepares us for careers where we can go head on with everybody out there."

Sorority membership offers women of diverse racial and ethnic backgrounds an opportunity to develop leadership skills and enhance their legitimate power. Some young women in this study indicated that they had first become leaders in their sorority and then used their skills and legitimate power as leaders in the sorority to branch out into other student organizations and to run for offices such as president or vice president of the senior class or of the student body. A few sorority women will continue to gain social power by becoming leaders of their sorority alumnae groups, even at the national level. Their prestige and prominence is established by their leadership positions, just as the sorority benefits from the "untiring efforts and wisdom" of the women who serve on the governing councils of the national organization.

For decades, some critics have argued that Greek-letter social organizations are dying out on college campuses and that those that remain have little effect on university life. This statement has not proven true as these organizations seem to go through periods of boom and bust somewhat like the U.S. economy, only to rise up again with a new strength as subsequent generations arrive on various campuses. This has certainly been true at the schools in this study. Moreover, elite women and men continue to believe that these organizations provide them with certain social advantages that will last long beyond the college years. As previously discussed, the leadership skills that are developed and the ability to exert social power outside of one's family that is learned in Greek-letter organizations are believed to be valuable lessons for adulthood. The friendships that are made, the dating and marriage patterns that develop, and the ability to call on another "Greek" for assistance when needed is seen as a powerful force in the upper-class lifestyle. The ability to list one's membership in such organizations beyond college serves as a code word to other elites that this individual has previously been accepted into the inner circle and thus has the right qualifications for professional and social opportunities usually restricted to other elites who have proven that they are "players."

However, despite their membership in prestigious African American sororities, many elite women of color do not receive the same kinds of access to the white power structure that some white sorority members may gain. Although people of color have made significant gains in educational, economic, political, and social arenas over the past fifty years, the parallel (separate but not necessarily equal) social spheres, including the so-called Greek system, in which they operate on college campuses, remain a limiting factor in their ability to achieve equal economic and social clout in the mainstream (white) "upper class" social structure.

Conclusion

Elite young women gain their earliest social power from their family ties. Many of the early experiences of elite young women can be traced to their families' ability to live in the most exclusive residential areas, the families' ability to pay to have their daughters attend the best etiquette classes, schools and colleges, and their families' social connections—frequently including the status of being "legacy"—that help the daughters get into top-tier Greek-letter sororities. By thus growing up in a wealthy residential enclave, having a "select" group of friends and acquaintances, and attending the most prestigious schools, elite young women gain social and cultural capital that is more difficult, if not impossible, for women in other classes to attain.

Since these elite young women are—almost from birth—surrounded by others who share similar attitudes and values, many of them do not question the norm of exclusivity or understand the fact that they live in a sheltered environment. It is simply something that is "there," like a birthright. When they are grown and raising their own families, these same women—in the name of tradition—will seek to pass the same sort of privilege and the same sheltered lifestyle on to their children and grandchildren, thus socially reproducing the upper classes.

Across racial and ethnic categories, the privileged lifestyle of elite young women makes it possible for many of them to gain social power and to achieve personal goals, such as entering a well-paid career and/or becoming a successful community volunteer. However, elite girls' experiences may also constitute a "brick wall" that obstructs their vision of other people and limits their interactions with those who come from lower-income or racial or ethnic minority backgrounds to people such as customers at a charity garage sale or thrift shop, or the people they hire to do domestic work in their home.[34]

The unique socialization experience of elite young women prepares them for community volunteerism and for participation in "high society" social events such as the debutante ball, a seemingly archaic ritual of the upper classes that is examined in the next chapter.

Notes

1. Although some young elites may grow up to follow in their parents' footsteps, others may rebel to the extent that they lose some or all of the economic and social assets that would otherwise accrue to them as a result of their families. As William A. Corsaro's (1997) study of children's sense-making process shows, children develop their own interpretations of situations. They engage in negotiations with others, and they frequently modify or transform the information that they receive from adults. Like children from other classes, elite children do not passively internalize the norms and values of their adult significant others. However, wealthy and privileged parents—who have more economic resources and advantages that they can offer their children from birth through college (or even beyond college) than do parents in other classes—can bring more of those resources to bear on socializing their children in a particular manner. Children who do not "learn the ropes" that would make them full-fledged members of the social elite run the risk of being estranged from families that typically place a high (but often unacknowledged) value on reproduction into future generations not only of the family itself but also of the lifestyle of the privileged classes in which the parents live.

2. Rothenberg 2000: 1.

3. Baltzell 1958, 1964; Cookson and Persell 1985; Daniels 1988; Domhoff 1998; Mills 2000 [1956]; Ostrander 1984.

4. Baltzell 1958: 174.
5. Graham 2000.
6. Higley 1995.
7. Graham 2000: 23.
8. Quoted in McCready 1988: Southwest Section.
9. Baltzell 1979: 278.
10. Cookson and Persell 1985.
11. St. Stephens 2001.
12. Cookson and Persell 1985: 30.
13. St. Stephens 2001.
14. Domhoff 1998; Mills 2000 [1956].
15. Cookson and Persell 1985: 19.
16. Cookson and Persell 1985.
17. Hagedorn 1996.
18. Graham 2000.
19. Graham 2000:59.
20. Domhoff 1998; Ostrander 1984; Daniels 1988.
21. Daniels 1988: 20.
22. Domhoff 1998.
23. Those filling out the legacy information form must indicate their own chapter and year of initiation and are informed that they are "prohibited from sending food or gifts of any kind to a chapter on behalf of a rushee," suggesting that such activities must have occurred in the past. Similarly, alumnae are admonished not to contact active members during rush or to call the family or the young woman (rushee) for information. Obviously, *who* gets into *which* sorority is very important to many of these women.
24. See Berkowitz and Padavic 1999.
25. Pi Beta Phi 2000.
26. Alpha Epsilon Phi, 2001.
27. Sanua 2000.
28. Ross 2000.
29. Giddings 1988.
30. Ross 2000.
31. Omega Phi Beta 2000.
32. Berkowitz and Padavic 1999: 546.
33. Lisa Handler, in a (1995: 236) study of sororities, concluded that "fraternal sisterhood" is a coping response that helps women deal with societal and professional gender bias. According to Handler, sororities encourage good relations among women, help them develop self-esteem, and make it possible for them to seek egalitarian status in the larger society. Although my research does not contradict this finding, it does suggest that norms of exclusivity within Greek-letter organizations may be harmful for some women while they are beneficial for others, and that values are promoted that are contradictory to widely held beliefs about philanthropy and community service.
34. Hondagneu-Sotelo (2001) provides a very insightful analysis of the relationship between wealthy women and Latinas who are employed as nannies and

domestic workers in their households. In her study, she found that very high income women, unlike their middle-class or upper-middle-class counterparts, wanted to distance themselves from their domestic employees. According to Hondagneu-Sotelo (188), very wealthy women who are the employers of domestic workers "prefer an American version of the 'upstairs, downstairs' segregation of master and servant. In part, this physical separation is encouraged by their palatial, mansion-sized homes. Spatial distance appears to facilitate emotional distance between employer and employee." From my study, I concluded that early socialization is also a factor in elite women's preference for physical and social separation from others whom they consider to be outside their group.

CHAPTER FIVE

$\sim$

Take a Bow:
Debutantes and Good Deeds

One way that some elite young women build their social résumés and establish their reputation as members of the upper-class social inner circle is through the debutante presentation. Being honored as a debutante is a source of prestige: Other individuals perceive that a young woman chosen as a debutante has access to social resources (those persons who recommended or chose her for the honor), economic resources (the ability to pay the many costs of participation), and the social and cultural capital (including the refinement, good manners, and "taste") to be a good representative of her family, and sometimes of an organization or community. The debutante gains social power because the ritual of the formal debut and the social season that accompanies it serve to establish that the young woman can wield important resources in interpersonal interactions.

Debutante presentations are a unique ritual of the upper classes, and elite women play a significant part in planning many of the exclusive charity balls where the young women are presented. Although, in many cities, some debutante balls are sponsored by prestigious men's organizations that have no community service requirement—and where the primary criteria for being selected as a debutante is having a father who is a member in good standing—many elite women's organizations that present debutantes require that the mothers engage in philanthropic activities if their daughters are to be considered for presentation by the group. In this way, elite women's organizations have power over their members and can ensure that they will have willing volunteers for the group's various fundraisers and community service projects.

Being chosen as a debutante by an elite women's organization is not something to be taken lightly by honorees. Women in elite volunteer organizations frown on young women—and sometimes their mothers— if the debutante designee does not take seriously enough the responsibility of representing her family and the sponsoring organization in a positive manner. For this reason, many young women spend time and energy carefully learning the rituals that surround their presentation. As I watched a debutante take her bow at a Texas presentation ball, I realized how much training and impression management goes into practicing for this event. Young women in formal debutante presentations wear a floor-length, "designer" gown and perform the Texas Dip, an athletic feat that must be successfully and gracefully accomplished in full view of thousands of people. Jeanine, a bow practice chair for a presentation ball, explained the technique to me as if I were the debutante:

> Well, first you bring your right foot around in an arc to the back. You have to make sure that you kinda drag your foot, so that you don't catch it in your petticoat. Then you have to sweep your arms out straight from the shoulder. Remember, you have a long bouquet attached to you in your left hand, so your back needs to be arched slightly and your arms fully extended so that you will look tall and graceful. Hold your neck straight and make sure that your head is centered. Then bend your left knee and lower yourself slowly to the floor. I usually recommend that the girls count to twenty as they do this, but sometimes I see their mouths moving as they count during practice, so I have to tell them to quit. Now, if you've lowered yourself successfully, you should be sitting on your right ankle. Turn your face slightly to the right and slowly bow your head deep into the gown with your forehead down. Be sure you don't get lipstick on your gown. Some girls actually touch the floor with their forehead or nose when they bow, but we don't require it. What is required is a "happy face," a continuous smile throughout. As you rise to a count of about fifteen, you really need to smile and look happy 'cause your parents will be watching proudly and photographers will be snapping your picture.

Why do members of the upper classes participate in rituals that may appear to outsiders to be archaic and meaningless?[1] What is the relationship between ritual and social power for elite women? This chapter examines the function of ritual in the maintenance of the upper classes, especially the function of the debutante presentation in that regard. It notes how such rituals create social networks and a power base that can be quite beneficial for the people who participate in them. The chapter describes the history of presentation balls and shows the growth of the parallel but racially or ethnically separate organizations that hold such balls. Finally, it takes a look at how participation in such events enhances the social power of elite young women and helps solidify their position in the next generation of social elites.

Rituals and the Reproduction of the Upper Classes

Sociologists argue that ritual stabilizes the current organization of cultural and social life because it "unites a particular image of the universe with a strong emotional attachment to it."[2] Upper-class rituals such as the formal debut convey such an image, particularly in regard to issues of race, class, and gender identity. They also involve strong emotional attachment through invoking the importance of "family values" and "tradition" in the rites of passage that publicly mark young people's acceptance as "insiders" by members of the social elite. Debutante presentations also convey specific images of racial/ethnic-, class-, and gender-based identities. In her study of U.S. elites during the Gilded Age (roughly 1870–1920), Maureen E. Montgomery notes that debutante presentations were of great significance to early elites because debuts, along with upper-class weddings, were the two "female-centered rituals that marked important stages in the female life cycle."[3] The debut introduced the young woman to society and brought her into contact with eligible marriage partners, whereas the wedding was a celebration of the "successful negotiation of the marriage market and a reaffirmation of the social order through the reincorporation of the individual into the 'tribe.'"[4] Even with many changes in the roles of women in society, elite young women today remain a part of the social reproduction process of the upper class. In her study of Coronation (the annual debutante pageant held in connection with the ten-day celebration of Fiesta in San Antonio), Michaele Thurgood Haynes described how this process works:

> A study of debutantes demonstrates the continued importance of young women as representatives of the family, the basic unit of the elite social class. Through participation in Coronation and its attendant social season, the royal women are keys to social reproduction: the families mark their continued membership among the elite, the social class reaffirms its group identity, and the next generation is assured through endogamous marriage.[5]

As Haynes points out, having a daughter presented as a debutante not only reaffirms the family's position among the elite but also reaffirms the identity of the upper class as a social group and encourages young people to marry other social elites.

Debutante presentations may also be a form of regional pride that is intertwined with class, as is the case of the previously described Texas

Dip. Young women in Texas who are formally presented typically do the bow where they go completely to the floor. According to Jeanine, a ball organizer:

> This is the Texas signature. Young women from no other state do this kind of bow. It's special in that it identifies the young woman as being from Texas. It takes special training, grace, and some degree of athletic ability. It also shows that she is aware of the contributions of those who have gone before her. And audiences love it: It's like Swan Lake in ballet . . . you know, the dying swan.

The Texas Dip is characteristic not only of white debutante presentations but of the more formal African American and Latina presentations in Texas as well. For example, young Latinas presented at the Colonial Ball of the Society of Martha Washington in Laredo perform a long, deep, and slow curtsy that one journalist referred to as like "having collapsed into a large debutante puddle."[6] Similarly, the annual presentation ball of one African American women's social club calls for debutantes to perform the Texas Dip. At that gala ceremony, the young women being presented make their way to the center of the stage to perform the Texas Dip and, as each debutante makes her way down the stage, the master of ceremonies describes her dress and her accomplishments for the audience. During the time of my study, the accomplishments recited for these young women were numerous, as Eunice, an African American ball organizer and debutante mentor described:

> The women our organization presents are among the finest in the country. They are not "Beauty Queens"! Over the past few years, we've had many debs who are on the dean's list at a major university; we've had officers in Pre-Law and Pre-Med clubs, and nearly all of them have been involved in such organizations as the NAACP, the Progressive Black Student Organization, the Black Student Alliance or Black Student Association, the Association of Young Black Educators, the National Association of Black Accountants, and I could keep naming others, but I think that makes my point. To be a part of our group, you've got to be a "do-er," not just a "pretty face."

Unlike the debutante presentations sponsored by elite white men's organizations—many of which do not require a community service component or active involvement in campus life as a prerequisite for being presented as a debutante—the presentation balls sponsored by most elite women's organizations, whether white, African American, Latina, or other, contain a specific community service or philanthropic requirement, which is important in the selection process of "royalty." Mothers, and sometimes daughters, are required to perform a certain number of hours of volunteer work, to serve on a specific number of committees, or to assume a leadership role in the organization before the daughter will be presented. Some elite families build or use existing social connections to have their daughters presented more than once, frequently in several cities. It is not unusual for a young woman to be presented during her freshman year of college by one organization and to follow this with one or more presentations by other groups during her sophomore and junior years. Kimberly, a white woman from an Old Name family, is an example:

Let's see . . . when and where have I been presented? Well, if you count the [high school presentation of the symphony], that's one. If you count the [medically related organization] presentation my senior year of high school, that's two. Then, there's [children's home benefit gala] for three; the [local symphony group] for four; the Cotton Palace in Waco, that's five; [elite men's social club] is six; and International in New York is seven. And, can you believe it, I did all those with only two dresses. We had to buy a new one after my freshman year [in college], when I gained the "traditional ten [pounds]" eating pizza in our dorm room.

Often, young women such as Kimberly consider a presentation sponsored by an elite men's organization to be more prestigious than a presentation by a women's organization. However, the cotillion sponsored by the women's organization may be a springboard for especially attractive and socially skilled young women to be selected for an exclusive men's presentation ball.[7] Girls who are not a "shoo-in for deb" (as one person referred to it) at a men's gala may rise through the debutante hierarchy by first being presented by a prestigious women's organization and then being invited to "come out" by one of the "old guard" men's organizations in the city. Some members of Society refer to the presentation by the women's groups as the "bush leagues" and subsequent presentation by the "old guard" men's groups as the "major leagues." A number of the white women in this study had patterns similar to the one described by Kimberly; however, most of them had been presented, at most, two or three times. Kimberly had been presented the most times, among the young women and mothers with whom I spoke; however, another young woman "held the record" for presentations the greatest distance away in that she had been presented in Paris, France, among other international locations.

I attended more than two dozen presentation balls sponsored by various elite men's organization's during the time I was gathering data, and this chapter will discuss presentation balls sponsored by elite men's as well as elite women's organizations. Although my primary focus is on how women's good deeds are related to exclusivity and social power, I believe that it is important to include debutante presentations sponsored by men's groups in my analysis because they work "hand in glove" (as one person stated) with elite women's organizations to preserve the seemingly archaic ritual of the debutante presentation. To gain a better understanding of how the formal debut became an important social ritual of the upper classes, it is important to look at the history of the debutante presentation.

The Class-Based History of the Debutante Presentation

The term *debutante* comes from the French word, "debuter," meaning "to lead off" or to "enter into society." Historically, the term meant that a young woman was of marriageable age and was old enough to participate in adult social activities without her parents being present. Although some historians trace the practice of introducing eligible virgins to possible suitors to the Old Stone Age,[8] the formal debutante presentations of today are more closely related to the class-based European tradition that originated when young women were presented at court to the monarch. During the era of the landed aristocracy who lived in country houses for most of the year, it was important for wealthy landowners to introduce a daughter of marriageable age to society so that a suitable husband of similar social standing could be found for her. Being presented at the Court of St. James was considered to be the most prestigious rite of passage available to aristocrats' daughters. At the beginning of the social season, young women were presented to the monarch, before whom they took the St. James Bow, starting a social season that ran from April to the end of July and afforded English elites with numerous opportunities to party together.[9]

The relationship between debutante presentations and philanthropy in the United States did not exist until early in the twentieth century. The origins of the U.S. debutante presentation can be traced to 1748, when fifty-nine colonial Philadelphia families held a Dancing Assembly, the forerunner of the Debutante Ball. Subsequently, the first "Southern" ball was held in 1862 by the St. Cecilia Society, an elite men's organization, in Charleston, South Carolina, the capital of the Plantation System between the Revolution and the Civil War, and for many years, the only debutantes in Charleston were the daughters of St. Cecilia members.[10] Prior to the Civil War, young women had often been introduced at private parties given by the girl's parents; however, by the 1890s, debutante parties had become elaborate balls and included a social season made up—as they are today—of receptions, teas, dinners, and other festivities.[11] Criticism of the lavishness of some debutante balls and the lives of conspicuous consumption exhibited by some of the women and their families produced a public outcry early in the twentieth century, and it was at this time that the formal debut and the idea of "do goodery" became firmly intertwined: Two New York debutantes decided in 1901 to organize a volunteer workforce made up of debutantes, and the Junior League was born.[12] Over the past century, the Junior League in many cities has continued to sponsor a debutante ball.

Historically, the debutante season has thrived in eras when there has been a strong emphasis on the traditional roles of women, such as during the Gilded Age when elite women were portrayed as models of True Womanhood.[13] Elite women were empowered with the responsibility of determining when their daughters should be presented to society. Mrs. Burton Harrison, a writer for the *Ladies Home Journal*, identified the mother's role as follows:

> The mamma determines the time when, by a proper celebration, her daughter shall be accepted by the world as a fully mature woman. . . . This ceremony should convey the information to the world that the young lady has been graduated in all the accomplishments and knowledge necessary for her uses as a woman in society. In fact, it should mean that she has been instructed in all that deft wisdom which will be required by a *belle* of her circle and a queen of a household, for which she is, as all women are, a candidate.[14]

Prior to her formal debut, the young upper-class girl was not permitted to attend public functions alone with a man or to mingle socially with adults. Thus, for an elite young woman, the debutante season marked the beginning of a greater degree of freedom (although there were still many restrictions) and her acceptance as an adult member of the upper class. In one of the few sociological articles regarding the formal debut, James H. S. Bossard and Eleanor S. Boll describe this ritual as follows:

> The debut is a ceremony observed among certain elements of the upper classes for the purpose of introducing young girls into society. This is a formal sign that a girl has ceased to be considered as a child whose prime duties are to "play" with her playmates, to be obedient to her parents, and to attend school. She is now considered as a young adult who will take her place in adult society, begin to assume responsibility for her own behavior and decisions, and be ready for a career, for college, or for marriage.[15]

The debutante presentation and its accompanying social season of parties, teas, and dances has been a part of the upper-class lifestyle for centuries. These events help elite young people get to know one another and create useful friendships and marital connections. Even during the late 1960s and early 1970s, when the custom of making one's bow to society was temporarily eliminated by some elite social organizations, debutante presentations in the Texas cities in this study continued. The persistence of this rite of passage has been attributed to its significant function in reproducing the social upper class. According to Domhoff, "The decline of the debutante season and its subsequent resurgence in times of domestic tranquility reveal very clearly that one of its latent functions is to help perpetuate the upper class from generation to generation."[16] Even though wealth and family name may be passed on across generations, the reproduction of the upper class as a social class with a specific identity and consciousness of kind must take place all over again with each new generation.[17]

The Road to Being a Debutante and Its Rewards

For generations, elite young women have been socialized to be "debutantes for life," as one woman commented. Domhoff suggests that how elite young people perceive upper-class rituals such as the debutante ball is one indication of how successful adult members of the upper class have been in "insulating their children from the rest of society."[18] Although some young elites may have no interest in participating in such rituals, their lack of enthusiasm does not reduce the significance of such events for those who do choose to participate, and it may further enhance the experience because it means that a "select few" will acquire this form of upper-class social capital.

Scholars have focused on the debut as a rite of passage and identified two meanings of the formal debut: (1) the girls being presented are ready to take their places in society as functioning members of upper-class social life, and (2) the girls have fulfilled the appropriate prerequisites for membership in a restricted and exclusive social circle. However, becoming a debutante is not something that happens suddenly. Bossard and Boll describe the lengthy socialization process that transpires on the way to becoming a debutante and accepting one's full place in society as an elite woman:

> The preparation for the introduction into society is a way of living and begins almost with the birth of the child. The pre-debutante must grow up in a debutante-producing environment. If her parents have assured social standing she will form her friendships with the children of her parents' friends and do the same things they do. She will go to the private kindergartens, preschools, and schools where they go. If her parents' standing is doubtful, but they are financially able to compete, she may be sent to those same kindergartens and schools, where the establishment of early and continued friendships with the acceptable children will tend to make her an integral part of the whole pre-debutante group and inseparable from them when the time for their common introduction season arrives. They grow up together "knowing the ropes" and being accepted as debutante material.[19]

Contemporary young women have many more opportunities than their predecessors to experience social autonomy and may have social lives outside the view of their parents and significant others, regardless of whether or when they are presented to society. However, such seemingly archaic rituals as a presentation ball, beyond merely pleasing their parents, provide young elites with a long-established tradition of exclusivity that may help them develop useful upper-class ties beyond their family, whether for the purpose of marriage and social connections, for business and political purposes, or for some combination of the above.

When I asked presentation ball chairs, mothers of debutantes, and debutantes themselves to describe the long-range benefits of participating in the debutante season, I received a variety of answers. Some indicated that the event was just for the fun of it, and that it doesn't really have much significance later on; however, most of the women cited examples of how young women or their escorts had developed or enhanced their social networks as a result of their involvement. Although elites generally downplay the part that the debutante season has in "matchmaking" for young affluent women and men, I heard numerous stories about how the young participants either met or developed a more personal relationship with those involved in the presentation ball. An example is Crystal and Nick, who previously did not know each other even though they lived in the same city. They had not attended the same high school and were enrolled in universities in different cities when they met at the Royalty Get Acquainted Party held by the organization sponsoring the presentation ball in which Crystal was to be presented and Nick was to serve as her escort. During the year of parties, rehearsals, and other debutante season-related events, Crystal and Nick began dating. They eventually married and had several children, uniting the two elite families. Crystal has followed in the steps of both her mother and mother-in-law, spending much of her time in philanthropic and community service work. In turn, her mother and mother-in-law were among the founders of a grandparents' club that raises money for the elite private school that their mutual grandchildren attend. Although the story of Crystal and Nick is only one example of how debutante presentations still introduce eligible young elites to one another for the purposes of marriage, it is not an isolated case. A number of other people described to me how their children met the person they married at the by-invitation-only events that accompany annual debutante presentation balls.

Some debutantes enhance their social and economic power by building important business connections through their participation in debutante rituals. Women who today are physicians, attorneys, and realtors described how the contacts they made when they were presented had served them well when they later applied to graduate or professional school or began a career. Marissa, a white woman in her early-30s explained how another debutante's father had helped her achieve her current position as an associate in a prestigious law firm. According to

Marissa, his assistance helped her to get started in a law career at a level higher than she believes she herself would have been able to manage:

> Judy's father offered me a job as a summer clerk in his law firm while I was in law school. The competition among students was tremendous that year; word was out that the bigger firms weren't hiring as many clerks, and we were really sweating it out to hear. I was really concerned I wouldn't get anything at all: I wasn't at [a top law school], and I was just doing so-so, somewhere midway in my class, although I did better later. Well, after working in his office for part of a summer (and living in the firm's condo for free!), I was able to put that on my resume, and other shareholders in other firms then said, "Look where she spent the summer." I have been very lucky in the firms I've been in, and I look forward to being made a partner soon.

Marissa might have had other contacts through her family that would have served her as well; however, because Judy's father lived in another city and initially met Marissa during the debutante season, Marissa believes that it is highly unlikely that they would have met under other circumstances.

What the stories of Crystal and Marissa show is that one's social circle of family and friends grows wider for elites—and can be useful in a variety of ways—as they create social networks and power bases across cities (and sometimes nationally or internationally) with others who are actively involved in the "debutante circuit" for one or more years. Being on the circuit means that similar rituals are replicated in most communities of any size in the United States, as well as urban centers around the world, and that those who participate constitute a relatively small core of social elites who not only experience a sense of accomplishment for their families but also develop ties to other social elites that may be personally beneficial. But, above all, debutantes and their parents emphasize the importance of the *ritual* that is involved in "coming out," not the social connections that are made or the conspicuous consumption that often transpires during the debutante season as lavish parties are planned and elaborate designer gowns and other attire are purchased by the debutantes and their parents. Members of the upper classes make effective use of rituals, ranging from infant baptisms and debutante presentations to weddings and funerals, to mark the individual's passage from one stage of life to another, but they also use these ceremonies as a time to mark their status as being in the top economic and social tiers of society. Social power is also important in the debutante selection process.

The Selection Process

Part of the ritual of the debutante presentation is the selection process that determines which of the eligible young women will be presented and who their escorts and other "royal" attendants will be. The importance of ritual in helping people make social connections is described by Catherine Bell, who refers to ritual as a tool for "social and cultural jockeying" and as a "performative medium for the negotiation of power in relationships."[20] Bell states that ritual activity serves to create reality through "redemptive hegemony," making the participants aware of the existing social order and how they can become empowered within it.[21] For example, debutante presentations and the organizations that sponsor them are hierarchically organized, allowing participants to move up through the ranks if they have the right credentials and fulfill the obligations associated with "succession" in the ranks. Women who work hard for the organization know that many of them will be rewarded by having their children presented as "royalty" or "junior royalty" at a formal ball. The presentation thus is an incentive to encourage women to join such organizations and to work hard not only for the cause but for their children. Susan, a former ball chair, described how the mothers' hard work fit into the selection process within her organization:

> I want each of our debutantes to have one of the most memorable nights of their life. The [presentation] ball means so much to our families and their friends. Members work on our fundraising projects for years knowing that some families will be honored by having their daughter chosen to be presented as "royalty." For a girl to be presented by our group, her mother must be an Active Member in good standing [meaning that she has fulfilled her membership obligations for the year] or an Associate [a long-term member who has made significant contributions in the past and continues to pay her membership dues] and the family must have "paid their dues."
>
> We have a committee that decides who our royalty will be. Committee members who select the girls who will be invited to be our [debutantes] use a summary sheet on "Eligible Royalty" that shows the financial contributions of the family and the amount of volunteer work the mother, or sometimes the grandmother, has done for [our organization]. Here's an example of the accomplishments of one mother whose daughter was presented: Juanita has been a member for fifteen years; she has served as a board member for ten years. During that time she was recording secretary, corresponding secretary, chairman of mailings, and frequently served as a meeting hostess. Juanita has served many hours on fundraising projects, and she and her husband are *major* contributors to [the organization]. Our members enjoy working on projects together for the benefit of [our organization], but it is also a real incentive knowing that their children might be selected for this honor.

As my interview with Susan suggests, elite women's organizations that sponsor annual debutante presentations have developed an elaborate set of procedures and appointed a committee to determine which young women will be selected as royalty and, from among those selected, who will receive the top honors as Queen, Diamond, or a similar designation. In other words, debutante presentations by elite women's organizations not only are significant to the young women themselves, but also are significant to the organization by encouraging elite women to actively participate and take leadership roles.

Elite rituals are more than rites of passage; they represent a form of parental in-group jockeying for prestige and for possession of the top status positions for their children, such as having a daughter selected to be Queen (or a princess or duchess). The selection process represents the norm of exclusivity in that these elite rituals set one's family apart from other elites who are not within the inner social circle. Second, having children selected as royalty sets the family apart from the ordinary people in the city. Coronation, the presentation ball associated with Fiesta in San Antonio, is an example. For many years, this formal event has been held by and for elites, where the system of rituals is "performed by blue bloods who use their manners and money to set themselves apart from the rest of San Antonio, including the city's nouveau riche."[22] Social analysts have shown that even mothers and fathers in Old Name families have worked diligently to ensure that their daughters will be selected as the Queen. According to one journalist, "Mothers and fathers wage phone and mail campaigns, seeking to build winning coalitions for their daughters. Tradition holds that such lobbying be performed with a certain finesse, although old-timers lament that campaigns are escalating to the point of poor taste."[23] According to one analyst, Old Name families ("blue bloods") typically win out in the long run, and these honors are often passed from one generation to the next. In a Queen of Coronation's family history in the late 1990s, for example, there had previously been twelve queens, six princesses, five mistresses of the robes,[24] and ten Order of the Alamo (the group sponsoring the presentation) presidents, making her a shoo-in for the top position.[25]

The Importance of Maintaining Tradition

Like Coronation, many other debutante presentation balls have intergenerational participants, and when this is the case, much is made of the fact that the mother, grandmother, aunt, cousin, or other relatives have been presented by the same organization. This constitutes one form of tradition and keeps this ritual viable: Children are socialized to want to follow in their relatives' footsteps, if for no other reason than to keep "family tradition" alive. The desire to maintain tradition is also important for ball organizers because, even when they adopt a "unique" theme for the annual ball, the overall procedure remains very similar from one year to the next. One woman used the rituals of the Episcopal church as an analogy:

> We have Rite I and Rite II in the Prayer Book; those who like one rite or the other best, come to the church service at the hour when that rite is being used. But they don't come in and find that everybody is swaying back and forth and saying things that are not in the ritual at all. That's why we're Episcopalians: We like the formal worship ceremony. The same is true for the ball: We don't want to see our children on the stage with tattoos and spiked hair dancing to some funky music. We want to see nice young men in their tuxedos and young women wearing their beautiful dresses who appreciate the honor and the rich symbolism of the occasion . . . plus, we want them to have fun. You're only young once, you know.

Tradition is important not only to the parents and the participants but also to the leaders of the organizations that sponsor the presentation balls. I learned that when there is discussion about doing away with a "traditional" practice or eliminating any of the symbolism, group "insiders" strongly protest, and their actions almost inevitably lead to the retention of the established way of doing things. One incident where a ball chair tried to "buck tradition" was described by Sally, a white woman in her mid-40s from a New Money family:

> Our ball has a long, time-honored tradition, and occasionally we get a feisty ball chairman who thinks she is going to change everything. I remember one year when we had a tall, thin dynamo who thought she was going to really make her mark on the ball . . . you know, give it a more "contemporary" theme and do away with some of the "stuffy old tradition," as she called it. What happened was that she had her first ball committee meeting and word got out about what she thought she was going to do. Well, the next thing you know, she had a swarm of old ball chairmen and several former presidents take her aside and say, "Look, we've been doing our ball for years. Everybody likes it the way it is. The local [debs] like it, the visiting [royalty] like it, the parents like it, and our major donors like it. Why change something that works for all of us just for the sake of changing it?" This woman got the message, but we've had several headstrong women who didn't heed our warnings and, as it got closer to time for the ball, they became frantic when they saw rebellion in the ranks. So, when a newly appointed ball chairman asks me what I think she should do, I say, "Follow the tradition— use the formula—then add your own touches or innovations."

As this example suggests, tradition and symbolism are important to women who are part of an organization's "permanent ball committee," which is made up of women who have power in the organization because they have served as an officer in the organization and have had their own daughters or sons honored as "royalty."

Racial and Ethnic Identity and the Debutante Presentation

As well as showing the importance of the selection process and the ritual involved in the debutante presentation, Coronation in San Antonio, sponsored by the elite men's organization, the Order of the Alamo, demonstrates how the intersections of race and class can be seen in the debutante ritual. Fiesta is an event held annually in San Antonio, a city with a large proportion of the population falling below the U.S. poverty line and an overwhelmingly Latino/Latina population. Although there is a week of festivities for people across lines of race, ethnicity, and class during Fiesta, the most prestigious and exclusive event is Coronation, which has as its participants and audience people who reside almost exclusively in a few wealthy enclaves of the city, such as Alamo Heights, Olmos Park, or Terrell Hills, which have been described as the "predominantly white, old-money enclaves close to downtown."[26]

In San Antonio and other cities that have prestigious debutante presentations, issues of race and ethnicity have been raised for a number of years. For example, some of the groups putting on Coronation have been subjected to criticisms such as "The point is that excluding people because of their race is wrong."[27] Some organizers of Coronation argue, by contrast, that there is representation of diverse groups of young women; for example, a Latina can be chosen as one of Fiesta's minority queens for the Battle of Flowers Parade and there are two kings, King Antonio, representing the white elite male organization (Order of the Alamo), and Rey Feo, who represents the Mexican American majority. According to one journalist, Fiesta organizers refer to this arrangement as "separate but equal," which brings me to an important question in my research: Is there such a thing as separate but equal in the social worlds of white Americans and people of color in the United States? How have separate debutante balls and other rites of passage become a way of life in a country that, in the twenty-first century, describes itself as diverse and inclusive? We turn now to an examination of the separate but perhaps not equal presentation rituals of racial and ethnic categories outside the "U.S. white mainstream."

White Ethnic Presentations: Italian Americans as an Example

Today, debutante balls are sponsored by a wide variety of "white ethnic" groups in addition to those comprised of white Euro-Americans (who trace their origins to Western Europe): Armenian Americans, Greek Americans, Jewish Americans, and Italian Americans in many regions sponsor debutante presentations for their daughters. So many come from more moderate income levels and less prestigious family backgrounds, but many have firmly established themselves as being among the more powerful and influential people in the cities where they reside. Italian Americans in Houston are an example.

While I was conducting an in-depth examination of debutante cotillions, I learned about debutante presentations that are organized as a way to preserve the heritage of Italian Americans in Houston. At the annual Italian American debutante presentation, the Italian Ball, about ten to twelve outstanding young women of Italian American descent are honored.[28] The Federation of Italian-American Organizations, which ties twenty-six Italian clubs together, sponsors the debutante presentation, where the Italian American surnames of family members, particularly the maiden names of mothers of Italian descent, are duly noted in programs and newspaper accounts of the ball. This event not only honors young women and their families but also serves as a major fund raiser for the Federation and its social and cultural activities in Houston.[29] Like Houston, other cities with substantial Italian American populations hold debutante cotillions for young women. One of the largest presentations is in Chicago, where a typical debutante's background is described as follows:

> Sabrina Passaglia's grandmother and aunt were on the board of the Joint Civic Committee of Italian Americans Women's Division for 15 years. Passaglia, 16, of Winfield, said she decided to be a debutante because "it's fun to be in the big dresses and dance. I'm meeting new people. We do charity things. And it's important to my grandma and my aunt, so it's important to me."[30]

Do debutante presentations mark the separation between people who are "in" socially and those who are "out"? According to one organizer of the Italian American cotillion in Chicago, "There is only one requirement to be a debutante, to be of Italian descent. If a girl wants to meet a really cute young Italian man, this is the place to come."[31]

Just as white Euro-American elites may use the debutante ritual as a sign of social acceptance into the inner circles and as an arena in which young elites can make important social connections, white ethnic groups such as Italian Americans may choose to preserve elite rituals in order to retain their cultural heritage and identity. Similarly, African Americans have achieved recognition while working for the "uplift of the black race" through debutante presentations.

African American Presentations
Through an extensive national search, I found only a few debutante presentations in which African American women were presented at historically white balls. In each case, only one or two African American women were presented out of a cohort of anywhere from ten to thirty debutantes.

These were the exception rather than the rule in 2000, when I was concluding my research, but I believe that it is important to note that seemingly "integrated" presentations do occur, typically with a headline noting that such an event has transpired. One example was the 1997 Kansas City Jewel Ball, sponsored by the Kansas City Symphony Orchestra and the Nelson-Atkins Museum of Art, in which debutante Allyson Lelia Ashley became the "first African-American young woman to be presented at the Jewel Ball since its founding in 1954."[32] Most of the cities in my study have yet to experience the first African American debutante being presented by an elite white social or philanthropic organization, but there are presentation balls for young African American women and in some cases, a Beautillion Ball that honors young African American men. Scholars have documented that high status African Americans have participated in debutante balls since the post-bellum era following the Civil War.[33]

To trace the history of debutante presentations among African Americans, some social analysts look back to the era of slavery and the early distinctions that were made between free and enslaved blacks. Since freed slaves and those who had managed to avoid the bondage of slavery were able to earn money and own property, they became the nucleus of the earliest black elites or "black aristocracy."[34] Between 1880 and 1940, black social clubs, fraternal organizations, and churches became the center of black social life, and it is in social organizations such as Jack and Jill of America, The Links, the Girl Friends, and the Boule, which were organized to focus on tradition and pride in family background and accomplishment, that we find the roots for the African American debutante presentation. According to Lawrence Otis Graham,[35] these groups and the elite rites of passage they sponsored were not a reflection of "white aspirations" among African Americans, as some have suggested, but rather these organizations and rituals were created around blacks' own traditions.

Prior to the 1970s, racial segregation of African Americans from whites perpetuated separate social circles and precluded the presentation of African American debutantes by any organization other than those formed by people of color. Today, racial segregation by law no longer exists, but racial *separation* is a social reality in many areas of contemporary life, including sororities—as discussed in chapter 4—and elite Society presentations of the next generation of young people. This racial separation is apparent today in newspaper and media coverage of the white debutante season as compared with that of presentation balls of other racial or ethnic groups. Although media coverage has been reduced from the years in which entire Society pages in many newspapers provided "the masses" with the elaborate details of elite galas,[36] there remains a steady flow of information in Texas cities about debutantes being presented at the most prestigious white cotillions. By contrast, coverage of presentations by other racial or ethnic groups is very limited, with the media providing, at most, small photos (displayed in high school year book format) of the participants and listing their parents' names.

Just as exclusivity and snobbism may occur within white Society and between white Society and black Society, exclusion also transpires within the black community as African American elites, like their white counterparts, strive to get their daughters presented by the "best" organizations[37] and to receive appropriate newspaper coverage of the event. This exclusivity has been documented by a number of scholars who have studied the practices that developed among elite African Americans as they began to make distinctions on the basis of education, skin color, material resources, and family background.[38] Adelaide M. Cromwell's study of Boston's black upper class between 1750 and 1950 found that the debutante presentation reflected the emergence of an accepted class structure among black elites in that city.[39] Resthaven Junior Club, an elite black women's organization, sponsored the premier African American debutante ball and carefully selected its participants from among the light-skinned, native born of Boston. Members of the Club were "all native Bostonians"—there were no southern-born or West Indian–born members; therefore, the debutante choices were based on "local origin, complexion, and family."[40] In other cities as well, African American debutantes were presented by black organizations that were considered prestigious within the African American community, thus creating a set of parallel structures whereby white debutantes were presented by white social organizations whereas African American debutantes were presented by black fraternal or social organizations. For example, when African Americans were excluded during the nineteenth century from the Carnival events associated with Mardi Gras in New Orleans, blacks started the Original Illinois Club, which has presented a debutante ball every year since 1895.[41]

Issues of skin color and appearance still exist within these organizations, as can be seen in the narratives of some African American debutantes, describing how their mothers or other relatives had attempted to influence their thinking and activities from an early age if they thought that the young women might be presented by a prestigious organization. Carrie, a wealthy African American woman, spoke of "the brown bag test—whether or not her skin was lighter in color than a grocery bag" and how important this was to her mother, who frequently warned her, "don't get out in the sun at all—period," for fear that Carrie's skin and appearance might not be acceptable to the debutante organizers whom she hoped would invite Carrie to participate. The fears of Carrie's mother may be an accurate assessment in some cases. While I was studying debutante presentations, one woman called my attention to the case of Michelle Barskile, a young African American woman who was not going to be allowed to participate in an Alpha Kappa Alpha sorority-sponsored debutante ball because of her hairstyle—dreadlocks. According to one news account:

> Seventeen-year-old Michelle Barskile could imagine her appearance at the Alpha Kappa Alpha debutante ball. All eyes would be focused on her as she waltzed with her father under the spotlight in the darkened ballroom. She planned to wear a pearly white gown purchased months ago for the special night and to have her black tresses sway to the music. But her coming-out experience isn't going to be anything like that. The Raleigh, N.C. chapter of the black sorority withdrew Michelle's invitation to the Nov. 27 ball, saying her hair was unacceptable. Michelle wears dreadlocks, long and thick ropes of naturally twisted hair that frame her bespectacled face and cascade down her back. The sorority sisters wanted her to wear her locks pinned up off her neck for the ball. "I'd look like Marge Simpson if I did that," Michelle says. . . . "When I refused, they said I couldn't be in the ball."[42]

Media accounts emphasize the importance this event held for Michelle, an honor roll student who had been accepted to five universities at the time of the controversy. For Michelle, the debutante ball represented a "public acknowledgment" of what she had accomplished in high school, and she saw her hair as an expression of her pride "in being a black woman."[43]

Some recent scholarly research on the African American debutante ball has focused on the part that dress plays in this rite of passage. Annette Lynch described how clothing is interwoven with personal and social identity at the African American ball. According to Lynch, debutante balls "must be interpreted as a part of a long history of African Americans using dress within public venues to display reconstructed versions of gendered identity."[44] Tracing the origins of this practice to the slavery period, Lynch describes the earliest balls, organized by slaves in urban settings in the 1850s, as being a venue in which women were able to display their clothing and enhance their social standing among other blacks. By the 1920s, a growing black middle class used clothing to show their heightened social position and created elite social events such as debutante balls to establish class boundaries within the African American community. As Lynch states, "the early African American debutante balls held within these communities, most often sponsored by African American professional men's associations, helped mark class boundaries as well as spotlighting the beauty, grace, and character of the daughters of prominent African American families."[45]

Katrina Hazzard-Gordon examined the relationship between African American debutante balls and the "uplift movement" that emerged in the post-emancipation period when African Americans sought to raise the quality of life for all free blacks. Debutante balls were a way to raise money for causes related to racial uplift, and these events also provided young African American women a venue in which they could receive the recognition that was categorically denied them in the dominant society, as well as by the organizers of "whites-only" elite balls.[46]

Comparing African American and white debutante presentations, two key differences can be identified: (1) African American women typically are presented at a younger age, often their senior year in high school, whereas white debutantes usually are at least in their first year of college, and (2) much greater emphasis is placed on the volunteer efforts and community service of African American debutantes than their white counterparts. Although white debutantes may be expected to fulfill some volunteer hours for an organization because they have been chosen for this honor, their selection typically is less dependent on their community service than on other criteria, such as the good deeds of their parents. By contrast, many African American debutante balls focus less on "presenting well-born daughters of men with high social standing" than they do on emphasizing the young women's accomplishments and community service.[47] An example of this difference is the annual presentation by the alumnae chapter of Alpha Kappa Alpha in a mid-sized city in my study that is located between two large metropolitan areas. The debutantes are high school seniors who are involved in community activities. In addition to the formal presentation, other events include a Mother/Daughter Tea and a series of weekly seminars that help the young women develop their personal and professional skills. At the presentation, one young woman is honored as Miss Debutante and receives a large scholarship. There are also second- and third-place scholarships and a Miss Congeniality award. Organizers of this event describe how becoming a debutante was a learning experience that would benefit the young women for the rest of their lives:

> We help guide the young women to be the best that they can be. They learn etiquette and know to do such things as to say "Please" and "Thank you" when they are around other people. They know to send thank you cards and to be nice to others—things that many people nowadays forget, or never knew to do in the first place.

One alumnae sorority member described her relationship to the debutantes as "like having a little sister . . . somebody I can give advice to and help make her path easier than mine has been." The young women presented by this and similar organizations are expected to donate hours of community service. Some of them raise money for charities; others do "hands-on" projects in the community. The enthusiasm of the young women is pronounced. with a number of them suggesting that they are following in the footsteps of older sisters or cousins: "All my sisters were presented, and I've been wanting to be a debutante since I was six so that I could wear one of those wonderful white dresses!"

The young women presented by the most exclusive African American women's organizations emphasize what an honor it is to be chosen for presentation and how much time and energy they are required to invest in preparation for this "special night." Chantelle, an African American debutante, described the period of preparation she and other debutantes went through before being presented by a prestigious African American women's sorority:

> I know we spent at least eight months getting ready. Every time I turned around I was learning new dance steps, being told about good etiquette, brushing up on our cultural history, and attending seminars on career development. I was really pressed for time because I was in school too, but after it was over, I thought to myself, "That was one of the most worthwhile things I've done. Look what I know now that I didn't know then."

At the end of our discussion, Chantelle stated that she was "happy to have had the opportunity to be a deb" because she knew of the deeply embedded history of prejudice and discrimination that had precluded many young women from receiving social recognition for their accomplishments. Anne, a friend of Chantelle and another debutante, agreed with her: "It was nice to have this special celebration with my parents. It was really a dream come true for me . . . and, I think, for them. My mother worked for years for [organization], and when I was on that stage I said to myself, 'This is Mother's payoff.'"

Latina Presentations

As I examined the presentation of young Latinas to society, I found two divergent paths were pursued, the formal debut, a strictly social event, and La Quinceañera, a combined religious and social event with participants from a wider diversity of income and class levels. La Quinceañera— the ritual celebration of a young Latina's coming of age—is different in two significant ways from the traditional debutante presentation: (1) the quinceañera is a religious and social celebration that includes a service in which the young woman reaffirms her religious faith—a practice that does not exist in the debutante season, and (2) young Latinas who participate in a quinceañera do not necessarily come from affluent families with high levels of prestige in the community. Sponsors, including members of the young woman's extended family and friendship groups, often help pay for the elaborate dress that the young women wear and for the party that typically follows the religious service.[48] One Latina college student referred to the quinceañera, or Sweet 15 (because it is celebrated on a young woman's fifteenth birthday), as "the poor girl's coming out party."

However, this description is not totally accurate: Some wealthy Latino families spend lavish sums of money on this event and view it as one of the most prestigious and exclusive social occasions in their city. A journalist referred to the celebration as "equal parts wedding feast, senior prom, and debutante ball," and emphasized that even the poorest of families held such an event, usually with the financial assistance of many "padrinos" and "madrinas" (sponsors) who provide money, food, and many other items to help make the event possible.[49] In turn, when their own children are eligible to participate in such rites of passage, they can rely on sponsors helping them to provide the same one-of-a-kind dresses, elaborate cakes, entertainment, decorations, and other things needed to put on the event. A complete analysis of this rite of passage is beyond the scope of my study, which focused on several "Hispanic" debutante presentations held in Texas.

In two cities in my study, upper-middle-class Latina debutantes are presented by organizations comprised primarily of "Hispanic elites" in their community. For example, the Hispanic Debutante Association in Fort Worth holds an annual debutante ball in which young Latinas make a formal bow to society in settings such as a ballroom at a private club. One debutante described the year she was presented:

> I remember that there was a large garden arch surrounded by flowers and, as I stood under the arch, I looked out to where I thought my parents and sister were and gave thanks for all of the people who had made that evening possible. We had been told that our presentation was a salute to the older generation, and I realized how true that was on the evening I was presented.

Similarly, the Dallas Pan American Golf Association—comprised of Latino golfers and others with an interest in promoting golf and junior golf—holds an annual Golfer's Ball that includes the presentation of Latina debutantes. Unlike some of the white (non-Hispanic) balls I studied, where as many as fifteen or twenty young women were presented, fewer women participated in the formal debut at the balls sponsored by Latino organizations. Four women were presented at the Dallas event; about ten or twelve are presented each year at the Fort Worth Hispanic ball.

Perhaps the most exclusive Latina debutante presentation in Texas takes place in Laredo where the Society of Martha Washington sponsors the annual Colonial Ball at which young women are formally presented to society. The ball has existed since 1924; however, today it is under the auspices of the Society of Martha Washington, which was organized in 1939 and held its first presentation in 1940. The Colonial Ball is part of a larger citywide Washington's Birthday celebration that takes place over a sixteen-day period and includes partying and patriotic parades. The most prized role for women at the Colonial Ball is that of Martha Washington, wife of the first U.S. president, for whom the organization is named. For men, the most prized role is to portray George Washington. The founders of the Society of Martha Washington and most of the early debutantes were white (Anglo) women, whereas contemporary group members and many of the young women presented as debutantes today are primarily wealthy Latinas.[50] Laredo has been characterized by intermarriage throughout its history, and today's Laredo elite is comprised of a tight bicultural, bilingual inner social circle of wealthy residents. A former president of the Martha Washington Society pointed out that Latinos "have always been among the dominant class" in Laredo, so it is no surprise that the debutante presentation has reflected the Hispanic and white non-Hispanic confluence over the years.

The exclusivity of the Society of Martha Washington's Colonial Ball is ensured by the closed membership of the organization, which is limited to two hundred people. New members mainly are legacy, those who have relatives in the group. According to a woman who had been involved with the organization for a number of years:

> Membership is limited to two hundred members, and we add members by invitation only. The invitations usually go to daughters or granddaughters of members because we have so few slots available. When a member dies, retires, or asks that her membership be moved to the sustaining membership category (this can only happen after twenty-five years of service to the Society), this opens a slot for new members. . . . We have many more women put up for membership than we can invite in each year. It's really an honor to be asked to join.

Just as the membership is closed, the young women asked to be debutantes or to portray Martha Washington are always the daughters or granddaughters of Society members, thus ensuing the continuing exclusivity of the group's debutante presentation.

Women who have served as Martha Washington or as other debutantes frequently describe the family tradition of being a part of the court at the Colonial Ball. Some recall the years when each debutante represented one of the thirteen original U.S. colonies, plus a representative of Nuevo Laredo (the sister city on the Mexican side of the border). Others remember the exact year when their mothers, grandmothers, or great-grandmothers portrayed Martha Washington or a member of her court. A newspaper account of this chain of legacy shows the interrelation of participants over the years since the Colonial Ball's start in 1924:

> The biggest chain of legacy, however, is in debutante Marcia Ann Powell's family. Marcia's mother, Josie Peña (Powell), was a deb in 1974 and was escorted by Marcia Ann's father, Lester Powell, while her paternal grand-

mother, Barbara Tucker (Powell) was presented as a debutante in 1948, escorted by Marcia Ann's paternal grandfather, William Richard Powell. The two grandparents also portrayed George and Martha in 1972. Then, Marcia's paternal great-grandmother, Hazel Kepley Powell, was Martha in 1941.[51]

Exclusivity and family pride in maintaining tradition are two of the compelling themes not only in debutante presentations featuring Latina young women but also in all of the presentations I have described. A highlight of elite women's volunteer efforts is seeing their daughters being presented as debutantes and/or their sons serving as escorts. The women typically view this as something they have earned and something to which members of their family are entitled. In other words, they do not see the bestowing of such honors on their family as a form of elitism or as a system that perpetuates the upper classes, even though the women who serve on the ball committee have literally created a special event where social elites gather. They have spent a year or more making sure that the rituals of the evening are carried out properly and that the event receives appropriate acknowledgment from other elites and from the community at large through publicity efforts directed at local and sometimes regional media outlets. I now turn to a brief examination of the amount of time and talent that elite women put into organizing these events, culminating in one "special night to remember."

A Year of Good Deeds:
Planning and Implementing the Charity Debutante Ball

I kept a diary of the year that I served as publicity chair for a major fundraising debutante ball held in one city in my study. The publicity chair typically has a relatively small job when compared to women in positions such as ball chair, debutante chair (who handles all of the communication with debutantes and their parents—both local and "visiting royalty"), and decorations chair; however, I spent approximately 160 hours, or the equivalent of four weeks' time, over the course of one year doing ball-related publicity. My tasks included writing press releases for each event associated with the debutante ball season, contacting members of the media and taking some of them to lunch to discuss the upcoming activities (in an attempt to secure adequate coverage of the events), and disseminating information about the debutantes and their parents to the newspapers. After the ball, I wrote thank you notes to members of the media who had provided good coverage for the ball, so that they would be eager to provide similar coverage next year.

While my tasks were relatively minor, women who chair a fundraising ball are making a major commitment, equivalent to full-time paid employment, for at least a year. Prior to her year as being chair of the ball, most women have served as chair elect, working as an understudy to other ball chairs before taking full responsibility for planning this important fundraising event. But the ball chair is not alone: More than fifty women chair various committees for this event and, in some organizations, most members have some ball-related responsibility to fulfill. In some cases this may be purchasing a specific number of tickets and in others it may be assuming a major responsibility for seeing that the ball is socially successful and economically profitable.

Amid planning for the festivities, the ball chair and other women who chair major committees know that they will be held accountable for how much money the event makes (after expenses) for the organization that is the designated beneficiary of the monies raised. Consequently, the women walk a "tight rope" between wanting to plan a lavish ball that will be "the talk of the town," as one ball chair noted, while at the same time raising more money than previous ball chairs have for the organization. Women who are the most successful at planning such events have a network of other women within the organization who want to see them succeed. The women take turns supporting one another as chair of the ball or of major committees, and an "inner circle" within the larger membership group often "controls the ball" for a number of years. Members of this in-group typically state that their control of the annual ball occurs by default: "If other members aren't willing to step up and do the work—to sacrifice the time we put into this event—we have no choice but to keep doing it— our ball is our major fundraiser; and we have to be sure that it isn't messed up," was one woman's explanation. Several women indicated that a core of women are responsible for the ball each year, with some newer members welcomed into their ranks, because of the number of members who now work full-time and have young children. However, one astute woman commented that eventually some of these women would become good ball volunteers: "Just wait until they have a daughter 'coming up' to the age of being a debutante: They'll be delighted to help out with the ball and serve on other committees in hopes of having their daughter selected to be a [debutante]." As will be discussed in chapter 6, the structure of the particular organization tends to perpetuate the "in-group" control of elite women's organizations and events.

The "Big Night"

A series of events lead up to the big night of the presentation ball in most cities. There are announcement teas and brunches where the young women to be presented are initially introduced to members of the organization. Some elite women's organizations sponsor fashion shows, children's and young people's events, and other parties in conjunction with their presentation ball. However, all the events lead up to, and build excitement for, the "big night" when everyone assembles at a specially decorated convention center, hotel ballroom, or other venue in which the formal debut is to take place.

The women volunteer many hours of their time, purchase tickets, and donate money to make the event a success. Perhaps of even greater importance, however, is the ability of the key players to get individuals and corporations to donate money, goods, and services to the events. Without major "outside" contributions, the events surrounding the charity debutante presentations sponsored by elite women's organizations would be impossible. "Ticket prices alone will not cover the expenses of our wonderful ball: If we aren't careful, instead of making money for the [organization], we'd go in the hole, which is a dreadful fate for the ball chairman," according to Sally, who had chaired several balls and served on many committees. This brings me back to a recurring theme in *The Power of Good Deeds*: The women's organizations that hold these presentation balls are groups whose stated purpose is to raise money—large sums of money—for worthy causes. To raise that sort of money requires having a certain "elite panache" that is incorporated into those events the organization holds to which only elite people (or at least primarily elite people) will be invited. Having a grand ball at which elite children are presented and their parents are recognized is a means of both raising money *and* promoting the elite status of the group.

Except for the location, decorations, and specific setup of the debutante ball, people who frequently attend such events claim they could walk into a similar event in any city and the ritual would be very similar. From the check-in point, or hospitality desk, to the evening's seating arrangements, presentation, and entertainment in its aftermath, the guests will feel at home because the structure of the events is similar across cities.

Upon arriving, ball guests find a lavishly decorated setting that reflects the theme of that year's ball. At Coronation in San Antonio and the Society of Martha Washington's Colonial Ball in Laredo, the themes are historical and may not vary as widely as those of debutante presentations sponsored by organizations in other cities. For example, Coronation has featured themes such as "the Court of the Napoleonic Empire" and "the Court of Heraldic Britain," whereas balls sponsored by women's groups in other Texas cities have had themes such as "Carousel of Dreams," "Night in Venice," "Carnival in Rio," "an Oriental Evening," and "a Scottish Fortnight." For a Scottish-theme ball, for instance, a bagpipe corps wearing kilts and playing traditional Scottish music greets guests as they arrive, live sheep stand nearby, and ball committee members are attired in clothing reminiscent of Scotland in previous eras.

Upon entering the presentation hall, guests see hundreds of tables draped with long flowing cloths, lavish flower arrangements, tall candelabras or candle holders, and other decorations. Prior to the presentation, guests mingle and visit with one another, as well as consuming drinks and appetizers. At the appointed hour, everyone takes a seat and the formal introductions begin. Anticipation grows within the audience, particularly among parents whose children are serving as the evening's royalty: "Will our daughter be able to make her formal bow correctly?" "Will our young son who is serving as a Royal Attendant do what he is supposed to do?" Trudy, a former ball chair, described the anticipation that builds as guests wait for the entry of the debutantes and their royal party:

> When people first sit down, they're still talking, laughing, having a good time. By the time the master of ceremonies and the trumpet announce the arrival of the first debutante, it is usually so quiet you could hear a pin drop (except for the occasional boor who doesn't know how to behave . . . or has had too much booze). It is really an electrifying feeling as each girl's name is announced and she slowly walks in, wearing a beautiful flowing dress or Queen's robe, escorted on the arm of her father who looks handsome in tux and tails. The overall effect is somewhere between English royalty and a really nice wedding. I get a lump in my throat every year . . . and tears in my eyes the year that it was my daughter's turn [to be presented].

As Trudy described, the grand entry of the debutantes begins when the first young woman's name is announced—"Princess Laura Allison [pause] of the House of Richardson"—and she enters wearing a floor-length formal gown. There is special significance to how the young women are introduced. One connotation is that she is royalty; the other is that she comes from a prominent family. In describing the presentation at Coronation in San Antonio, one researcher has noted how "Breaking the name into two sections, the first and middle names followed by the surname preceded by 'house of,' emphasizes the middle name, often the mother's maiden name."[52] If a young woman comes from a prominent Old Name family or if her mother is well-known as a community volunteer, the introduction makes the debutante's lineage apparent to any ball guests who otherwise might not make the connection. However, most guests at presentation balls are "insiders" who typically are well aware of who the young women are and to whom they are related.

When the young woman is introduced, all eyes—and sometimes a spotlight—are on her. The formal attire worn by a debutante varies depending on the type of presentation at which she takes her bow. Some presentations require that all the young women wear period costumes, especially if the debutantes represent historical figures such as Martha Washington, at the Laredo celebration, or historical periods of time, such as at the Cotton Palace Pageant in Waco. Some period costumes are very elaborate and cost as much as $25,000. "Royal seamstresses" design and create elaborate robes and dresses, which are made of chiffon, tulle, or satin and adorned with beads, jewels, or lace. At some balls, the debutante designated as the Queen or Diamond wears an elaborate robe and a full-length white gown, while those designated as Duchesses or Princesses simply wear a formal dress. At other balls, the local royalty will wear white gowns while the visiting royalty (debutantes from other cities) will wear dresses in colors that match the theme of the ball. Over the past one hundred years and continuing today, the most typical debutante attire is the all-white gown, white shoes or "Cinderella slippers," long white gloves, and pearl earrings and necklaces.

As the debutantes' names are called and they make their slow progression up to the stage on the arm of their father or another male escort, two images are evoked: the entry of royalty and the beginning of the wedding procession. The illusion of the wedding procession is further established where the father or an older male escort walks with the debutante to the staging area and then relinquishes her to a younger man, who will serve as her escort for the rest of the evening (in the surrogate role of the "groom"). The young woman and her escort then move to the middle of the staging area, sometimes an arch or a gazebo, for example, where the debutante performs the Texas Dip or the appropriate bow or curtsy for that ball. After her bow, the couple may take their place in a tableau on the stage (with King and Queen enthroned and members of the "royal court" standing nearby) or slowly walk around the room as others admire them. After all of the debutantes have been presented, the young women are escorted to the dance floor and have the first dance with their father (similar to the post-wedding ritual). Next, they will dance with their escort, marking the end of the formal presentation. At this time, some older guests leave while others head for the bars and buffet lines. Gradually, as the evening wears on, the character of the festivities may become more lively to make sure that the younger people enjoy the gala.

Conclusion

To outsiders, the formal debut may appear to be an archaic ritual of the upper class; however, to insiders, this ritual establishes participants as "elites" and distinguishes them from "ordinary people." Elites have the money to purchase the clothing and pay for the parties that show their friends that they are modern-day "royalty" or that they are related to "royalty." By attending expensive, by-invitation-only fundraising events such as the debutante ball, elites avail themselves of the companionship of others who are similarly situated in the inner social circle. The possibility of having their daughters presented or having their sons serve as escorts at such rituals encourages elite women to work on behalf of the nonprofit organizations to which they belong—not just the ones that have such presentations, but also other elite women's groups that demonstrate that the woman is a team player in the overall landscape of philanthropy.

Thus, ritual helps maintain the upper classes while it enhances the social power of the women who participate in such rites of passage. Ritual helps the "next generation" learn its role and earn its status as part of the upper class. Privileged young people learn both family and class solidarity from such rituals; they also begin to forge networks with other elite young people. The rituals become a source of pride. The outcome, according to organizers, is that everybody benefits: the charitable cause benefits, the parents benefit, and the children benefit.

There is, however, a downside to such elite rituals. Almost by definition, the presentation of the next generation to Society means that people who are not elite are excluded from these activities and do not gain access to influential social networks. Upward social mobility is limited for those who do not have the "right connections" for getting ahead. As described in this chapter, these rituals also have profound racial and ethnic implications, as evidenced by the separate groups that have been organized to present young people of a different racial, ethnic, or religious heritage. The leadership of the separate organizations that hold rituals such as the debutante presentation are aware of this, and that awareness carries over into their maintenance of the structure of the groups to which these women belong, as I describe in the following chapter. Although members of predominantly white, black, or Latina organizations typically describe the composition of their group as being based on preference or the comfort zone, much more lies beneath the surface of these separate—and not necessarily equal—organizations and the influence they have on social relations in the larger community and society.

Notes

1. When I told sociologists and other individuals outside the "social elite" about my study of debutante presentations, they frequently asked me, "Do *they* still have those things?" When I reassured them that "they" did, the typical response I received was "How archaic!" or "How elitist." Several people suggested that I shift my topic to something of greater relevance: "Who cares anyway?" one sociologist asked. I find comments such as these baffling because so little is known about how elite families not only manage to remain in positions of economic and political power but also to control social power that can be used to gain the ends the family desires, such as good educational and career connections and being in the "inner circle" to influence the decisions of powerful people. How do young people who grow up "having it all," at least in the material sense, come to sub-

scribe to the same norms and values that their parents hold? Is it apparent to them from early childhood that the norm of exclusivity preserves their way of life? Do they have an inherent desire to replicate their parents' lives? Questions such as these bring us to an analysis of the social construction and reconstruction of the upper classes and the part that rituals, including rites of passage such as the formal debut and the wedding, play in the social reproduction process.

2. Stoeltje 1996: 15.
3. Montgomery 1998: 41.
4. Montgomery 1998: 41.
5. Haynes 1998: 8.
6. Thomas 1996.
7. Although white debutantes may be presented at a number of balls, most of the African American debutantes that I interviewed had been presented only once. When asked about this, the general response was that they could see no need for this because the one event had been significant enough "to last a lifetime."
8. Birmingham 1990.
9. San Marino Women's Club 1999.
10. Birmingham 1990.
11. Montgomery 1998.
12. Birmingham 1990.
13. Marshall 1997.
14. Quoted in Montgomery 1998: 46–47.
15. Bossard and Boll 1948: 247.
16. Domhoff 1998: 95.
17. Domhoff 1998.
18. Domhoff 1998: 95.
19. Bossard and Boll 1948: 250.
20. Bell 1997: 79.
21. Bell 1997: 136.
22. Herrick 1997.
23. Herrick 1997.
24. The mistress of the robes, the only woman in the hierarchy of the Order of the Alamo, designs the dresses for each of the duchesses and the Queen, as well as supervising the actual construction of the dresses. It is also her job to keep the debutantes and their parents happy throughout debutante season (Haynes 1998).
25. Herrick 1997.
26. Herrick 1997.
27. Herrick 1997.
28. *Houston Chronicle* 1996.
29. Strong 1990.
30. Rotzoll 1999.
31. Rotzoll 1999.
32. Hockaday 1997.
33. See Gatewood 1990; Mack 1999.
34. Graham 2000.
35. Graham 2000.

36. Neighborhood newspapers in affluent enclaves and "City" magazines have picked up the slack in coverage of debutante presentations, and some now provide in-depth coverage of such events, including numerous photographs of white debutantes performing the Texas Dip and dancing the first dance with their father. In fact, one pronounced difference I found in several Texas cities was how the media covered debutante presentations sponsored by "white" organizations as compared to those honoring people of color.
37. Graham 2000.
38. See Cromwell 1994; Mack 1999.
39. Cromwell 1994.
40. Cromwell 1994: 155.
41. Kolb 1995.
42. Fulwood 1998.
43. Fulwood 1998.
44. Lynch 1999: 82.
45. Lynch 1999: 86.
46. Hazzard-Gordon 1992.
47. Lynch 1999: 88.
48. Davalos 1996.
49. Hastings 1991.
50. Rodriguez 2000.
51. Owen 2000.
52. Haynes 1998: 83.

CHAPTER SIX

Members Only: Organizational Structure and Patterns of Exclusion

We had a major fight at the board meeting over bylaws changes regarding how new members are selected. One woman (who thought she really knew all about parliamentary procedure) kept calling out "Point of order" and correcting the president and others. We finally got so tired of her, I thought somebody would surely choke her. She was relatively new to our city, having moved here from [a larger city in the state], and she thought she was "Miss High and Mighty." [Our organization] is made up of a great group of women, but sometimes one gets in the door that we'd as soon live without. . . . This one transferred in from another [chapter] and we've been stuck with her ever since. All the more reason to be sure that we admit only those who are compatible with us as new members.

With this example from her own experience, Sally described the concern that many women in elite organizations feel regarding any proposed changes in the rules establishing how "outsiders" become members of the group—a concern that only "compatible" people be invited to join. Although the image that Sally conveys—a "major fight"—is quite different from how most people would envision what happens at board meetings of elite women's volunteer organizations, proposed changes in rules relating to membership in these groups can be a contentious issue.

Many elite women seek to exercise legitimate power in the nonprofit organizations in which they engage in philanthropy. They gain legitimate power when they are elected to the board of directors or serve as appointed officials of these organizations. Those with legitimate power are able to exercise influence over others and to make decisions, such as with

regard to rules pertaining to membership, that have long-term consequences for the organization. In elite women's organizations, leaders can
exercise their skills and be more assertive with others than they believe
they can in organizations dominated by men.[1]

Historically, elite women's volunteer groups have been viewed as informal structures somewhat akin to a coffee klatch. For example, a number of years ago a male executive with the American Symphony Orchestra League said, "Give me six women, a tea pot and a handful of
cookies—and I will give you a symphony orchestra."[2] Even though elite
women volunteers in the past may have casually sat around a table, de-
vising ways to raise money to support orchestras and other nonprofit
causes, many contemporary women participate in volunteer organizations that are much more formally organized. The membership practices
of these bureaucratically structured organizations are set forth in written bylaws that have been voted on and approved by the membership.
As we will see in this chapter, these bylaws can be used in a manner that
excludes entire categories of other women—even on the basis of race or
religion—although on their face, the provisions do not appear to have
that purpose. However, spokespersons for organizations such as the Junior League and women's orchestra volunteer groups emphasize that
their groups have been restructured in recent years to change their "elitist" public image. An example is this comment by a member of the New
Orleans Junior League:

> [Our members] took off the white gloves and put on the work gloves. But
> people often have a warped view of the Junior League. Many people think
> of the organization as exclusively for wealthy New Orleans women who sit
> around all day sipping tea in lush, perfectly manicured gardens. We're not
> just ladies who lunch. We have lawyers, doctors . . . women who are busy
> working during the day. [The Junior League] is run by women, and women
> do all the work.[3]

Another example is this statement by the president of the Junior
League of Dallas:

> We have an open admission policy. Definitely not a little social club. [We]
> are dedicated [and] welcome anyone who is willing to work. To join, you
> have to have a sponsor. You can pick up a sponsor form at the Junior League
> office. You may not think you know someone to sponsor you, but you'll find
> there are Junior Leaguers in your church, your company, your PTA and
> many other organizations.[4]

Similarly, a recent publication by the American Symphony Orchestra
League's Volunteer Council emphasized that orchestra volunteer groups
are assessing the effectiveness of their organizations, structures, and

image in regard to issues such as membership diversity. Do these statements reflect a new attitude and direction or do some organizations continue to do things the way they have "always been done"? My observations indicate that a little of both is true: Although some organizations I have analyzed are in the process of making major changes, this process is slow in some groups and virtually nonexistent in others.

To understand how elite women's organizations operate in the twenty-first century, it is necessary to examine the historical roots of such groups.

Past Practices with Current Relevance: The History of Exclusion in Elite Women's Organizations

Many of the earliest elite women's clubs in the United States were organized for purely social purposes, and the formal organizational structure blocked from membership all women but those who were in the inner social circle or who otherwise were acceptable to established members. For example, the Colony Club in New York City and similar clubs in Boston, Philadelphia, and San Francisco were founded by white socialites who required that any new member be from a family listed in the *Social Register*.[5] When the Junior League was founded in 1901, all of its members were debutantes or former debutantes. Criticized for their seemingly frivolous lives of partying and conspicuous consumption, the founders of the League decided to start an organization that would combine social activities with community service work so that the members could show that they were accepting their social obligation to the community.[6] Consequently, the Junior League for the Promotion of the Settlement Movement—the organization's original name—started settlement houses to improve child health, nutrition, and literacy, particularly among recent immigrants.[7] Racial-ethnic and class distinctions between the members of the League and the beneficiaries of their largesse were great: The recent immigrants frequently did not speak English, were poor, and lacked the social skills that League members prided themselves on possessing.

The founding of the Junior League and the subsequent changes in this organization show how white women of the upper classes have largely maintained the exclusivity of many of their organizations while, at the same time, doing good deeds that serve a diverse clientele that would not be invited to membership in the group itself. From its origins, the Junior League practiced exclusivity in its membership, a fact that contemporary organizational leaders have worked to diminish in significance. Some African American members of local branches of the League are aware that racial discrimination historically was a fact in their organization. One African American woman who has served as a League president in a southern city referred to it as the League's "unwritten, cultural ban" against nonwhite members until the mid-1970s.[8] The organization today is quite different from its original debutante membership and it no longer has unwritten racial or religions bans, allowing more Jewish, African American, and Latina women to become members. Changes in racial and ethnic composition are most apparent in a few of the League's leadership positions, such as the presidency of the national organization, the Association of Junior Leagues International, where some recent presidents have been Cuban American or African American. Similarly, among the 285 Junior Leagues, an estimated two dozen African American, Latina, and Asian American women have served as president.[9] However, about 96 percent of all Junior League members are white Americans, and even the women of color who serve as officers of the international organization and of the local Leagues fit class-based criteria typical of its white (Anglo) officers, such as having a successful career or a prominent family.

The norm of exclusivity remains strongest in elite women's social/community service organizations where there are many members who fit the Old Money or Old Name family categories. Women whose families have resided in the same city for many years and whose relatives have been active in elite women's and men's organization often believe that membership in these prestigious organizations should continue to be restricted. Judith, a sustaining member of the Junior League in one city, expressed her concerns about changes in her local League:

> Now, don't get me wrong. I'm not a snob, and I don't think that the League should shut its doors on anyone. Discrimination is bad, and our community projects are planned to benefit people all over town. But, I will say that things have changed on the membership front over the past years. We have gone from having our "first Jewish member" to bringing in new members who are Hispanic or black. Several "old timers" were commenting the other day that we used to know everybody in the League and now there are so many new faces that we don't recognize. I know that diversity is good, but I don't know that bringing more people [of diverse racial and ethnic groups] into the organization actually means that we talk to each other a whole lot more. At the earliest meetings black provisionals [women who are new members] mingle with everybody and don't all sit together. But as the year goes by, they start doing everything together like "peas in a pod." They sit together at meetings, work on the same projects, and generally "hang out" together. It seems that several of the black women were members of the same sorority, and apparently they enjoyed being together. But what's more important than all of this is that our organization is very successful and that we make a significant contribution to [city] each year through the groups we support, and that's what really counts, isn't it?

In some cases, when women believe that it has gotten to where "just anybody" can become a member of their formerly exclusive organization, the women either quit participating or form a new group where they be-lieve they can exert more control over who becomes a member or an offi-cer of the club. For example, some members of Junior Leagues stated that they believed that "political correctness has overtaken the League," giv-ing other exclusive women's organizations a greater chance to recruit members who would like the prestige of being a member of a highly se-lective organization more akin to those elite men's clubs that have res-olutely held onto the sanctity of "Members Only" and have protected their membership rosters from outsiders. However, other members be-lieve that elite women's organizations such as the Junior League that have welcomed greater diversity in their membership and leadership ranks are "on the right path"—that "change was long overdue"—but that these groups still have far to go before they are actually seen as welcoming mi-nority women into the organization.

Due to the existence of other, parallel organizations, being seen as "welcoming" minority group members into an organization does not nec-essarily mean that those individuals would want to join previously all-white groups, or conversely that whites (Anglos) would want to join a previously all-African American organization.

How Racial Exclusion Led
to Parallel Elite Women's Organizations

A number of elite women's organizations, including the Junior League, were founded on patterns that denied membership to women—either in-tentionally or unintentionally—on the basis of race, ethnicity, religion, and/or class. Throughout the United States, women who were identified as white ethnics (such as Irish Americans and Italian Americans), mem-bers of religious minorities such as Jews or Catholics, and African Amer-icans were categorically excluded from membership in elite white women's organizations. Even women from prominent families, such as Rose Kennedy (wife of Joseph Kennedy and mother of President John F. Kennedy), were refused membership in the Junior League for reasons such as being a Roman Catholic.[10] Because of these patterns of overt dis-crimination, parallel women's organizations comprised of women from excluded racial, ethnic, and religious categories were founded in many cities. New Haven, Connecticut, for example, was home to seven different Leagues or their equivalent when August B. Hollingshead conducted a study there in the 1950s. According to Hollingshead's classification:

> The top ranking organization is the New Haven Junior League which draws its membership from "Old Yankee" Protestant families whose daughters have been educated in private schools. The Catholic Charity League is next

in rank and age—its membership is drawn from Irish-American families. In addition to this organization there are Italian and Polish Junior Leagues within the Catholic division of the society. The Swedish and Danish Junior Leagues are for properly connected young women in these ethnic groups, but they are Protestant. Then too, the upper-class Jewish families have their Junior League. The principle of parallel structures for a given class level, by religion, ethnic, and racial groups, proliferates throughout the community.[11]

As Hollingshead's work shows, parallel structures of elite volunteer organizations were founded by women from somewhat similar class positions who did not have access to membership in the most prestigious women's organizations. One of the earliest parallel organizations founded by African American women was the National Association of Colored Women's Clubs (NACWC), which was created by an 1896 merger of the national Federation of Afro-American Women, the Women's Era Club of Boston, and the Colored Women's League of Washington, D.C. The NACWC had as its stated goals advancing the education of women and children, improving conditions for family living, and promoting understanding so that justice might prevail. The NACWC was similar to the Junior League in that it sought to unite women for service to the community; however, the NACWC has particularly emphasized the importance of improving the quality of life in the black community. Its motto is "Lifting as We Climb," and the group focuses on improving the condition of people of color who are the victims of race- and class-based oppression.[12]

Other elite African American women's organizations have structures and functions similar to those of the predominantly white Junior League. The Girl Friends, founded in New York in 1927, has about forty chapters that sponsor fundraising events such as debutante cotillions and provide many hours of community service.[13] Jack and Jill of America, a membership-by-invitation-only social group, was founded in 1938. Although it is the mothers who are invited to membership, this organization primarily benefits middle- and upper-class African American children.[14] Today, the 220 chapters of Jack and Jill constitute a national network for African American children and their families, providing them with opportunities for social service, education, and other projects.[15] African American college students I have talked with about this organization fondly—or not so fondly—recall how much emphasis their parents placed on attending academic awards dinners and parties sponsored by Jack and Jill. As one young woman stated, "With my parents, it was be-there-or-else when it came to Jack and Jill."

The Links, Inc., another prestigious African American women's organization, has been described as the "the black equivalent of the Junior League."[16] Founded in Philadelphia in 1946, The Links has a membership of over 10,000 women in 270 chapters located in 40 states and several other nations. The Links defines itself as "a group of friends committed to civic, educational, and cultural activities, with the singular purpose of serving community needs for the improvement of life and the pursuit of excellence."[17] Members estimate that, during the more than fifty years of this organization's existence, the group has donated more than $15 million to various charities and programs, and its members provide more than one million hours of volunteer service annually.[18]

Membership in The Links is considered by many elite African Americans to be an exceptional honor. Briana, a professional African American woman in her late 30s, described it as follows:

> I'm proud to be a member. Links is well organized. We have elected officers at the national level, and they're excellent. One recent president was an attorney, and believe me, she's a dynamic public speaker. At the national level, the president and former presidents are top notch, and they keep the organization running smoothly, along with the members of the Executive Council. Because of the national organization we have shown our concern for people in African countries as well as the U.S. We've been at the cutting edge on programs to revitalize African American families and communities. We've also worked with education and programs promoting good health. I could go on and on . . . but I'd sum this up by saying that we've done as much as the Junior League, but we are not as well known because we don't get all the publicity they do.

Statements by women like Briana have been expressed by other members of the African American community such as author Lawrence Otis Graham, who provided the following account of how happy his family was when his mother was invited to join The Links:

> As my mother and every other woman in her crowd would have told you, getting accepted into the Links was a big deal, and it was not something you'd ever need to explain if you were in the company of the right kind of people. In this case, some would say the right kind of people didn't include whites or blue-collar blacks.[19]

According to Graham, membership in The Links is so valuable because:

> For fifty years, membership in the invitation-only national organization has meant that your social background, lifestyle, physical appearance, and family's academic and professional accomplishments passed muster with a fiercely competitive group of women who—while forming a rather cohesive sisterhood—were nonetheless constantly under each other's scrutiny. Each of the 267 local chapters brings together no more than fifty-five women, most of them either professional, socialites, volunteer fund-raisers, educators, or upper-class matrons, and is added to only when a current member dies or moves to another city.[20]

As Graham's statement suggests, one of the reasons membership in The Links (or other elite women's organizations) is so valuable is because of its scarcity—not everyone who wants to become a member will be invited to join. The history of The Links's intraracial practices of exclusivity—and sometimes exclusion—has been described by social historian Stephen Birmingham, who notes that even in the 1970s its membership was restricted by covert practices such as an emphasis on skin color: "Most Links are so fair-skinned that some blacks wonder why Links call themselves a black group at all."[21] Despite the many positive contributions The Links has made to improving the quality of life for the African American community and the society at large, organizational leaders have felt a need in recent years to try to shed the group's appearance of elitism, just as some predominantly white women's organizations have sought to do. Patricia Russell-McCloud, a recent national president of The Links, stated the problem as follows:

> I think that because membership in this organization is by invitation only, it creates an aura of mystique, and it lessens the knowledge and understanding of the mission. Therefore, the stereotypical portrayal that gets attached relates possibly, and unfairly, to an upper middle class that is insensitive to the greater needs in the community. But our record speaks for itself, and in the past and now our purpose has been demonstrated, our commitment firm.[22]

According to Russell-McCloud, Links members have been stereotyped as rich ladies who wear white gloves and sponsor teas and socials, whereas she views the organization as an activist group involved in many domestic and international projects.[23] The concerns that this former president expressed remain an issue with some members of The Links, as well as with women who were not invited to join the group. Cassandra, an African American college student, described her mother's frustration when she learned that her nomination for membership had been turned down:

> [A local chapter of Links] really hurt my mamma's feelings. So, I'm not going to have anything to do with them when I graduate even though my [sorority] background would probably make it easy for me to get in. My mamma does lots of good things in [city] and she is somebody you can always count on. But she isn't fancy. She doesn't wear those expensive designer clothes—even though she could afford them if she wanted to—and she wasn't in the "best" sorority, but they had no good reason to tell her sponsor "no."

Like other elite women's organizations, the membership practices of The Links may vary somewhat from city to city; however, the racial and ethnic composition of the group has remained largely unchanged, and parallel organizations of elite white and African American women volunteers remain in the cities in my study.

It has been more difficult to trace the development of parallel organizations of elite Latinas, perhaps because patterns of exclusion of Latinas have been somewhat different from those applied to African American women. In some cities, affluent Latinas have been welcomed into elite white women's social/community service organizations more readily than have African American women. In cities where there is a large population of Mexican Americans, Cuban Americans, or other groups that trace their origins to Latin America, many elite Latinas fully participate in previously all-white organizations such as the Junior League. In a few cases, affluent Latinas have succeeded white (Anglo) elite women as leaders of prestigious groups previously associated with Anglo elites. An example is the Society of Martha Washington in Laredo, Texas—which (as discussed in chapter 5) holds a lavish annual debutante presentation. Originally, this prestigious group was composed primarily of affluent Anglo women; however, in a city that is currently about 95 percent Latino/a, the board of directors, many members of the group, and the "royalty" honored at the annual Martha Washington debutante ball are affluent Latinas or women who are married to Latinos. A recent president of the Society of Martha Washington, for instance, was Libby Casso, an Anglo who married her college sweetheart, Alfonso Casso, Jr., and who identifies her three children as being "Hispanic."[24] At the annual ball, many of those chosen to be royalty, including those chosen to portray George and Martha Washington, are now Latinos and Latinas, whereas in the past this organization and its fundraising events were considered to be social events for rich Anglos.[25]

At the national level, Latina leaders of formerly all-white (Anglo) women's organizations such as the Junior League have also emerged in recent years. An example is Clotilde Dedecker, the Cuban American president of the Association of Junior Leagues International, who was the first Latina to hold that post. As president of the League, Dedecker described her organization as being so inclusive that it now advertises in newspapers and on billboards for new members;[26] however, others have disputed this claim because League chapters, like other elite women's organizations, have bylaws stating that new members must be proposed by several existing members of the organization. Women who might be interested in joining but do not know current members may be unlikely to pursue their interest and thus turn elsewhere for their volunteer work. But current members defend the membership policies that exist as a part of the organization's bureaucratic structure.

Joining the Club: Bureaucracy Maintains Barriers

In the past, a symphony fundraising group may have been started by a group of women meeting over cookies and tea at someone's home, but this is no longer the way in which elite women's symphony leagues and other charitable groups are structured. At the local, state, and national levels, the organizational structure of women's community service and fundraising groups have all of the characteristics of other bureaucratic organizational structures. Sociologists have utilized Max Weber's ideal type construct of bureaucracy in research involving for-profit and governmental organizations. As the following discussion will show, this model can also be applied to nonprofit organizations, particularly those that have not only local chapters or affiliates but also regional and national associations.

To Weber, bureaucracies are the most rational and efficient means of attaining organizational goals, and certain ideal-type characteristics are found in bureaucratic organizations: (1) standardization through the application of specific rules and procedures; (2) a division of labor (specialization); (3) a hierarchy of authority (chain of command); (4) impartiality in personnel matters; and (5) employment based on technical qualifications, resulting in recruiting experts who have a career pattern.[27] The first three of these are most applicable to the structure of elite women's organizations because these characteristics help them to attain goals that would not be possible if the women acted individually or conducted the group's activities informally. The latter two characteristics are inapplicable to these groups themselves, although they are true of the paid staffs that support these organizations.

Evidence of the bureaucratic organizational structure in elite women's organizations can be found in the way in which the groups have formalized their relationships, not only with one another (within the umbrella of national and regional organizations) but also under the law. The women in these organizations have incorporated their groups and established a board of directors that is held responsible for the fiscal management and administrative operations of the organization. The women in volunteer organizations would agree with Weber's emphasis on the importance of efficiency in getting the job done and in achieving organizational goals in a timely manner, because most of the women are involved in a variety of competing activities that also vie for their time and attention. Although some elite women are "full-time moms," or are otherwise not employed outside their own household, a growing number of elite women volunteers are employed either full or part time and have young children living in their household. Consequently, across class lines, today's women volunteers want the time they donate to an organization to be well used, and, in some cases, they want the organization to log the number of hours they have worked, to show the significance of their nonpaid contributions to the charity or arts organization.

Bylaws as the Ground Rules for Membership

The seemingly neutral bylaws of some elite women's organizations establish the guidelines by which new members are selected. It is the manner in which existing members use those provisions, however, that determines how inclusive of outsiders the group actually is. Most elite women's organizations are corporations created under relevant state law, in this case, under the Texas Non-Profit Corporation Act. One major reason for being incorporated is to prevent any of the women from having personal liability for the actions or obligations of the organization itself. Thus, the corporation has liability for its debts, yet—as long as the women adhere to the requisite "corporate formalities" prescribed by state law—the members and officers will have no such liability. However, adhering to corporate formalities requires written articles of incorporation (a "charter") that are filed with the state government. It means having written bylaws, having a board of directors or trustees, and having elected officers. These written, formal documents become the basis for the rules and procedures of the organization itself.

The bylaws of the organization are, among other things, the ground rules for membership categories, including the rights and responsibilities that go with each of the membership categories (such as who may be elected to an office and—if the group holds debutante presentations—which category or categories of members are eligible to have their children selected as "royalty"). According to Weber, rules are standardized and are provided to members in written format, so that clear-cut guidelines are established. For this reason, most elite women's organizations publish their bylaws in their annual yearbook and provide a copy to all members.

When a question arises, such as how to propose a person for membership, existing members are referred to the bylaws and are told to fill out the appropriate form. After completing the membership proposal form, the current member is responsible for getting the requisite number of signatures—sometimes as many as four—from other members in good standing who are willing to sponsor the candidate. The form must be submitted to the membership chair by a specified date in order for the candidate to be considered. The membership chair, who typically serves on the organization's board of directors, holds one of the many elected or appointed positions that are set forth in the bylaws. Although positions such as membership chair and provisional- or new-member chair have little meaning in the for-profit organizational environment, these are very influential positions and serve as a source of social power in many elite women's groups.

The bylaw provisions have an effect on the kinds of people who are invited to become new members. The "admission to membership" section of the bylaws of one organization sets forth, for example, the deadline by which membership applications must be submitted and who is eligible to sponsor a candidate for membership:

> An active member in good standing [who has completed the requirements for new members and fulfilled her annual membership obligations] may sign her name on four applications per year. Her name may appear only twice as the main proposer. Associate members [who have served eight years as active members in good standing and have requested a change to associate status] may second two candidates. One of the sponsors of a candidate must attend the sponsor orientation meeting prior to the candidate being considered for admission by the committee. If the candidate is found to have the required qualifications, the Admissions Committee shall vote upon her eligibility for membership. Upon a favorable vote of at least four members of the Admissions Committee, such a candidate shall be issued an invitation to join the organization.

The nomination form for membership in this organization requires that proposed candidates have an interest in the organization, a commitment to volunteerism, and have demonstrated previous interest in the organization by donating time and money to its fundraising projects. However, other factors are also taken into consideration. The form asks the sponsoring member to indicate the following: "How long has this woman lived in the city?" and "Does she have a personal acquaintance with her sponsors?" New member proposal forms typically ask for information about the candidate's membership in other groups such as alumnae sorority organizations, other nonprofit boards, and evidence of "active" participation in school and church work. In all of the organizations I examined, the membership process included at least the following steps: (1) a membership proposal form must be completely filled out, (2) the candidate's sponsor (who is a member) must get from two to four signatures (depending on the organization) from other members in good standing, (3) the candidates for membership are discussed and voted on, sometimes one at a time, by a membership committee and, in some cases, by the full membership at one of its monthly meetings, (4) candidates who are approved by the membership committee must also be accepted by the organization's board of directors, (5) the candidate is notified that she will be "invited to membership" if she is willing to assume all the responsibilities and fulfill all the requirements for active membership in the organization as set forth in the bylaws and other rules, (6) the organization holds an announcement party or new members luncheon and prints biographies of the women in the organization's newsletter, and (7) new members serve out a provisional year in which they are more closely scrutinized to see that they fulfill the obligations of their new status before officially becoming an "active" member of the organization.

Bylaws and informal group "understandings" pertaining to membership—regardless of their original intent—partly determine what type of women will be invited to become members of elite organizations. According to some women in these organizations, explicit membership rules have the following positive functions: they typically state the various categories of membership and what the expectations are of women in each of these categories; they state the number of women who can be in some categories (e.g., active members) at any one time, thus limiting membership to a workable size; and these membership caps give women the distinct impression that they are fortunate to be one of the "chosen" because membership in the organization is a finite resource not necessarily available to all who might desire to become members. This practice reinforces the referent power of the group because scarcity of membership positions enhances the group's social attractiveness to other women. However, most members would not justify the membership limits in those terms. Rather, they would agree that capping the membership at a specific number and not admitting new members beyond this point has the function of ensuring that the organization does not grow so large that it is "unwieldy," as one organization's president stated:

Just because our membership is limited to [a given number], does not mean that we try to keep anybody out. It just means that we don't have houses large enough for monthly meetings with more women than that. I'm sure that somewhere in the past, our leaders decided on what they thought was a good number, and we've stuck with it because it works for us.

However, as another women implied, this membership cap can be used to exclude women deemed to be "unacceptable" candidates:

I like it that our bylaws state a set number of members: If we have a candidate who is not accepted for membership, we can tell her sponsors that there were only a few "open slots" that year and that the competition was real stiff for those.

For some women, exclusivity is an important incentive for joining voluntary organizations. In her study of upper-class women's social clubs, Susan Ostrander found that exclusivity of association was particularly important to those women who wanted to associate only with those who have similar interests and values.[28] Today's members may be

more subtle when they express the same concern, framing their preferences in terms of finding new members who are "congenial" and will
"fit in with the rest of the group."

As noted above, there are potentially exclusionary effects of bylaws
pertaining to membership because these rules set parameters regarding
who may, or may not, become a member. Requirements that women be
put up for membership by existing members limits the access of other
women, particularly individuals from other racial, ethnic, or religious categories, from consideration for membership. Then, members can truth-
fully state, "Well, no African American women were nominated for membership this year, so we have no new black members."

Since the bylaws are the formal means by which women's organizations establish the number and composition of their membership, perhaps
it is no surprise that "bylaw fights" such as the one described at the beginning of the chapter may take place in some organizations if individuals seek to modify existing rules and procedures. However, the bylaws of
women's groups that operate under the "umbrella" of a larger (state, regional, national, or even international) organization may be encouraged
to have a more "open door" admissions policy at the national level because gaining a wider diversity of members not only brings new people
and ideas into the group but also sends a message that the organization is
not racist or elitist.

Division of Labor: Who Decides Who Gets to Join

Like organizational rules and procedures, division of labor—another of
Weber's ideal characteristics of bureaucracy—plays a central part in
membership policies and practices. Division of labor refers to the process
of dividing up tasks so that they are performed by different people and
thus are performed in the most optimal manner. Because elite women volunteers are not paid employees or career professionals in a for-profit work
environment, a clear statement of the division of labor—what important
tasks must be accomplished and who is responsible for doing them—is integral to the organization's success. As found in the organizational rules,
the division of labor includes the titles of officers and the heads of standing committees and in what the specific duties of each shall be. By dividing the tasks into a variety of unpaid administrative duties—such as the
treasurer and the newsletter chair—and into leadership positions relating
to specific fundraising projects, the women can specialize in certain tasks
within the organization. Chairing the membership committee is an example. Although many guidelines for membership are set forth in writing,
other factors considered by the typical membership committee are more
nebulous (such as how well a candidate is known by other women and

how suitable she is for membership). Barbara, a white woman in her 50s, described her duties as chair of a membership committee:

> I am honored to chair this committee because when you get right down to it, the decisions we make are crucial to the lifeblood of the [organization]— we help the general membership select those women who are best suited to become "one of us." Because of the needs of our constituency and the time-consuming fundraising projects we have each year, we need to be able to count on dedicated volunteers who, if they say they'll be there, will indeed *be there with bells on*, ready to do their jobs with a smiley face. Compatibility with existing members is really important, too. You can let in one or two bad apples, and it really sours the feelings of other members, especially if the newcomer is a gossiper, griper, or doesn't have good manners. When you work in close proximity on important projects and events, going along to get along is essential.

In Barbara's organization, the membership committee can strike a candidate from the list of potential members who will later be voted on by the entire membership. In other organizations, the membership committee makes the final choices about new members and reports its decision to the larger constituency. Women selected to chair the membership committee are trusted, often long-term members. According to Hallie, the former president of one elite women's organization:

> If you ask me, heading up the membership committee is one of the most important tasks we ask members of our group to take on. The year I was president-elect, several members of the board told me to be really careful who I appointed to that position because she needed to be "balanced." I decided that they meant the membership chair had to balance the needs of the organization against the wishes of membership candidates and their sponsors.

As Hallie's statement indicates, elite women's organizations typically have individuals such as members of the board of directors or other long-term members who provide suggestions to incoming officers and, sometimes from behind the scenes, provide direction for people who take on leadership positions in the organization. In other words, as the division of labor becomes established in elite women's organizations, a core of women emerge who "run" the organization and have coercive power over others because they have the ability to "punish" them (at least in limited ways) if they do not fulfill the "core's" expectations as to how other members and potential members should behave. Organization leaders possess coercive power in that they can mete out negative sanctions, such as harsh criticism, rejection of a member's proposed new membership candidate, or refusal to vote for a member's daughter to be presented as a debutante. This "core" group of influential members is often described as "running the show" by some newer members and by longer-term members who consider themselves to be "outside the loop" when it comes to the decision-making process. Audrey, a relatively new member of a prestigious women's volunteer organization, referred to this phenomenon as the "outsider on the inside" feeling:

> My husband and I had moved to [city] about two years before I become a member. My mother had old friends here, and she asked them to put me up for membership. Apparently, there wasn't any problem because the next thing I knew I was being invited to join and come to a new member orientation. The women are very cordial, and I've attended a number of the meetings. However, one day I noticed that there were a lot of "insider" jokes among the women, and that these same women were the ones that everybody was always praising. If some major decision had to be made, they'd say, "We've got to ask so-and-so. She'll know what we should do." After I had been a member long enough to nominate a woman for membership, I asked questions about how to do this. When I asked how membership decisions were made, I was told: "It's like magic . . . it either happens or it doesn't happen. After the committee meets you will be told whether or not your candidate was accepted." When I asked if I could put in a good word for her in addition to the letter of recommendation I had written, I was told rather curtly that the organization worked best if members who weren't on the board just let other people do their jobs. My friend didn't get in that year, and I was told that there just weren't enough places for all of the outstanding candidates for that year.

As described by Audrey, the division of labor in some elite women's organizations is firmly established, serving as a source of power for the women in the "core" group, and challenges to their power are discouraged.

Hierarchy of Authority:
Pressure for and Resistance to Change

Division of labor in elite women's organizations is intricately linked to the organization's hierarchical structure—Weber's ideal-type hierarchy of authority. By definition, hierarchy of authority means that each lower position in an organization is under the control and supervision of a higher one, with the further proviso that all of the persons in the chain of command need to recognize the necessity and legitimacy of the higher positions. In elite women's groups, committees responsible for fulfilling various organizational functions do not operate in isolation, with the chair and committee members making their own plans and establishing their own budget. For a lavish fundraising event such as a debutante ball, wine tasting dinner, designer showhouse, or "luxury" holiday bazaar, for example, the chair is told how much of the organization's money she can spend on the project and, in some groups, it is understood that committee chairs and members who exceed the budget will be responsible for making up the difference out of their own pockets.

In addition to a hierarchy of authority at the local level, many elite women's organizations have state and/or national associations that are a part of the larger organizational bureaucracy. State and national associations of elite women's organizations have elected officers (who typically are unpaid volunteers), paid staff members, and numerous advisory boards and councils made up of delegates from local chapters or leagues. The Links, Inc., an elite African American women's organization, is an example. Established more than 50 years ago, The Links has more than 10,000 members in 270 chapters located in 40 states, Washington, D.C., the Bahamas, and Frankfurt, Germany. The local chapters are mainly supported by membership dues and fundraising activities that benefit scholarship programs and community service projects. In 1949, members of local Links chapters established a national organization that holds annual meetings, has elected officials, and oversees the National Foundation of The Links, Inc., the philanthropic arm of the organization.

Predominantly white elite women's organizations such as the Junior League and symphony orchestra leagues have state and national bureaucracies. Local Junior Leagues participate in the Association of Junior Leagues, Inc. (AJLI), the umbrella organizations for the 285 Junior League chapters located in four countries. According to a recent president of the AJLI, "Our Association is . . . about growing something: It is about growing our collective future. The Leagues add value to the communities; the Association exists to add value to the work of the Leagues."[29] Although state and national organizations of The Links, the Junior Leagues, and symphony orchestra leagues serve in an advisory capacity to the local organizations, this hierarchy influences how local chapters conduct their business. Generally, the national groups want to bring about at least the appearance of greater openness in membership; however, at the local level, some members are resistant to change, especially if it means that they have less control over membership decisions that determine with whom they will associate.

How do women's volunteer associations reach out to a wider diversity of people and meet their fundraising goals while also providing elite women with a "comfort zone" in which they associate primarily with others like themselves? One answer has been the tiering of volunteer groups under larger umbrella organizations such as the American Symphony Orchestra League. The volunteer groups that are to be "less selective" and thus less exclusive often indicate their presence on Web sites where visitors can find information on "how to get involved" or "volunteer opportunities." Some have membership forms that can be filled out on the Web site, and people are invited to fill out a survey form indicating areas of interest in which they would like to help out.[30] However, a visit to some Web sites reveals the tiers of membership and what demographics are included in each group. An example is the Dallas Symphony Orchestra League (DSOL) Web site, which states: "Membership is open to anyone interested in supporting the Symphony through special projects and committees." The Web site visitor learns that the demographics for this group are: "Women, generally over the age of 40. Open to anyone. Daytime meetings." The fundraising projects of the DSOL include a Neiman Marcus Fashion Show and Luncheon, a Presentation Ball, the Junior Symphony Ball, and the Dallas Symphony Derby. With daytime meetings and these fundraisers, this group largely appeals to older, nonemployed women. By contrast, the Junior Group of the DSOL has this requirement for membership: "Candidates are recommended for membership. Active membership must be proposed and is limited to 225 women under 45." The Junior Group requires that members purchase symphony tickets, attend three general meetings a year (which are held in the daytime), and participate in a variety of fundraising and service activities each year. While the DSOL and the Junior Group follow the more traditional model of elite women's organizations, two "professional" groups are open to business and professional men and women; one has luncheon meetings whereas the other has evening meetings.

The formal organizational structure of some elite volunteer organizations has been modified to bring in a greater diversity of people; however, other groups remain relatively resistant to change. It is in these organizations that we find vestiges of past exclusionary practices based on race, ethnicity, religion, or class that now are perpetuated in a different way. Informal networks within elite women's organizations are a primary way in which officers and others in the established "inner circle" are able to maintain social power. They gain control of the organization and restrict membership to those with whom they think they would be compatible. An example of how the informal network may control membership is Trudy, a white woman who was rejected by an elite white women's organization because it was believed that she "would not fit in." One member of the group described the situation as follows:

> I knew that [women's names] were putting [Trudy] up for membership, but when the new members were announced, she wasn't among them. I didn't think much about it until the same thing happened two years in a row. When I asked [other members] about it, one of them said that [the membership committee chair] had asked them not to propose [Trudy] again next year. [The chair] told them the general consensus of the membership committee

was that Trudy "would not fit in," given that she was a known trouble-maker in another organization. Apparently, she had started arguments and spread rumors, and wasn't a "team player." She was described as too loud . . . flamboyant . . . and that her hair style was "too much" for the organization. Personally, I think some members saw her as a "climber" even though she had been a hard worker for [another organization].

During several years of participant observation, I learned that Trudy was not invited to join several of the most prestigious women's volunteer organizations in her city. It was interesting to observe that she had a number of skills but that many of the "older guard" did not want to be associated with her on a more permanent basis as a member of their club. Trudy's case is not the exception; women in other organizations with "closed" memberships described similar situations but nearly always emphasized that none of these had to do with race, ethnicity, religion, or how much money a particular woman has.

Most members are aware that their organizations have a statement such as this in their bylaws: "The Club shall not discriminate on the basis of race, color, religion, national origin, age, or disability in the admission of candidates to membership." However, requirements for sponsorship of new members and numerical restrictions to membership serve the latent purpose of limiting membership to "friends," "friends of friends," and others who are similarly situated in terms of class and race/ethnicity. For example, the phrase that follows immediately after the "nondiscrimination" clause in one organization's bylaws states, "Active membership shall be limited to 150." This membership limit serves as an official way to restrict the size of the organization and, in an unofficial way, to limit changes in the composition of its membership. A woman who has been proposed for membership may not be invited to join because of any number of factors, but her sponsors may be told that there are simply no new member slots available this year or that those who are invited to become new members have been on a waiting list for several years.

The formal organizational structure of many elite women's groups is carefully guarded by those who have been members of the club for long periods of time and by newer members who believe that they benefit from the norm of exclusivity. Although some women attempt to maintain the status quo through existing bureaucratic channels, other women typically work through informal networks to maintain exclusivity and to gain social power. Informal networks serve as an integral part of elite women's organizations and have a significant influence in the "formal" decisions that are made by the group.

Like other sectors of the society, some elite women's organizations may decide that it is desirable to have racial and ethnic diversity in the membership. Based on the overall membership figures for elite, previously all-white women's organizations, however, it appears that women of color are very limited in their overall numbers in such groups. Likewise, white (Anglo) women typically are not members of traditionally black elite women's organizations. In elite white women's organizations, highlighting the few members who are from diverse racial, ethnic, or religious categories—particularly those who have risen to the top positions in the organization's hierarchy—makes it possible for the group to convey the appearance of diversity while maintaining the elitist, essentially all-white prestigious organization that controls privileged ties and rituals. Similarly, the most prestigious organizations for women of color may exclude women based on their family background, skin color, appearance, or other attributes that are not strictly within the scope of organizational bylaws and other policies.

Conclusion

For many women at the top economic tiers of society, being invited to join a prestigious women's philanthropic organization has a special meaning that might not be easily understood by nonelites. The women I interviewed and the observations that I recorded show a similar pattern: Many elite women gain social power and personal rewards through their membership in by-invitation-only women's groups and, for these women, those rewards equal—or exceed—the rewards they might receive in paid employment. Across racial and ethnic categories, these organizations are a source of empowerment for privileged women, and they provide a setting in which they can interact with like-minded women "who will understand who I am and why I want to participate in the betterment of my community," as one woman stated.

In both historically white and historically black organizations, certain commonalities are apparent. Primary among these is the bureaucratic structure that makes it possible for the women to accomplish major fundraising and community service projects. However, the same bureaucracy also provides the women with the means whereby they can retain the exclusivity of the organization's membership and "hand-pick" new members. Rules and policies, the division of labor, and a hierarchy of authority may serve as a buffer against incursion by "outsiders." Requirements that new members be recommended by existing members may exclude some women who would desire to participate in the group's beneficial community service projects but fear rejection by the members if they seek to join.

Within elite organizations, change-oriented women quickly learn that organized resistance will be mounted against the changes that they propose. Those who resist changes in membership policies, for example, can use the existing bureaucratic structure to fight proposed changes. Women who resist change can also use their informal social networks to subvert change. Buffy, a member of several elite women's organizations, described how she had used existing rules to maintain the status quo in a group:

> Some women have no sense of tradition—they always want to throw out the baby with the bath water—"Let's change the bylaws!" is what they say when someone says "The bylaws won't let us do that." But instead, I say, "If it ain't broke, don't fix it." We need to have a really good reason to make a change, and frankly I've seen very few in my many years on boards.

Women such as Buffy resist change in the organizations where they consider themselves to be the "grande dames." Less-established members come to realize that they can suggest changes in the organization only at the risk of frustrating—and frequently angering—more long-term members who are deeply entrenched in the organization's leadership and advisory roles.

With resistance to change—and the fact that some women may believe that no change is necessary—it is not surprising that there are racially and ethnically separate elite women's organizations and that change, if at all, comes very slowly despite changes in the demographic composition of the population throughout the United States. Although opening up the membership of elite historically white women's organizations to greater diversity has been an issue among privileged white women, the women of color I interviewed or observed were less concerned about this topic with regard to historically black organizations. Those who were involved in The Links, The Girl Friends, or similar groups saw themselves as uniquely related to other women of color because of shared goals of racial uplift and a common "history of discrimination that is not easily understood by those who have not experienced it," as Viola stated.

Are separate, parallel organizations of elite white women volunteers and elite women of color problematic for individuals? Do these parallel structures offer equal social power for participants? Do parallel structures maintain and perpetuate racial and ethnic divisions within the next generation of social elites? These issues will be examined in the final chapter.

Notes

1. See Carli 1999.
2. Quoted in Winzenried 2001: 72.
3. Quoted in Ermann 1997: 37.
4. Quoted in Schwartz 2000.
5. Birmingham 1968.
6. Birmingham 1968.

7. Association of Junior Leagues International 2000.

8. Yeomans 2000.

9. Yeomans 2000.

10. Bumiller 2000.

11. Hollingshead 1952: 685–686.

12. NACWC 2000.

13. Birmingham 1977; Graham 2000.

14. Graham 2000.

15. Graham 2000.

16. Birmingham 1977: 74.

17. Columbia Chapter of The Links, Inc. 2000.

18. *Jet* 1996.

19. Graham 2000: 102.

20. Graham 2000: 102.

21. Birmingham 1977.

22. Quoted in *Ebony* 1996: 112.

23. Graham 2000.

24. Rodriguez 2000.

25. Rodriguez (2000) states that, among the Laredo elite, intermarriage between non-Hispanic whites and Latinos/as has become the rule rather than the exception, thus giving Anglo newcomers a bicultural, bilingual society into which they tend to assimilate.

26. Bumiller 2000.

27. Weber 1958.

28. Ostrander 1984.

29. Dedecker 1999.

30. Winzenried 2001.

CHAPTER SEVEN

෴

Societal Implications of the Contradictions in Elite Women's Good Deeds

I want every woman who wants to join our organization to feel welcome. We don't discriminate against anybody—race, nationality, religion, it doesn't matter as long as you want to help us with our community projects. But, I will say this: I think we don't get more interest from minority women, even though some of our activities benefit minority kids, because of the comfort zone. Psychologically, people hesitate to step outside their comfort zone. They fear the unknown. They fear failure. We reach out to all women as much as we can, but our top priority has to be holding successful fundraisers that will help us support [a specific charity].

> —A former president of an elite women's organization that, by reputation, has one of the most selective membership processes in a large Texas city

I might be interested in joining [the elite women's organization described above] if anyone showed that they really wanted me to be a member. I have worked for many years for [a sorority alumnae group], [a museum], and [various arts, educational, and musical groups], but I've never felt particularly welcome in groups where there are no other minorities. When people say, "You're different. You're not like *those* people," it gives me the feeling that they are not too comfortable having people like me around. Despite what they say to reporters, some groups are not actively recruiting African American and Mexican American women: A small group of white women run several of these organizations, and I'll give it to

165

them—they do a lot of fine things, but the racial divide still runs
wide in this city.

—An African American community leader, explaining why
women of color are not members of several elite white volunteer organizations and are underrepresented in others

As the statements of these two women demonstrate, there is a wide di-
vergence of opinion among elite women as to the extent to which the organizations discussed in this book are open to people of all races and ethnicities and as to the reason why their memberships are not more diverse.
These prestigious volunteer organizations perform beneficial services for
individuals and organizations in their communities; however, these
groups adhere to membership policies that reinforce the norm of exclusivity and maintain patterns of racial and ethnic segregation. This is one
of the contradictions that I have noticed in these elite women's organizations. Although their leaders typically state that the group welcomes all
women who fit the membership criteria, my observations and interviews
do not support this assertion. Thus, although elite women's volunteer organizations—across racial and ethnic lines—provide millions of hours of
community service and raise large sums of money for worthy causes,
pressing questions remain about the ways in which these groups may reinforce patterns of classism and racial segregation in the United States. In
this chapter, I assess the societal implications of patterns of classism and
racial segregation in privileged women's volunteer organizations, including how elite philanthropy is one of many mechanisms used, either intentionally or unintentionally, to protect elite privilege and uphold its legitimacy across classes and racial or ethnic categories. This chapter also
describes how, at the societal level, the status quo with regard to race and
class inequalities is perpetuated by women who themselves are subordi-
nated by systems of gender inequality in society.

Many people might believe that the racial and ethnic composition of
elite women's voluntary organizations is of little or no concern, that these
are simply rich women with time on their hands and charity in their
hearts, but that is an incorrect assumption. Like women in other classes,
elite women remain in a subordinate position when it comes to power. Although elite women today control more of the nation's wealth and political power than they have in the past and may also have more control over
their own economic resources than they previously had, most of them
have less political and economic power than do the men in their lives:
their fathers, husbands, and the other men with whom they associate.
However, elite women do have social power: the power to get things done
in their own lives, in their families, and in the larger society. I have described the sources of social power that are made available to elite women

through their membership in prestigious invitational volunteer organizations. These organizations make it possible for elite women to possess and utilize reward power, referent power, expert power, legitimate power, and (to some degree) even coercive power.

In my study, the five sources of power identified in French and Raven's typology[1] are not all of equal importance, but each of them has some relevance with regard to how elite women participate in philanthropy, set the framework for their children's entry into elite circles, and establish networks through which the women derive recognition and esteem as a result of their volunteer activities. Through membership in elite organizations, privileged women gain power that they do not possess as individuals. By establishing and maintaining racially separate parallel organizations, African American, Latina, and white women may have more opportunities to gain social power than might be available if the separate groups did not exist. In other words, the women may have no interest in bringing about greater inclusion in volunteer organizations because the existing structures allow them to impress and gain status with other elites they consider to be equal to or above themselves in the social order.[2] This pattern of separation, however, has implications that reach far beyond the boundaries of the organizations themselves.

Using Social Power as a Mechanism for Enforcing Class and Racial Privilege

As I have shown throughout this book, elite women use their social power to enforce class and racial boundaries and to protect and enhance privilege, either intentionally or unintentionally. My study shows how some forms of power are based on social relationships and not merely on the possession of economic or political power. Referent power, for example, is personal in that it is based on a feeling of identification with other people and is a form of power that can be used even by people who lack access to other forms of power.[3] Both referent and reward power are evident in the types of fundraising efforts—ranging from thrift shops and garage sales to lavish charity debutante presentations and multimillion dollar showhouses—that are sponsored by elite women's organizations. Only women who are high in these forms of social power can organize successful "high-brow" fundraising parties that serve as a social setting where elites can enjoy the company of others in their inner circle. Using their expert and legitimate power as successful fundraisers and community volunteers, elite women also organize "low-brow" events that may be used as a statement to the general public that the group's goals relate to helping others, not to promoting the members' own interests. In this way, members of an elite women's organization can engage in seemingly

contradictory practices such as hosting a charity ball where guests purchase expensive tickets, wear designer gowns and tuxedos, drink cham-
pagne and cocktails, and enjoy a multiple course dinner while thinking of
themselves as philanthropists who help disadvantaged categories of people such as children from poverty-level, dysfunctional families.

Elite women in the Old Money and Old Name family categories typically have possessed social power almost from the moment of their birth.
These women are socialized to accept the role and social power of the elite
woman. At an early age, they learn that they must go to the right schools,
have the right friends, join the right clubs and sororities, take a bow at one
or more debutante presentation balls, and marry another member of the
upper class. In this way, they and their parents can be reassured that their
position in the inner circle of social elites will be secure. These "traditions"
or social practices also ensure that the biological and social reproduction
of the upper class will continue into future generations. As a latent effect,
these women also learn how to use their "grace, beauty, and charm" to get
men to do what the women want them to do. Although many feminist analysts would view this as a sign of the women's continued subordination
to the men of the upper classes, most of the women in these elite groups
view it as a form of dominance that they exercise over others.

Women who are not born into the upper classes may marry into elite
circles or enhance their social power and become part of the social elite
through their own efforts as Worker Bees who produce desirable results
for charitable organizations. Frequently, these women are resocialized—
by their mothers-in-law or other "old guard" elite women who serve as
their membership sponsors in elite women's organizations—to speak and
act as a "true member" of the upper class, including recognizing the importance of maintaining the status quo. Women who were not born into
the upper classes may experience subordination not only to upper-class
men but also to the upper-class women who serve as their mentors and as
leaders of the volunteer organizations.

Most elite women tend to support the status quo, including inequalities based on race and class, even if they have no intention of being "snobbish" or "elitist." The structure of elite women's organizations makes it
possible for the women to maintain social power and establish membership boundaries without individually taking any overt action that appears to exclude others. Elitism and the norm of exclusivity are simply
built into the rules of the organization, which are maintained in the name
of promoting the worthy goals of the organization itself.

A matrix of privilege—a source or basis of privilege—is created in
these organizations that gives elite women and their families an advan-
tage over people in other classes.[4] Women who possess reward power can
maintain control over social interactions by making it advantageous for

others to do what they want them to do. By limiting membership in these organizations through membership "caps" and highly selective admissions procedures, privileged women ensure that their organizations will be composed primarily of other women like themselves—women who will share the same goals, attitudes, and beliefs. Elite women organize fundraising events that are planned and implemented with other elites in mind, providing them with the opportunity to demonstrate their largesse and to socialize with one another and, in the process, the organization reaffirms its goals and maintains its prestigious image. In the end, group membership and involvement appear to be an act of benevolence on the part of the elite women rather than one that reflects self-interest.[5] For elite white women, racial separation in organizations typically gives them advantages over elite women of color.

Elite Women's Organizations and Issues of Access to Opportunities

Previous sociological research has clearly established that elite white men work through "old boy networks" to gain information, enhance their social connections, and develop leads to opportunities in business and social settings.[6] As this book has shown, elite women likewise establish networks to gain information, enhance their family's social connections, and develop opportunities that otherwise might not be available to them. But are these same opportunities available to elite women regardless of their race or ethnicity?

Parallel organizations that are created and maintained along lines of race and ethnicity maintain a separation of elite women volunteers and typically do not provide equal access for all of the women to powerful people who might offer "insider" advantages to select groups of individuals, nor are the charity fundraisers and social events of predominantly minority organizations viewed as being as important or as prestigious as those activities sponsored by elite white women's organizations. Eve, an African American professional woman, identified ways she believed that privileged women of color in elite African American organizations were, in her terms, "not very privileged at all" because they lack certain types of access that women in elite white organizations possess. First, according to Eve, elite women of color lack access to an information base that is available to the white women and includes "insider facts" about important activities that are occurring, about whether it would help a person to participate in those activities, and about who might be present at those events. Although women of color have information sources, Eve believed that her resources were often limited to what she referred to as the "black news network." Second, Eve said, elite women of color lack crucial connections to white social networks. According to Eve, "if you are invited to a charity function sponsored by [an elite white women's organization], you are supposed to buy tickets, bring your black friends, blow air kisses at the [white] women who invited you—and are sitting at another table—and not stay too late, be too loud, or otherwise be seen as a nuisance." Third, elite women of color have more limited access to "leads" about opportunities to better their own position or to do something that would benefit other members of their family. This same lack of access—and the rewards that access brings—would also apply to people in other social classes, regardless of race or ethnicity. As Eve's statements suggest, the norm of exclusivity in elite women's volunteer organizations and the sources of social power that are primarily available to elite white women are a reflection of larger social inequalities in U.S. society and may serve to reinforce those inequalities.

Although Eve identified these as being three distinct areas in which many elite women of color remain out of the social "mainstream" despite their membership in exclusive African American organizations—or even in a few elite, predominantly white groups—each of these sources actually intersects and interacts with the others in a way that benefits those who have access to these sorts of information and social connections. Two examples illustrate this point. In my study, one white woman who is married to a medical doctor gained access to high political circles in her community through her involvement, first as president of the local Junior League, then as a participant in various city and state leadership programs, and then by being appointed to a major state commission. Were it not for this woman's information base and her social networks, largely gained through her leadership roles in elite women's organizations, it is unlikely that she would have gained access to the position she currently holds. A second example is an older white woman who has been involved for many years in the most prestigious elite women's organizations in her city but is also a realtor by occupation. As a result of her sources of information, largely gained through her "friends" and "friends of friends" in women's organizations, she knows what houses are going to be on the market, often before the houses are even formally listed for sale; as a result of her social ties, she has close connections with both individuals who want to sell and individuals who want to buy residences, and she gets the business of many of those people. Her connections serve her even "beyond the grave": When members of her own peer group die, she is often at the funerals as a close friend of the family—and the next generation of the family often lists the decedent's house with her for sale.

These examples are not isolated cases: My research shows that such "connections" to community, state, and national elites is an important factor in privileged women's social power. Thus, who is admitted to the most prestigious women's volunteer organizations and to their inner circles is psychologically, socially, and economically important to the women and their families. When elite women help their own children gain social power that others do not possess, the women participate in the maintenance and reproduction of the upper classes and engage in practices that may limit other people's opportunities to gain access to that class standing. In so doing, elite women serve as gatekeepers to the upper classes and their social institutions,[7] and their children may view their privilege as an entitlement. Interestingly, some privileged elite children may view the "entitlements" (such as a social "safety net") claimed by people in lower social classes as "welfare" to which those "other people" are not entitled.

Whether women of color believe that they are excluded from, or not actively recruited to participate in, elite white women's organizations, and whether or not they believe that they lose some sources of social power as a result, wealthy women of color nonetheless do participate in elite volunteer groups, gain and exercise social power in elite black social circles[8] in many of the same ways described in my two examples regarding white women, and pass this same social power on to their own children.

If the patterns of racially segregated elite organizations, whether women's volunteer groups or Greek-letter college sororities, continue largely unchanged from their present state, what are the implications for future philanthropy of the types I have described in this book? Some analysts might write off these endeavors as archaic activities that will soon disappear; however, the remarkable persistence ("tradition") of events such as the charity debutante balls and other Society fundraisers that I have described suggests otherwise. Many elite women and their families have resources to devote to charitable giving and volunteering, and they gladly give of those resources, although perhaps because of the benefits that they and other members of their family can derive from such endeavors. The amounts that they can raise for charitable causes are much greater than the amounts that people with less wealth can raise and give, thus maintaining community support for their endeavors.

Implications of Elite Women's Volunteerism for the Future of U.S. Philanthropy

Through volunteerism and funding of the arts, education, health care, and certain organizations that assist the "less fortunate," women of the upper classes provide the general population with certain valuable resources. However, we should not assume that elite women's by-invitation-only volunteer groups actually provide large-scale human welfare services or that they advocate, or in the future might advocate, changes in social policies in order to benefit people in other economic classes. As prior studies have found, the philanthropy of the wealthy typically serves to sustain upper-class interests, including the organizations and institutions from which elites derive specific benefits.[9] Similarly, the human welfare services that elite women provide are usually available only to limited numbers and categories of people, such as teenaged mothers or abused children.

Although many of their volunteer activities raise money for causes favored by the advantaged in society, privileged women do not envision that it is their groups' mission to provide a "safety net" for disadvantaged people because (in their view) other agencies or organizations—perhaps the United Way or a religious organization—should provide such services to those who are deemed to be "deserving" of assistance. This is in keeping with Ostrower's finding that philanthropy by wealthy donors is closely connected to broad themes in American society: "Individualism, private initiative, suspicion of governmental power and bureaucracy—these are the underlying values and attitudes in terms of which philanthropy takes on meaning as a social institution."[10] From this perspective, elite giving and volunteering must be viewed as distinct from other forms of altruism or helping behavior that takes place primarily for the benefit of other people: Elite women's volunteerism often is a mark of class status that binds elites together while differentiating them from people in other classes.

The irony of this distinction is that, although elite women and their families contribute much-needed money and volunteer time to nonprofit organizations that provide some economic resources and cultural capital-enhancing opportunities for children and adults who otherwise would not have them, any significant effort to change the social conditions that produce problems or to introduce a large-scale "safety net" for those who are in need typically is outside the scope of elite women's volunteer work. In sum, people who are already in the inner social circles or those who aspire to move into those circles may be the people who benefit the most from the charitable giving and volunteer activities of elite women.

Although some elite women in my study were willing to "get their hands dirty" at charity garage sales, thrift shops, and other fund raisers, these privileged women belong to exclusive organizations that either guarantee that the members will do only as much hands-on work as they choose or that require such activities only during the women's earliest years of membership. Many long-term members fulfill their volunteer responsibilities by serving as board members or by working in other ways that do not involve direct contact with people of other classes and the clients of the organizations.

Elite women volunteers typically think of themselves as working *with* an exclusive organization rather than as working *for* the benefit of the recipients of their largesse. Their primary identity is with the group ("I'm a member of the Junior League") more than with the individuals who are assisted by the various charities the elite women support. An example is the women who raise money at an elegant Christmas charity bazaar so that they can award grant money to an assistance agency that helps individuals as contrasted with the elite women providing direct services to that agency's clients. This is quite different from how nonelite volunteerism is done and what purpose it serves. Studies of nonelite charitable volunteerism have described volunteers as serving on the front lines with the poor, the homeless, and others who are in need. By contrast, elite women's volunteerism primarily focuses on raising money or serving in a decision-making capacity rather than on actual participation in activities such as serving food in a soup kitchen or working at a shelter for the homeless. Activities among nonelite volunteers typically involve direct aid to people in need of assistance, and these endeavors have been described as pursuits that build a sense of community or help people develop "moral selves" through service to the disadvantaged;[11] however, similar terminology is generally not used in discussing most elite fundraising projects. Due to the exclusive nature of elite women's volunteer organizations, only certain forms of philanthropy are compatible with the goals and traditions of those groups and as such, their members are interested in participating in only limited outreach activities in the community.

Implications with Regard to
Social Inequality Based on Class and Race

Elite volunteerism is both a reflection and a perpetuator of larger social inequalities in the United States. Inequality is perpetuated in many ways in a class-based society such as ours. Economic inequality persists and sometimes grows wider because the wealthy control resources such as the ownership of stocks, bonds, and businesses that "make money for you even while you sleep," as one woman stated when describing her ownership of a radio station. Elites are able to pass such economic advantages on to their children, putting those children ahead of other children, not only financially but also in the quest for cultural and social advantages.

The "American Dream" is based on the assumption that anyone who works hard enough can move up the class ladder in the United States; however, the reality of social stratification suggests otherwise.[12] Families with wealth and social power are able to maintain their position at the top of the stratification hierarchy, and they are in a distinctly advantaged position to do so because they control the process of *sponsored mobility*—a very selective recruitment process that ensures that those individuals who possess the requisite wealth to be acceptable candidates for inclusion in the inner social circles of the upper classes will be compatible with those already in those circles and that these newcomers will be supportive of those practices that maintain elite privilege.[13] Only those individuals who meet this prerequisite will be actively sponsored by existing members for inclusion in their clubs, organizations, and interpersonal networks.

For the upper class to remain in a position of control, elites and nonelites alike must subscribe to an ideology that supports class-based inequality. Elite women volunteers help maintain this status quo by serving as gatekeepers and caretakers of the upper-class social institutions that restrict interclass mobility and promote intraclass marriage. The presentation of debutantes, for example, creates an entire season of activities at which elite young people develop their own social networks and identify other elites as potential business or marriage partners. However, upper-class women's gatekeeping activities are not restricted to the next generation: Through their elite organizations, these women participate in the process of sponsored mobility for others in their own age cohorts. Aspirants to the inner circles of social elites are given an opportunity to show that they are worthy by participating in social events where current "inner circle" members determine how well these individuals might fit in with other members of the group.

The "closed circle" created by elite women's invitational volunteer organizations not only protects the longer-term elites from "social climbing" newcomers but also influences nonelites to believe that the elevated position of the privileged class is justified. As such, privileged women serve in the macrolevel process of class-based legitimation, a practice that creates "a belief on the part of a large majority of the populace that institutionalized inequality in the distribution of primary resources—such as power, wealth, and prestige—is essentially right and reasonable."[14] According to legitimation theorists, people in subordinate positions may accept as inevitable the dominant position of the upper classes because elites consistently depict their own favored status as emanating from their higher levels of intelligence, greater determination and hard work, or continuous demonstration of noblesse oblige toward the "less fortunate" in their community. Elite women tend to legitimate class-based inequality by making nonelites aware of the good deeds that these women (and, thus, their families) do through their volunteer organizations. In my study, for example, some low-income mothers who shop at a thrift store or a charity garage sale describe the elite women volunteers who organize these events as "angels" or "kind club ladies" who want to help them. These lower-income women typically do not associate these privileged women's activities with the positions that elite women's husbands—and sometimes the elite women themselves—occupy in the capitalist economy. The wife of a banker may be chair of the charity garage sale, for instance, while, across town, her husband is refusing loans to low-income families. Or, when the privileged woman is not fulfilling her community-service duties, she may serve as a corporate director on a board that demands a better rate of return on stocks, resulting in an employer laying off thousands of factory workers and producing a corresponding increase in shoppers at the next charity garage sale.

Class-based inequality is not the only issue raised by elite women's volunteerism because, as we have seen, race-based segregation is also perpetuated by elite women's organizations. The intersections of class and race in elite volunteer organizations raises an important issue about the potential for greater racial equality in the United States. Most of the women of color in my study have wealth and are members of the capitalist or corporate upper classes—those who own the means of production or control the major means of production[15]—but most of them do not possess equal access to the social networks of the white upper class. In essence, money and other economic resources alone are not enough to guarantee affluent women of color inclusion in the social organizations that benefit members of the dominant white upper classes. Race remains a salient feature in determining who will gain access to those organizations and the extent to which individuals who are invited to join will gain full acceptance in these previously all-white, tradition-bound organizations.

Once separate elite women's organizations are established on the basis of race or ethnicity, this racial separation continues indefinitely despite changes that continue to occur in the larger society. Racial segregation such as that found in the more prestigious college sororities and fraternities, elite clubs, and other upper-class volunteer organizations is often justified by elites of all colors as nothing more than a reflection of the participants' right to choose with whom they will associate. Moreover, elites argue that, in a democratic society, everyone is entitled to establish his or her own "comfort zone" of acquaintances. However, an alternate sociological interpretation is that the racial separation evident in elite women's volunteer organizations can be identified as yet another form of institutional discrimination—the everyday rules and practices of institutions and organizations that result in differential treatment of individuals and groups, based on ascribed or achieved attributes such as race, ethnicity, class, or gender.[16] Through such patterns of organizational discrimination, individual elites do not have to be accountable for decisions that disadvantage others and limit their social power. Whether intentional or not, this form of discrimination in elite women's organizations may adversely affect not only women of color but also other people who have experienced generations of class- and race-based inequality. Although some analysts explain the racially separate nature of elite women's organizations on the basis of the divergent needs of the groups' members and their constituents, the continuation of these racially separate organizations serves to legitimate divided, racially segregated communities in which even affluent whites, African Americans, and sometimes Latinos/Latinas do not cross racial and ethnic barriers in their most prestigious organizational memberships. This racial division among elites indicates to all people that full racial integration is not attainable—and perhaps not desirable—even among those in the top economic tiers. This, in turn, suggests that our nation remains divided along racial and ethnic lines, even among those individuals who supposedly are living the "American Dream."

Although members of the U.S. upper classes tend to espouse the virtues of the "American Dream," that dream remains elusive for many people in this country. Inequalities based on race and class continue to increase, and many who possess economic and social power do little to level the playing field so that others can gain economic and social opportunities. It is ironic that elite women, some of whom acknowledge that they have experienced sexism and gender-based discrimination within their own families and in their communities, are hesitant to acknowledge—or to seek to change—the detrimental effects of class- and race-based discrimination.

The women I have described throughout this book do many good deeds for others; however, they could make a significant contribution toward bringing about greater equality and wider inclusion of diverse categories of people if they chose to do so. By taking a stand for social change in and through their organizations and volunteer activities, these women could set an example for others to follow. The power of good deeds should carry with it a corresponding obligation to make the "American Dream" truly available to *all* people in this nation.

Notes

1. French and Raven 1959.
2. Domhoff 1998; Ostrander 1984; Ostrower 1995.
3. Carli 1999.
4. Estelle Disch (1997) suggests that, like the matrix of domination identified by Patricia Hill Collins (1990), there also is a matrix of privilege that makes life easier for those who possess it and disadvantages those who do not possess it. Privilege in the United States includes being male, heterosexual, upper class, white, or possessing other characteristics or attributes of the dominant power group in society.
5. My findings in this regard are similar to those of Ostrower (1995), who described the charitable endeavors of wealthy philanthropists in New York as benefiting both themselves and the causes they support. Both studies confirm the importance of peer recognition and approval in the process of elite philanthropy.
6. See, for example, Baltzell 1958, 1964; Domhoff 1970, 1974, 1998; and Kanter 1993.
7. Domhoff 1998.
8. See Graham (2000) for documentation regarding the social power of elite African American women within the "black community."

9. Odendahl 1990; Ostrander 1984; Domhoff 1998.
10. Ostrower 1995: 132.
11. See Allahyari 2000; Putnam 2000; Wuthnow 1991, 1998.
12. See Wright 1979, 1997.
13. Domhoff 1998.
14. Della Fave 1980: 955.
15. Useem 1978.
16. Feagin and Vera 1995: 7.

Preparatory Schools

All Saints' Episcopal School of Fort Worth, Fort Worth, Texas
Episcopal High School, Bellaire, Texas
The Episcopal School of Dallas, Dallas, Texas
Fort Worth Country Day School, Fort Worth, Texas
Greenhill School, Addison, Texas
Groton School, Groton, Massachusetts
The Hockaday School, Dallas, Texas
The John Cooper School, The Woodlands, Texas
Keystone School, San Antonio, Texas
The Kincaid School, Houston, Texas
Lamplighter School, Dallas, Texas
Miss Porter's School, Farmington, Connecticut
St. Andrew's Episcopal School, Austin, Texas
St. John's School, Houston, Texas
St. Mark's School of Texas, Dallas, Texas
St. Mary's Hall, San Antonio, Texas
St. Stephen's Episcopal School, Austin, Texas
Vanguard College Preparatory School, Waco, Texas

APPENDIX TWO

⤳

Rush Information Form

Rush Information Form (RIF)

(To be used by alumnae members only.)

Name of Rushee: _____

College Attending: _____

Home Address: _____

City: _____ State: _____ Zip: _____

Year in College: ____ Freshman ____ Sophomore ____ Junior ____ Senior

If transfer student: College attended _____ College GPA ____

High School attended _____
                          (Name, City, State, Zip)

Class Size _____ Rank _____ GPA _____ SAT/ACT (if known) _____

Parent or Guardian _____

Pi Beta Phi Relatives _____
                        (sister, mother, grandmother)

Other Greek Affiliated Relatives _____

Please check ONE of the following:

_____ Wish to highly recommend _____ Wish to recommend

Please check ONE of the following:

____ Known personally by an alumna (if so, how long?) _____
____ Only factual information included. Source of Information _____
____ Other _____

Signed _____
                    Individual Pi Beta Phi Alumna

Chapter _____ Year of Initiation _____

Address _____
            Street   City   State   Zip

Telephone _____ Date _____
            Area Code   Number

LIST SCHOOL AND COMMUNITY ACTIVITIES AND HONORS: (Attach another sheet if needed.) Comment on special interests, talents, leadership qualities, personality.

References

Addams, Jane. 1999. *Twenty Years at Hull House: With Autobiographical Notes*. New York: Signet.

Allahyari, Rebecca Anne. 2000. *Visions of Charity: Volunteer Workers and Moral Community*. Berkeley: University of California Press.

Alpha Epsilon Phi. 2001. "History." Retrieved July 7, 2001, from http://www.duke.edu/web/AEPhi/

American Heart Association. 2001. "Austin Heart Ball." Retrieved June 4, 2001, from http://www.americanheart.org/tx/austin/heartball.html

Association of Junior Leagues International. 2000. "AJLI History." Retrieved October 29, 2000, from http://www.ajli.org/hisotory.html

Baltzell, E. Digby. 1958. *Philadelphia Gentlemen: The Making of a National Upper Class*. Glencoe, Ill.: Free Press.

———. 1964. *The Protestant Establishment: Aristocracy and Caste in America*. New York: Random House.

———. 1979. *Puritan Boston and Quaker Philadelphia*. New York: Free Press.

Barnes, Michael. 2001. "Dells Donate $10 Million to Arts Center." *Austin American Statesman* (February 13): A1, A9.

Bell, Catherine. 1997. *Ritual: Perspectives and Dimensions*. New York: Oxford University Press.

Berkowitz, Alexandra, and Irene Padavic. 1999. "Getting a Man or Getting Ahead: A Comparison of White and Black Sororities." *Journal of Contemporary Ethnography* 27, no. 4 (January): 530–557.

Birmingham, Stephen. 1968. *The Right People*. New York: Little, Brown.

———. 1977. *Certain People: America's Black Elite*. New York: Little, Brown.

———. 1990. *America's Secret Aristocracy*. New York: Berkley Books.

Blomme, Anita. 2001. "First African-American Association of Junior Leagues President to Visit City." *Carolinian* (January 15). Retrieved June 6, 2001, from http://www.ajli.org/deborah_aaa.html

Bossard, James H. S., and Eleanor S. Boll. 1948. "Rite of Passage—A Contemporary Study." *Social Forces* (March): 247–254.

Bourdieu, Pierre. 1984. *Distinction: A Social Critique of the Judgement of Taste.* Trans. by Richard Nice. Cambridge: Harvard University Press.

———. 1986. "The Forms of Capital." Pp. 241–258 in J. G. Richardson (ed.), *Handbook of Theory and Research for the Sociology of Education.* New York: Greenwood Press.

Bumiller, Elisabeth. 2000. "The Refugee from Cuba Who Grew Up to Head the Junior League." *New York Times* (August 24): A15.

Cable, Mary. 1984. *Top Drawer: American High Society from the Gilded Age to the Roaring Twenties.* New York: Athenium.

Carli, Linda L. 1999. "Gender, Interpersonal Power, and Social Influence." *Journal of Social Issues* (Spring). Retrieved September 18, 2001, from http://www.findarticles.com/cf_0/m0341/1_55/54831711/print.jhtml

Columbia Chapter of The Links, Inc. 2000. "Purpose and Projects. " Retrieved November 30, 2000, from http://www.midnet.sc.edu/links

Columbia Encyclopedia. 2001. "Philanthropy." *Columbia Encyclopedia* (6th ed.). Retrieved March 24, 2001, from http://www.battleby.com/65/ph/philanth.html

Cookson, Peter W., Jr., and Caroline Hodges Persell. 1985. *Preparing for Power: America's Elite Boarding Schools.* New York: Basic Books.

Corsaro, William A. 1997. *The Sociology of Childhood.* Thousand Oaks, Calif.: Pine Forge.

Cromwell, Adelaide M. 1994. *The Other Brahmins: Boston's Black Upper Class 1750–1950.* Fayetteville: University of Arkansas Press.

Daniels, Arlene Kaplan. 1988. *Invisible Careers.* Chicago: University of Chicago Press.

———. 1995. "Gender, Class, and Career in the Lives of Privileged Women." Pp. 115–132 in Judith R. Blau and Norman Goodman (eds.), *Social Roles and Social Institutions: Essays in Honor of Rose Laub Coser.* New Brunswick, N.J.: Transaction.

Davalos, Karen Mary. 1996. "'La Quinceanera': Making Gender and Ethnic Identities." *Frontiers* 16: 101–128.

Dedecker, Clotile. 1999. "President Dedecker's Annual Speech." Annual Conference 1999. Association of Junior Leagues International. Retrieved June 5, 2000, from http://www.ajli.org/clotilespeech.html

Della Fave, L. Richard. 1980. "The Meek Shall Not Inherit the Earth: Self-Evaluation and the Legitimacy of Stratification." *American Sociological Review* 45 (December): 955–971.

Diggins, John Patrick. 1999. *Thorstein Veblen: Theorist of the Leisure Class.* Princeton, N.J.: Princeton University Press.

Disch, Estelle. 1997. "General Introduction." Pp. 1–18 in Estelle Disch (ed.), *Reconstructing Gender: A Multicultural Anthology.* Mountainview, Calif.: Mayfield.

Domhoff, G. William. 1970. *The Higher Circles.* New York: Random House.

———. 1974. *The Bohemian Grove and Other Retreats.* New York: Harper & Row.

———. 1998. *Who Rules America? Power and Politics in the Year 2000.* Mountain View, Calif.: Mayfield.

Ebony. 1996. "The Links: Women's Organization Celebrates 50th Anniversary." *Ebony* 51, no. 9: 108–112.

Edwards, Tamala M. 1999. "The Power of the Purse: More and More, It's Women Who Control the Charity." *Time* (May 17): 64.

Ermann, Natalie. 1997. "A League of Their Own: Two Women's Groups Celebrate Anniversaries." *New Orleans Magazine* (December): 37–39.

Feagin, Joe R., and Clairece Booher Feagin. 1999. *Racial and Ethnic Relations* (6th ed.). Upper Saddle River, N.J.: Prentice-Hall.

Feagin, Joe R., and Hernán Vera. 1995. *White Racism: The Basics.* New York: Routledge.

Frankenberg, Ruth. 1993. *White Women, Race Matters: The Social Construction of Whiteness.* Minneapolis: University of Minnesota Press.

French, John R. P. Jr., and Bertram H. Raven. 1959. "The Bases of Social Power." Pp. 150–167 in Dorwin Cartwright (ed.), *Studies in Social Power.* Ann Arbor, Mich.: Institute for Social Research.

Fulwood, Sam III. 1998. "Black Sorority Splits Hairs by Barring Teen with Dreadlocks from Debutante Ball." *Buffalo News* (November 21). Retrieved January 24, 2000, from http://www.northernlight.com

Gatewood, Willard B. 1990. *Aristocrats of Color: The Black Elite, 1880–1920.* Bloomington: Indiana University Press.

Giddings, Paula. 1988. *In Search of Sisterhood: Delta Sigma Theta and the Challenge of the Black Sorority Movement.* New York: Quill/William Morrow.

Goffman, Erving. 1959. *The Presentation of Self in Everyday Life.* Garden City, N.Y.: Doubleday.

———. 1967. *Interaction Ritual: Essays on Face to Face Behavior.* Garden City, N.Y.: Anchor.

Graham, Lawrence Otis. 2000. *Our Kind of People: Inside America's Black Upper Class.* New York: HarperPerennial.

Hagedorn, Katie. 1996. "And the Walls Come Tumbling Down." Pp. 135–137 in Tim Hillman and Craig Thorn IV (eds.), *Social Home: Life in a Boarding School.* Gilsum, N.H.: Avocus Publishing.

Handler, Lisa. 1995. "In the Fraternal Sisterhood: Sororities as Gender Strategy." *Gender & Society* 9, no. 2: 236–255.

Hastings, Karen. 1991. "Sweet 15: The Passage to Adulthood Is a Lavish One for Many Girls on the Border." *Houston Chronicle* (January 13). Retrieved July 29, 2001, from http://www.houstonchronicle.com/archives

Haynes, Michaele Thurgood. 1998. *Dressing Up Debutantes: Pageantry and Glitz in Texas.* New York: Berg.

Hazzard-Gordon, Katrina. 1992. *Jookin': The Rise of Social Dance Formations in African-American Culture.* Philadelphia: Temple University Press.

Herrick, Thaddeus. 1997. "Party On: Beneath the Fun and Pageantry of San Antonio's 10-day Spring Bash Are Rifts of Race and Class." *Houston Chronicle* (April 13). Retrieved July 29, 2001, from http://www.houstonchronicle.com

Higley, Stephen Richard. 1995. *Privilege, Power, and Place: The Geography of the American Upper Class.* Lanham, Md.: Rowman & Littlefield.

Hill-Collins, Patricia. 1990. *Black Feminist Thought: Knowledge, Consciousness, and the Politics of Empowerment.* London: HarperCollins Academic.

Hine, Darlene Clark. 1990. "'We Specialize in the Wholly Impossible': The Philanthropic Work of Black Women." Pp. 70–93 in Kathleen D. McCarthy (ed.), *Lady Bountiful Revisited: Women, Philanthropy, and Power.* New Brunswick, N.J.: Rutgers University Press.

Hockaday. 2001. "Welcome: 1999–2000 Fact Sheet." Retrieved January 12, 2001. from http://www.hockaday.org/welcome/fact.html

Hockaday, Laura R. 1997. "Jewel Ball Sets Precedent." *Kansas City Star* (June 29): FY1. Retrieved February 15, 2000, from http://www.kcstar.com/newslibrary/

Hollingshead, August B. 1952. "Trends in Social Stratification: A Case Study." *American Sociological Review* 17, no. 6 (December): 685–686.

Hondagneu-Sotelo, Pierrette. 2001. *Doméstica: Immigrant Workers Cleaning and Caring in the Shadows of Affluence.* Berkeley: University of California Press.

Houston Chronicle. 1996. "Italian-American Debutantes" (photo). (November 10):10F.

Jet. 1996. "The Links, Inc. Celebrates 50 Years of Service." *Jet* 90, no. 12: 12–14.

Kanter, Rosabeth Moss. 1993 [1977]. *Men and Women of the Corporation.* New York: Basic.

Kolb, Carolyn. 1995. "Waltzing Through the Century: The Original Illinois Club at 100." *New Orleans Magazine* (February): 59–61.

Lewin, Tamar. 2001. "Women Profit Less than Men in the Nonprofit World, Too." *New York Times* (June 3): 23.

Lynch, Annette. 1999. *Dress, Gender and Cultural Change: Asian American and African American Rites of Passage.* New York: Berg.

Mack, Kibibi Voloria C. 1999. *Parlor Ladies and Ebony Drudges: African American Women, Class, and Work in a South Carolina Community.* Knoxville: University of Tennessee Press.

Marshall, Susan E. 1997. *Splintered Sisterhood: Gender and Class in the Campaign against Woman Suffrage.* Madison: University of Wisconsin Press.

McCarthy, Kathleen D. 1982. *Noblesse Oblige: Charity and Cultural Philanthropy in Chicago, 1849–1929.* Chicago: University of Chicago Press.

———. 1990. "Parallel Power Structures: Women and the Voluntary Sphere." Pp. 1–31 in Kathleen D. McCarthy (ed.), *Lady Bountiful Revisited: Women, Philanthropy, and Power.* New Brunswick, N.J.: Rutgers University Press.

McCready, Anne. 1988. "Teaching the Cotillion: When You Cut In, Don't Say 'Beat It.'" *W* (March 21–28): Southwest Section.

Mills, C. Wright. 2000 [1956]. *The Power Elite.* With an afterword by Alan Wolfe. New York: Oxford University Press.

Montgomery, Maureen E. 1998. *Displaying Women: Spectacles of Leisure in Edith Wharton's New York.* New York: Routledge.

NACWC. 2000. "National Association of Colored Women's Clubs, Inc: A Legacy of Strength." Retrieved November 25, 2000, from http://expert.cc.perdue.edu/~wov/NACWCHistory.html

Nelson, Margaret K., and Joan Smith. 1999. *Working Hard and Making Do: Surviving in Small Town America.* Berkeley: University of California Press.

Newman, Katherine S. 1999. *No Shame in My Game: The Working Poor in the Inner City.* New York: Alfred Knopf.

Odendahl, Teresa. 1990. *Charity Begins at Home: Generosity and Self-Interest among the Philanthropic Elite.* New York: Basic Books.

Oliver, Melvin L., and Thomas M. Shapiro. 1995. *Black Wealth/White Wealth: A New Perspective on Racial Inequality.* New York: Routledge.

Omega Phi Beta. 2000. "Our Founders." Retrieved December 3, 2000 from http://www.omegaphibeta.org/founders.htm

Ostrander, Susan A. 1980a. "Upper-Class Women: Class Consciousness as Conduct and Meaning." Pp. 73–96 in G. William Domhoff (ed.), *Power Structure Research.* Beverly Hills, Calif.: Sage.

———. 1980b. "Upper-Class Women: The Feminine Side of Privilege." *Qualitative Sociology* 3 (Spring): 23–42.

———. 1984. *Women of the Upper Class.* Philadelphia: Temple University Press.

Ostrower, Francie. 1995. *Why the Wealthy Give: The Culture of Elite Philanthropy.* Princeton, N.J.: Princeton University Press.

Owen, Chuck. 2000."Celebration's Marthas, Debutantes Share Special Heritage." *Laredo Times.* (February 8). Retrieved November 9, 2000, from http://madmax. lmtonline.com/mainnewsarchives/020800/s12.htm

Pi Beta Phi. 2000. "Historical Highlights." Retrieved March 27, 2001, from http://www.pibetaphi.org/ourfr/herfram.htm

Putnam, Robert D. 2000. *Bowling Alone: The Collapse and Revival of American Community.* New York: Simon & Schuster.

Raven, Bertram H. 1988. "Social Power and Compliance in Health Care." Pp. 229–244 in S. Maes, G. D. Spielberger, P. B. Defares, and I. G. Sarason (eds.), *Topics in Health Psychology.* New York: Wiley.

Rodriguez, Gregory. 2000. "We're Patriotic Americans Because We're Mexicans." *Salon.com* (February 24). Retrieved November 9, 2000, from http://www. salon.com/news/feature/2000/02/24/laredo

Ross, Lawrence C., Jr. 2000. *The Divine Nine: The History of African American Fraternities and Sororities.* New York: Kensington.

Rothenberg, Paula. 2000. *Invisible Privilege: A Memoir About Race, Class, and Gender.* Lawrence: University Press of Kansas.

Rotzoll, Brenda Warner. 1999. "Debutante Cotillions Are Flourishing." *Chicago Sun-Times* (September 5). Retrieved July 28, 2001, from http://www.northernlight.com

St. Stephens Episcopal School. 2001. "Academics." Retrieved February 24, 2001 from http://www.ststephens-texas.com/site/PageServer?pagename=academics

San Marino Women's Club. 1999. "The History of the Debutante Season." Retrieved September 2, 1999, from http://www-bcf.usc.edu/~clingerm/rules.html

Sanua, Marianne R. 2000. "Jewish College Fraternities in the United States, 1895–1968: An Overview." *Journal of American Ethnic History* (Winter): 3–30.

Schlenker, Barry R. 1980. *The Self-Concept, Social Identity, and Interpersonal Relations.* Monterey, Calif.: Brooks/Cole.

Schwartz, Marilyn. 2000. "Joke's On You: Junior League Has Grown Up." *Dallas Morning News* (May 11). Retrieved June 6, 2001, from http://ajli.org/ jokesonyou.html

Simmel, Georg. 1971 [1908]. "The Stranger." Pp. 143–149 in Donald N. Levine (ed.), *On Individuality and Social Forms: Selected Writings.* Chicago: University of Chicago Press.

Snow, David A., and Leon Anderson. 1993. *Down on Their Luck: A Study of Homeless Street People.* Berkeley: University of California Press.

Stoeltje, Beverly. 1996. "The Snake Charmer Queen: Ritual Competition and Signification in American Festival." Pp. 13–29 in Colleen Ballerino Cohen, Richard Wilk, and Beverly Stoeltje (eds.), *Beauty Queens On the Global Stage: Gender, Contests, and Power*. New York: Routledge.

Strong, Sally. 1990. "Groups, Events Preserve Italian Heritage." *Houston Chronicle* (September 9): 16. Retrieved July 29, 2001, from http://www.houstonchronicle.com

Thomas, Cynthia. 1996. "Curtsies, Knickers and Jalapenos: George Washington Never Slept Here, but Laredo Treats His Birthday like a Presidential Affair. *Houston Chronicle* (April 7). Retrieved July 29, 2001, from http://www.houstonchronicle.com

Tilly, Chris, and Charles Tilly. 1994. "Capitalist Work and Labor Markets." Pp. 283–313 in Neal Smelser and R. Swedberg (eds.), *Handbook of Economic Sociology*. Princeton, N.J.: Princeton University Press.

Useem, Michael. 1978. "The Inner Group of the American Capitalist Class." *Social Problems* 25: 225–240.

Veblen, Thorstein. 1994 [1899]. *The Theory of the Leisure Class*. Introduction by Robert Lekachman. New York: Penguin.

Weber, Max. 1958. *From Max Weber: Essays in Sociology*. Translated and edited by H. H. Gerth and C. Wright Mills. New York: Oxford University Press, pp. 196–244.

Wilson, John, and Marc Musick. 1997. "Who Cares? Toward an Integrated Theory of Volunteer Work." *American Sociological Review* (October): 694–713.

Winzenried, Rebecca. 2001. "Not Your Mother's Volunteer Group." *Symphony: The Magazine of the American Symphony Orchestra League* (July–August): 72–80.

Wright, Erik Olin. 1979. *Class Structure and Income Determination*. New York: Academic.

———. 1997. *Class Counts: Comparative Structure in Class Analysis*. Cambridge: Cambridge University Press.

Wuthnow, Robert. 1991. *Acts of Compassion: Caring for Others and Helping Ourselves*. Princeton, N.J.: Princeton University Press.

———. 1998. *After Heaven: Spirituality in America since the 1950s*. Berkeley: University of California Press.

Yeomans, Jeannie. 2000. "Junior League Remakes Itself for the 21st Century." Retrieved June 6, 2001, from http://ajli.org/remakes.html

Zweigenhaft, Richard L., and G. William Domhoff. 1998. *Diversity in the Power Elite: Have Women and Minorities Reached the Top?* New Haven, Conn.: Yale University Press.

Index

Americans and, 145; Asian Americans and, 146; community service before being invited to join, 15; first African American president of, 50; helping the disadvantaged, 40; history of, 145, 147; Latinas and, 146; operation of charity thrift shops by, 59; working to dispel stereotypes, 31, 144

Lady Bountiful, stereotype of, 30
Latinos/as: families considered to be "old guard," 8; parallel social organizations of, 151; participation in primarily white organizations, 8; presentation balls, 116, 132, 133, 135; sorority participation of, 105. *See also* Hispanic Debutante Association; La Quinceañera
legacy: defined, 35; as factor in sorority participation, 101; as hereditary form of social power, 92
legitimization, process of, 174
less fortunate, groups that support the, 40
The Links, 28, 58, 148–50, 159; helping the disadvantaged, 40
Lynch, Annette, 130

Martha Washington, Society of, 133, 134, 137, 151
McCarthy, Kathleen D., 24
medical schools, volunteer efforts on behalf of, 38
medically related causes, 38; boards of trustees of, 40; women's groups that support, 40
Montgomery, Maureen E., 73, 115
Musick, Marc, 26

National Association of Colored Women's Clubs, 148
National Coalition of 100 Black Women, Inc., 43
neglected children, groups that support, 41

noblesse oblige, 92; elite children learning concept of, 83
norm of exclusivity, 19, 25, 52, 97

Odendahl, Teresa, 24
Original Illinois Club, 129
Ostrander, Susan A., 7, 17, 24, 56, 73
Ostrower, Francie, 22n5, 25, 34, 44, 52n3, 172, 176n5

Padavic, Irene, 105
Persell, Caroline Hodges, 35, 53, 95, 96
philanthropy, 25; age as factor in involvement, 49; benefit to wealthy, 25; debutante presentations and, 118; defined, 23; gender, class, age, and race in, 44; relationship to upper-class lifestyle, 23; relationship with upper-class lifestyle, 24, 166; rising influence of women in, 25; sororities and, 105; as source of social power, 23; as vehicle for upper-class lifestyle, 24
presentation balls, 67, 136, 137; community service requirement, 113, 116; comparison of weddings to, 139; fashion shows and, 66; history of, 115, 118, 119, 139, 171; Latino/a, 116; planning and implementation of, 135; social hierarchy of, 1, 70, 117; training of debutantes for participation in, 114; types of, 67. *See also* charity balls
prestigious schools: brick wall syndrome and, 96; cultural capital and, 95; diversity of women who support, 36; factors in determining participation in groups that support, 35; highly-regarded public schools, 92; as locus of children creating social networks, 94; parental satisfaction with children's education, 36; parental selection of schools their children attend, 93; recurring themes at, 95; relationship to upper-class lifestyle, 35; represented in this study, 35, 95;

165, 169, 171, 175; factors in selecting which to join, 31; future of, 171; hierarchical arrangement of, 26; medically related causes and, 38; membership caps, 155, 161; necessity of recruiting new members, 29; parallel social organizations, 51, 58, 147, 148, 162, 169, 175; pressure to raise large sums of money, 29; racial and ethnic empowerment and, 42; segregated nature of, 8, 15, 18; social change and, 158; social power and, 113; structure of, 143, 151–53, 155–57, 159–61; white ethnics and, 147; working to dispel stereotypes, 31, 150

Zweigenhaft, Richard L., 54n51

About the Author

Diana Kendall is associate professor of sociology at Baylor University. Her research and teaching interests include social theory and race, class, and gender. She is the author of several widely used textbooks, including *Sociology in Our Times* and *Social Problems in a Diverse Society*.